DROP AND GIVE ME TWENTY!

First published in 2006 by

WOODFIELD PUBLISHING
Bognor Regis, West Sussex, England
www.woodfieldpublishing.com

© Rob Novak, 2006

All rights reserved.
No part of this publication may be reproduced
or transmitted in any form or by any means,
electronic or mechanical, nor may it be stored
in any information storage and retrieval system,
without prior permission from the publisher.

The right of Rob Novak
to be identified as Author of this work
has been asserted in accordance with
the Copyright, Designs and Patents Act 1988

ISBN 1-84683-022-2

Drop and Give Me Twenty!

*Mischievous Memoirs
of a former RAF Mechanic*

Rob Novak

*This book is dedicated to
Emma Louise
who brought true meaning to my life and un-
conditional love*

CONTENTS

Acknowledgements .... *ii*

Introduction .... *iii*

1. Early Days 1
2. Gas Chamber 13
3. It's Not a Gun 21
4. On the Range 29
5. MFT 39
6. Pass-Out Parade 45
7. Jock and Pat 49
8. Train Mischief 63
9. Buffoon Apprentice 73
10. Tyres, Bikes and Bollockings 87
11. Lubrication Bay 95
12. Winter Games 105
13. A Christmas 'Do' 117
14. Main Hangar 129
15. Assessments 141
16. A Day in the Life at Cranwell 145
17. A Day Out at Her Majesty's Expense 159
18. Islas Malvinas: Willies, Poo and Piss! 167
19. Man Overboard 185
20. Zippy 201

Epilogue 207

Acknowledgements

Sincere thanks go to the following people:

The staff at Houghton-le-Spring library who tolerated my to-ing and fro-ing as I researched the book and got in contact with ex-service comrades through various websites.

The staff at Houghton-le-Spring Job-linkage and Back Up North East who contributed financially to the production of my first ten books that went out for review.

To family and friends who read the book and offered constructive criticism, encouragement and some positive quotes.

And finally, to all the members of Houghton-le-Spring writers group, 'Writers For Fun' who have been a constant source of enlightenment, encouragement and wisdom during the time of writing.

Introduction

It is March 1981 in the small ex-mining community of Houghton-le-Spring, situated halfway between Durham City and Sunderland in the north-east of England. Joe Dolce's 'Shaddap Your Face' is at number one in the hit parade and is playing on the radio in a naive boy's bedroom as he gets ready to begin a life-changing journey. Was this an omen of what was to come?

At seventeen he's more like thirteen – had many girlfriends but never actually 'done the deed'. Released from mother's apron strings for the first time, he ventures into the big, bad world of Her Majesty's Royal Air Force.

The image below is of my very last day in the Royal Air Force. The story begins on my very first one...

1. Early Days

10 March 1981 – 0530 The lime-green alarm clock, which I had placed in an empty biscuit tin, with its Roman numerals and massive bells on top, announced that it was time to haul my tubby little arse off the mattress. I had perfected the skill of jamming my finger between the bell and the clapper until I could clutch the clock to my chest and switch it off.

Getting up at this time was something I was definitely not accustomed to doing, the previous night's nerves and anticipation having taken their toll. Attempting to go to bed early and awaken bright eyed and bushy-tailed, I had placed the clock in the tin for maximum effect. Hours of tossing and turning (more tossing than turning) had elapsed and I stared at the ceiling like a barn owl on speed.

Today was to be the beginning of ten years of piss taking and practical jokes on a grand scale.

Today I became a fully enlisted member of Her Majesty's Royal Air Force. The nation slept safe in their beds knowing they were being defended by Britain's finest! Three days earlier I had graduated to the ripe old age of seventeen; having left school with ten CSEs, I was certain to secure a future in the big bad world. What I had failed to realise was that a grade five in arithmetic ruled out a career in accountancy, a grade four in mathematics had the same effect, and a three in metalwork was not about to gain me a scholarship into the field of mechanical engineering. My best mark, a grade two in physics (of which I was extremely proud), was not the precursor for a career in nuclear science.

However, the weeks spent in the science lab with my hand on top of the 'Van der Graaf' generator made for hours of endless fun as I electrocuted every passer-by with approximately ten thousand volts of static electricity. This gave many entertaining moments, including the most prim-and-proper female prefects blurting out obscenities of which I could only dream, followed by a wave of purple embarrassment, which manifested itself in a high flush and the pertest nipples I have ever seen.

In my final years at school I realised that I had developed a talent for making people laugh, with impressions of teachers, ridicule and self-ridicule, jokes and funny voices. The one thing that does strike me now is the length to which I was prepared to go, and the trouble I got into, to secure a hearty laugh.

After I had finally managed to prise my hand off my knob long enough to stop the incessant rattling of the clock, I could feel the warm vale of sleep returning. In a desperate attempt not to go back there, I swung my legs at right angles to the bed; my feet landed on my furry bedside rug (mmm, soft and gentle) and I scrunched my toes up through its fluff.

It's one thing to sit naked with your head in your hands – to look down and see your willy, which has developed a mind and will of its own, looking back at you was depressing enough – but to face that dash to the bathroom, hoping no one would see what little morning glory I had, was another matter. Do I attempt the stealth approach and risk getting caught in a ridiculous stalking pose with my pointy white Y-fronts, or the 'I've-got–diarrhoea' ploy? I think the latter.

Returned, relieved and refreshed from the bathroom, I padded my way downstairs with the alertness, speed and agility of a three-toed sloth, rubbing my eyes on the way down. I would soon be ready for my journey to the Royal Air Force Recruiting Office, 10 Ridley Place, Newcastle-upon-Tyne. I caught the 39 bus and wrote rude words in the condensation of the windows on the top deck – !REKNAW A SI YTTOCS – knowing I would be passing Scotty's house on the way. He was still in bed, but his Dad saw and I peered in horror through the steamed-up window, hoping that I wouldn't be recognised. The bus lurched as it rounded the tight corner and up the steep incline into Worsick Street depot, next to the fire station. I picked up my folder and went to rub the words off the window; then I thought no, bollocks: I was too proud at being able to write it backwards, and thought it should stay there. I glanced back up at it as I got off the bus and had a small chuckle to myself.

The smells of diesel fumes and cigarette smoke in the depot were overwhelming on this cold March morning; there were old men coughing their lungs up, reading half-folded newspapers and smoking Woodbines. I asked one of the many conductors the way to Ridley Place and was duly pointed in the right direction: past the fire station and up into the town. I was quite fascinated by the huge stone buildings as I made my way into the recruiting office.

I was given a warm welcome, much as I was in Sunderland's recruiting office – that was, until I told him I was there for my attestation (official joining up); then I was just another lamb to the slaughter and was directed towards the waiting room.

I gazed around the small sea of faces; everyone looked so much older than me. There were no seats left, so I just trembled in the corner trying to look hard – all five feet four of me.

'You joining up?' one of the faces said, dragging a 'rolly' out of his mouth and spitting a bit of 'baccy' out.

'Yeah,' I said, trying to sound unflustered.

'What yer ganna dee? There's nee jockeys in the Air Force, yer nar.'

The room filled with laughter, and all I could manage was one of those inane grins. The door opened and someone in a uniform beckoned us upstairs. It was here, after yet another round of form filling, that we were to swear allegiance to Her Majesty the Queen and all who sail in her.

'Place your right hand on the bible and repeat after me,' the officer said.

'I, your name,' and there's always one twat who actually says the words 'your name' instead of his own, causing a good deal of head shaking and then the task being made clear. As it turned out, it was the lad with the 'rolly'. Now that we were enlisted we became the property of HM Forces, and our lives as we knew them ceased to exist; requests became demands: 'YOU WILL report to Newcastle railway station at 0900 hours on Tuesday the sixteenth of March, 1981.'

~ Early Days ~

We met on the platform: long-haired 'yobbos', hippies, punks, snot-nosed mummy's boys and, of course, the all-knowing, streetwise geezer. We boarded our train to Newark (which I later found out was an anagram of wanker, after I'd been called one by one of the lads for being naïve about something – probably sex). I was as green as grass and still, very definitely, a 'cherry boy'. I was the youngest, at seventeen and three days, and listened in utter disbelief at the exaggerated stories about who had had the most shags, and I was fascinated by the different names people had for things. I had never heard of a girl's parts being referred to as 'poon-tang' or 'hairy pie'; as far as I was aware it was just a plain old 'fanny'. There were tales of who could drink the most and what people were going to do – why, where and when.

The most I'd ever managed was a bottle of Pomagne and a six-pack of Snowballs from the off-licence, and even then I couldn't keep them down and was sick all over my girlfriend. It soon became apparent that whenever you have a gathering of people, you will always get a 'natural-born leader', a smelly twat and a thief, and our group was no different (although I hasten to add that as both my parents were ex-RAF, I had had a decent upbringing with manners, kindness and courtesy, so did not fall into any of the aforementioned categories).

There was an air of both excitement and trepidation as to what we could expect at the other end. Tales of 'short back and all off' were bandied around, and the rumour that they put bromide in the tea to stop you getting a 'hard on' were beginning to unnerve me. After all, this was a grown man's air force, and I was just a boy at heart.

The journey took about three and a half hours and was quite an adventure for me. We rolled into Newark at about 1330 hours and were greeted by a civilian coach driver, who remarked how lovely our hairstyles were, given that there were a couple of hippies in the ever-growing group as the train collected recruits along the way. I tried to imagine them without any hair. Our driver ushered us towards an old SB3 coach, the type you see on those black-and-white films, with the whining petrol engine that groaned and spluttered the eight or so miles from Newark Northgate to RAF Swinderby, home of recruit training. The banter was getting louder and louder, as the piss taking had already begun. We got a great view of the airfield as we turned off the A46 and onto the camp roads.

'Hey look, there's one of Smithy's socks blowing on that pole.'

'Nice colour too,' someone else remarked.

'Yeah, it'll go with his ginger bollocks,' a third said.

It was, of course, the windsock, as on most airfields.

The guard at the gate grinned knowingly as he lifted the red-and-white pole which gave us access to what was probably considered the worst six weeks of our lives.

We grabbed our bags and left the bus to be organised into one straight line: 'Tallest on the left, shortest on the right, go!' And then it dawned on me that this was my first direct order and I strangely enjoyed complying with it, even though I was the shortest, on the right. The one long line was then reorganised into three rows, ready for marching.

~ Drop and Give Me Twenty! ~

This was our first encounter with Corporal Wild, our drill instructor (DI), and if you've ever wondered about the validity of the 'by name, by nature' adage, it was certainly applicable here. Stockily built, about five-foot eight, this bundle of wind and piss was to be our mother, father, aunty and uncle for the next six weeks. The peak of his cap was 'slashed' so as to point down at an angle of 45 degrees, completely obscuring his eyes – which was probably just as well because to 'eyeball him' was a fate worse than death. He had a thick, bushy, black moustache that accentuated the strange shape of his nose, which I thought was due to his cap resting on it for all those years; but no, we later found out that all the cartilage had been removed for some obscure reason.

I think I must have started daydreaming, because I was not prepared for the shock that was about to follow.

'WHEN I GIVE THE COMMAND, MARCH!'

I had never heard a voice so loud and intense in my life, and practically shat my kidneys out with the surprise.

'You will move forward with the left foot, swiftly followed by the right; this is commonly known as marching.'

I had a quiet laugh to myself and thought of 'It ain't 'alf hot, mum' and how he was surely going to burst a blood vessel if he carried on like this. How wrong can ya be? 'Shortest on the right' meant that I was always going to be at the back of the queue.

I felt like a straggling fart in the back of someone's trousers while the rest of the pants moved off in front of me. Still, it meant I was obscured from the corporal for the most part. So when the command 'By the left, quick march' was given, there was a great deal of pushing and shoving, as we all set off at different times and speeds, people standing on the backs of others' shoes. I managed to get the shoes off the lad in front of me so many times that he was forced to articulate the sentiment of 'ripping my head off and shitting down my neck', which I hadn't heard before, and thought 'I must remember that one.' At least we were on the move, although to call it marching would have been a little adventurous. We were on our way to the most sadistic place on the whole station, 'the camp barber's'; and although we didn't know it, there were going to be some huge transformations as at this point the hippies were still in possession of their locks.

'WHEN I GIVE THE COMMAND, HALT!'

There it was again, that booming voice, and I thought, 'Steady on old chap, no need.'

'When I give the command "halt", it will be when your left foot touches the ground. You will take a further two steps, then come to a complete stop.'

It all sounded so simple; what could possibly go wrong?

'PLATOON, HALT!'

The three lads at the front stopped immediately and the rest of us shunted into them like a set of runaway carriages. I definitely thought I was going to get punched this time as the lad in front of me had to pull the backs of his shoes up again.

~ Early Days ~

'ARE YOU FUCKING DEAF?' the Corporal enquired; and I thought that was a bit steep. If only I'd known we were to become farts, faggots, nancys, pansies, mummy's boys and (I quote) 'half-fucked ferrets'. I myself progressed to being a 'short, fat, humpty-backed toad' on a good day.

The barber practically wet his pants with excitement as the number one attachment came out. Hair piled up around his knees with ever-growing speed, and we barely recognised each other as the hippies emerged from the building, stroking the tops of their heads lovingly. Well, at least we were beginning to look like airmen now, or 'sprogs' as we were more affectionately called. Back into our lines of three again and off towards our accommodation, or 'block' as it was known. Each room of about fourteen to sixteen men was given a flight number, and we were 'Fifteen Flight' of Hansen Block.

The blocks were in an 'H' configuration, ground and first floor; parallel living quarters with an adjacent connecting corridor containing showers, toilets and drying rooms.

They were absolutely spotless; never a thought was given that it was going to be us that had to keep the place like this. We entered through the front doors, something we were to do only twice in the whole six weeks' training – usually because twice was enough to take off the gleaming shine the previous entry had left us with and replace it with deep scuffs and scars. All, of course, would have to be polished out again with a good deal of 'elbow grease'; but then, that was the general idea.

'Fifteen Flight, you are in room two; find a bed space and stow your gear. I will be back for you at 1600 hours.'

We all looked at each other blankly until one of the older lads said, 'It means four o'clock.' Still none the wiser, we nodded enthusiastically.

Each room and flight was allocated a 'senior man' and deputy senior man, someone who would generally look after the lads – usually the oldest and/or most experienced, or the biggest, so he could knock seven bells out of you if you fell behind.

The more experienced lads launched themselves at the beds as far as possible away from the door and the loudspeaker located above it. I was slow to pick one and ended up just two beds from the door, on the right-hand side of the room. Four mistakes here: 1. The right-hand side of the room was forward facing and looked out onto the road, so the noise and the light both hit my bed just beautifully. 2. In a room with fourteen men, that left thirteen other people who would wander backwards and forwards at all hours of the night for a piss, and after a night on the beer that could be quite tiresome. 3. The most important – with all the to-ing and fro-ing it was practically impossible to have a wank without getting caught. Oh, I almost forgot – 4. When 'reveille' sounded at 0600 hours the following morning, it was understandably a good deal louder at this end of the room than the other. To add to this there was always the danger of being struck by low-flying shoes and keys as they were aimed at the loudspeaker.

The Corporal arrived on the dot of 1600 hours and bellowed from the road: 'OUTSIDE, FIFTEEN FLIGHT!' which was shortened to just 'Fifteen' later on.

We all thundered out like a herd of wildebeest through the front door, scuffing the shiny floor even more.

'NOT THROUGH THE FUCKING FRONT DOOR. YOU HAVEN'T EARNED THE RIGHT TO USE THE FRONT DOOR. GET ROUND THE FUCKING BACK!'

And the herd did an about-turn and ran back through the front doors and out of an exit halfway down the connecting corridor; this was now to be our only means of entry and exit from the building. We lined up in our rows of threes and began to march to the 'Airmen's Mess' (canteen/restaurant). It was here we sampled that very individual style of RAF cooking, and the old adage came to mind of 'The exams for becoming an RAF cook must be really difficult, as no one has managed to pass them yet.' Sorry, cooks – but the rubber eggs, frazzled sausages and cold bacon did nothing for my introduction to service food.

After the meal we were allowed to wander over to the NAAFI (Navy, Army and Air Force Institute), which consisted of a small shop, run by the only female we had seen; built like a brick shithouse with the mouth and attitude to match, she had no worries. The shop sold items like soap, toothpaste, towels, etc. – heavy on the cleanliness issue at what I considered to be grossly over-inflated prices – and sweets and pop, of course.

Attached to that was the main club – a bit like a 'Workingmen's Club', only better decorated and with cheaper beer. Oh, cheaper beer – and I thought of the 'Homer Simpson' drool: 'What better way to recruit new trainees? Come and join the Air Force, fly to faraway exotic countries, meet new and exciting people and shoot them; but don't forget the cheap beer, mmm!' After a few pints and reflecting on the day's events, we drifted back to the block in dribs and drabs and retired to bed thinking we would get a decent night's sleep; after all, I'd been up since five-thirty am, had had my head shaved, had been threatened with decapitation and defecation and was absolutely knackered. There was still a feeling of excitement, though, as I was part of a very big organisation.

I can't think for the life of me why I expected to get a good night's sleep with thirteen strange men only feet away, when I was used to my own room at home. I can honestly say that I have never heard such a collection of burping, farting, sneezing and snoring in my entire life, with the low mumble and chatter that marched on into the night. I just had to listen in case I missed something, but eventually the vale of warm sleep drifted over my weary eyes and I was gone, for what seemed like thirty seconds.

'REVEILLE, REVEILLE, REVEILLE! THE TIME IS 0600. REVEILLE, REVEILLE, REVEILLE!'

I couldn't believe my ears; it couldn't be time to get up yet, could it? Then the flock of low-flying shoes, keys and rucksacks bounced off the speaker from the ones who had stayed that little bit later at the NAAFI.

Some people had made the conscious decision to leave already; to quote one lad: 'Fuck this for a game of soldiers,' which was quite apt for the situation we were in – and sure enough he wouldn't last the week.

The dents and the cracked plaster were evidence that the previous entry had gone through the same motions, but what never ceased to amaze me was the fact that at least half of the lads had managed to sleep through the whole thing.

~ Early Days ~

I peered over my blankets and thought, 'Bollocks, I'm not going to be first up; don't want to appear too keen.' Some drifted back off to sleep, only to be awoken by what can be described as the end of the world.

'HANDS OFF COCKS, FEET IN SOCKS. COME ON YOU LAZY BASTARDS, MOVE IT, MOVE IT, MOVE IT!'

This snarling entity of snot and spit was definitely too early in the morning. Every time Corporal Wild spoke, something – or more often someone – would get showered in body fluids; he would rub his nose, which without the cartilage would spring back into position like a rubber mask, and I wished I'd been the one to have done it. He had a 'Cliff Richard' face, you know? One you would never get sick of slapping, like a bulldog chewing a wasp. With that slashed peaked cap, I often wondered how he knew where he was going; all you could see was his 'Roman' nose, roamin' all over his face! He was always immaculately turned out, though, and I couldn't imagine how many hours had gone into shining those boots to that degree; crisp, starched creases like razors – he knew every trick in the book and then wrote a few more.

I swear I must have leapt vertically at least three feet in the air – no one was expecting him to be up at this time – and we launched ourselves towards the bathroom, or ablutions as they would come to be known. They were of the communal type, five sinks back to back. Ten sinks, fourteen blokes: it doesn't take a lot of working out that someone's going to be late. We were all running around like headless chickens, sleep in our eyes, bumping into each other, trying to get to a sink before anyone else.

I'm not sure if you've ever given any thought to people's toiletry habits, especially this early in the morning. A good deal of farting and snorting went on in the five lavs which were all side by side; some people, regular as clockwork every day, occupied the same cubicle for the same length of time. It must have really come to something when you had to get up earlier to enjoy a quiet crap.

The lengths people would go to so you couldn't hear the 'plop' were amazing. The old-fashioned toilet-roll holder, with its wooden centre, that compressed inside itself when the need for a new roll was necessary, rattled as it dispensed approximately twenty sheets of tracing paper, like someone trying to kick-start an old Triumph, da da da – da da da – and then came the crunching sound as it was screwed up and deposited in the bowl. This was the only way to make it soft enough to use effectively.

Once washed and awake, we were marched down to the mess for a spot of 'brekkies'; you could have as much of the damn' stuff as you liked, including the bromide-enriched tea, which did have a curious taste, I have to say. And it was a chargeable offence (disciplinary action) NOT to have it – the breakfast that is, not the tea. Again you couldn't have found a finer selection of burnt offerings, including sausages, raw on one side and cremated on the other, genuine rubber eggs, and cooked bacon you'd think had come straight out of the fridge – all washed down with a large helping of the aforementioned tea/coffee.

We were not sure if bromide had actually been put in the water, but we were led to believe so. For those of you who have never encountered bromide, the dictionary tells us it is a derivative of 'bromine', which is used in the photographic and pharmaceutical industries. It comes from the Greek word *bromos*, 'a stink'; 'a dose of sodium or potassium bromide given as a sedative'. Quite why the RAF would want us drowsy was beyond me. It was alleged that it was a substance that, for want of a better description, 'stops your willy getting hard' and suppresses your libido. Why the hell they would need to put that in the drinks was baffling; there weren't any women on the camp anyway, except for the permanent staff whom we hardly ever saw, and of course the lone NAAFI girl – and believe me, there would be no requirement for bromide there! She managed that all of her own accord.

We weren't told about the tea until a couple of weeks into the training, and a sigh of relief echoed from the boys. 'Thank Christ for that, I haven't had a "stiffy" for a week,' said big Jock, although I'm sure it was psychosomatic. After breakfast we marched across the camp to stores, where we were issued our 'individually tailored uniforms' – trousers, jumpers, raincoats, shoes and socks. Lots of socks.

'Sea socks, long, white, one pair,' the lad behind the counter said, which begged the question: where are my sea socks, short, white, one pair? But I didn't ask, as there was a lot to get through.

'Socks, woollen, two pairs, black. Socks, nylon two pairs, black,' he started again. I thought, blimey, I've only been in the RAF a day and I've got five pairs of socks – more than I ever had at home and all without 'toe holes'. I put them to my nose and sniffed.

'Mothballs, mate,' he said.

'Mothballs to you an' all,' I replied.

'No, that's what you can smell,' said one of the lads. 'My Dad's a tailor; he has loads of them.'

'Oh!' I said, wondering where I might store that fabulous piece of information in my already overflowing memory. In amongst all this kit were our individually sized, 'Stanley Matthews' PT shorts, dark blue in colour and coming in three sizes – racing snake, fat bastard, and somewhere in the middle. The plimsolls were like canoes; if I stopped quickly in them, my feet would slide to the front and I would disappear. They would have made better flippers than running shoes any day of the week.

Once our kit was safely stored in our lockers and we had on our 'number two uniform' – light-blue shirt and black tie, standard woolly jumper, trousers, socks nylon, shoes and beret – it was time for our first spot of 'square bashing' (marching and drill practice); but before we went anywhere, the Corporal suggested we might like to … 'PUT YOUR FUCKING BERETS ON PROPERLY.'

I gather he said this to every new entry, no matter what, after a few minutes of being shown how to put it on properly.

'The badge will go over the left eye, pulling the rest of the beret down and to the right,' the Corporal said, and we were sorted.

I remember thinking, 'This bloke doesn't half make a fuss, and it's only a hat.' We were then given our welcome speech, which went something like this:

'You are now what is known as Fifteen Flight. From now on, i.e., whenever you hear the word "fifteen" that means you.'

'I'm with ya so far,' I thought; 'this is a doddle.'

'For the next six weeks we will turn you shower of shit into military machines. If you have a problem you will come to me. NOT FUCKING NOW – PUT YOUR HAND DOWN. My name is Corporal Wild, spelled G-O-D. You will address me as Corporal.'

For one minute there I thought he was going to suggest we actually called him God.

'You will not call me Sir, Staff or Corps. Corps are fucking dead things, which is what you will be if you call me that – am I clear?'

There was much nodding of heads in agreement.

'Stand fucking still; you look like something I've got in the back of my car.' I immediately thought of the 'Churchill dog'.

So, in the crisp March morning air we moved to the parade ground, which was on the other side of the camp, the same side as the airfield, separated by a road that effectively split the camp into two halves. On our arrival a couple of polar bears were throwing snowballs at the penguins. Fuck, it was cold.

'Is anyone cold?' asked the Corporal.

A fair question I thought, so I said 'Me, Corporal.' Big mistake!

'Can you see that fence in the distance?'

'Yes, Corporal.'

'Well, run there and back – twice.'

'Oh bollocks,' I thought; this six weeks is gonna seem like a lifetime if I learn every lesson this way.

After the first trip he asked, 'Warming up, are we?'

'Yes, Corporal,' I replied. 'Thank you!'

'Come on; get those porky little chipolatas moving, Novak. Open your legs, man, your bollocks won't fall out. They wouldn't get damaged even if they did – your arse is too close to the ground.'

When I'd finished, my face was burning from the cold air, which made me cough uncontrollably. The corporal flicked one of my ears; I thought it had shattered into a million pieces and fallen to the ground.

'Are we learning yet?' he peered up my nose and tilted his head to 45 degrees.

'Yes, Corporal,' I coughed, writhing from the pain of my flicked lug. I thought of the school janitor and how one day you were gonna get the bastard. I planned Corporal Wild's death a hundred different, excruciating ways.

'Stop that coughing,' he said.

Now as far as I know, coughing is usually involuntary and you don't have any control over it. As I tried holding my mouth shut, I kept inflating like a South American bullfrog, much to the amusement of all concerned. After about an hour of screaming and shouting at us, much standing on toes and people facing in different directions, Corporal Wild was getting as pissed off as we were and decided that a spot of PT was just the thing to wake us up. So, back to the block we go and get changed into our PT kit, a quick jog to the gym, and then a five-mile run in driving hailstones through a quagmire forest. Yes, I thought, this is the life for me – bollocks! The racing snakes and anorexic whippets disappeared into the distance, while us real individuals did as little as was possible to get away with. I loitered at the back, thinking the only time I'd run before was when the 'last orders' bell went at the local boozer, and it was then that the real power of camaraderie was demonstrated.

'Come on, Novak; if you're last, the whole flight will go round again.'

Holy shit! Little old me being responsible for another five miles of this torture? One of the lads dropped back from the front to give me some encouragement...

'I'll pull your arms off and bash ya to death with the soggy ends if you make us do this again, ya fanny.'

We didn't have to go around again, but I got the message. A new dilemma was just around the corner; back to the gym for a shower (this was compulsory), but there was always one smelly bastard who was allergic to soap and did his utmost to avoid it. The showers, like the individually sized plimsolls, were as advanced as Neolithic man, and had two settings: freezing and 'Aaaaargh!' Like someone flushing the toilet or turning on the washing machine back home whilst you were still under the water. Now if you've never showered in a group before, let me throw some light on the subject. The first thing is, NEVER get caught looking at someone else's 'tadger', no matter how big it is – although sheer curiosity will get the better of most people.

Secondly, try to stretch your own willy, without being seen, as you have been out in the cold and it has retracted to just a head; and finally face the wall if your pubic region, like mine, was not dissimilar to Kojak's head.

As I mentioned before, whenever you get a gathering of people you always get a smelly twat, a natural-born leader and someone on the same level as pond life. Characters and nicknames soon appeared, and one particular chap just couldn't get anything right; the Corporal christened him in Latin *'semper'*, meaning always, and *'excreta'* meaning, just that: 'Always in shit'. The DIs (drill instructors) knew every trick in the book and were rarely surprised, as 'Semper' soon found to his bemusement and detriment. Mounted on the corridor wall, near the back doors of the block, was a public telephone, so we could phone home and tell everyone what a terrible time we were having.

'Someone has written a telephone number on the wall, next to the phone; WHO WAS IT?'

No answer, came the stern reply.

'It wouldn't have been you, would it, Semper?'

'No, Corporal,' he replied confidently,

'SO WHY, OUT OF THE WHOLE OF FUCKING ENGLAND, WOULD SOMEONE GIVE ME YOUR NAME WHEN I DIALLED IT?'

'Semper's' arse fell out, and he had an attack of the Elmer Fuds, a wer, a wer: I wonder how that could have happened? Needless to say he spent his first weekend cleaning the walls. The blocks we lived in were a gleaming, dust-free environment, with polished brass and shiny chrome everywhere; the floors were the same, highly polished like glass. They had to be – they were inspected every day, and if you've seen them on TV with the 'white gloves' looking for dust, it was exactly like that. We walked around in our socks so as not to scratch the floors; this made for hours of endless fun, 'polish as you go'. Remember the

~ Early Days ~

blocks being in an 'H' shape? The ringing tones of Corporal Wild's voice echoed, as God summoned me to the other side of the block.

I flew up the stairs and along the corridor in my stockinged feet; it was like something from 'Tom and Jerry'. My feet were going like bee's wings and as I neared the Corporal, I suddenly realised that with the speed I had built up I was going to need a small runway to stop. As I glided gracefully past the Corporal and into the fire bucket full of sand at the end of the corridor, I really didn't think it was possible to fit so many insults into such a small space of time.

2. Gas Chamber

As time moved on and we settled into a routine, the time came for the dreaded Gas Chamber. The very mention of these words would strike fear into the hearts of even the natural-born leader; we never again would see so many macho men turn into gibbering idiots, the gibbering idiots turn into pond life and hence a new breed of 'Terrorfidius Shit Scaredius' was born. It was, like most things, fear of the unknown.

The basic idea was for us to get a 'small' whiff of the gas (CS gas is an irritant which attacks the eyes, nose and soft, damp, fleshy parts of one's body, and is used for crowd control).

The term 'small' can be defined in many ways; in practice and in the way it was used, I should just like a similar 'small' win on the lottery. The reality was for us to inhale vast quantities of the damn stuff and snort, sniff and fart our way out of the chamber. We'd heard stories of people diving through windows and punching corporals – this would be the perfect opportunity to stick one on God Wild; alas, as time went on we realised he was there to help and not to hinder us. We donned our 'snug'-fitting respirators (yes, you guessed it, snug as a pea in a tin) and checked each other for leaks.

All satisfied, we entered the chamber; the Corporal lit two (whoops, four) CS tablets and we were ordered to walk around the room, circulating the gas. 'No ill-effects yet,' I thought; my heart was pounding in my chest so hard I could feel it in my ears, neck and head – not only this claustrophobic feeling of the mask, but gas as well. I cannot begin to overestimate the sheer panic and fear felt in that room; if someone had said 'Boo!', Andrex would have had to take on additional staff to cope with the extra demand, but as we circled our confidence grew. Aha! – not as bad as it was made out to be, until ...

'During time of war, you will be required to change your canister' (the filter element screwed onto the side of the respirator).

'This can be made easier by changing each other's canisters.'

All sorts of scenarios flew through my mind – the 'what-ifs'.

'Pick a partner to change with and prepare,' the Corporal said. Everyone picked their closest buddy with lightning speed and I was left with 'Semper'!

Oh fuck! – fuck, fuck and more fuck, piss, shit and bollocks! I could well die, right here in this chamber!

'So on the command "change canisters", you will take a deep breath and unscrew your partner's canister, pass it behind your back and then replace it.'

Sounds simple enough, I thought, and so we did. I took 'Semper's' off; he took mine off with remarkable skill for one so inept, and refitted it. I, on the other hand, dropped his while it was behind my back. With all the confusion and gas, I couldn't see a thing, and it was made worse by the rest of the lads playing football with his canister. There was a splendid slurping and farting noise coming from 'Semper's' corner, as he gulped lungfuls of gas and I pissed myself laughing; after a while the Corporal refitted his canister and sent him outside. We thought that was it – piece of piss – until ...

'On the command "Respirators off" – you will take three deep breaths and remove your respirators; you will then state your name, rank and number before leaving the chamber.'

This sounded well dodgy, and I thought, 'I've fucking done it now.' We all started breathing more deeply immediately – it sounded like a porn film (not that I've seen any; it's just what I've heard, you understand). We all took our respirators off at the same time and started to recite our names, ranks and numbers.

This was fine if you were at the correct end of the queue; fortunately, by some strange coincidence I was near the door, so:

'Novak, Airman P1234567,' I spluttered, and thought that was it: freedom city.

To my absolute horror the Corporal said, 'Sorry, Novak, I didn't quite catch that – can you say it again?' I had already used up all my air thinking I was home free; there was nothing for it – a short gulp and my head was on fire, lips burning, eyes streaming, snot flowing, but I managed it and off I went; and if you think that was bad, there were another twelve blokes behind me.

After we had all performed impressions of airplanes, arms outstretched and weaving from side to side to allow the air to flow around us outside, it was back to the shower – a nice, hot shower. We looked like we'd just won the world onion-peeling championships. Kit off and into the shower, red hot. Do you remember the bit about the soft, damp, fleshy parts? Well, the hot water rained down like acid on my poor trouser snake (or trouser worm, at least).

I tried to cool the temperature down, but what I didn't mention is that there was only one control for the whole of the showers. I tried to adjust it gently, but the control was stiff; it shot across to 'cold' and snow came from the shower heads. That small error of judgement led to a severe whipping on the arse and legs from thirteen towels, one rough 'thwack' catching me right on the edge of my 'love spuds' and causing me to yelp like a scalded pup.

Back on the parade square, and more shouting. One thing I just couldn't grasp: whenever you're stood still for any period of time, the brain becomes bored and says, 'I'll have a quick snooze,' and the body starts to gently sway. I remember seeing this – and so did the Corporal.

'Stand fucking still; you is not a daffodil blowing gently in the breeze – passing out and fainting are not allowed.'

It happened to the lad next to me, so I went to steady him.

'Novak, what the fuck are you doing?'

'I was just going to ...'

'You was just fucking nothing; get back in rank.'

I could see he wasn't well at all as he tilted gracefully towards the ground; the nose usually contacts the concrete first, followed shortly by the rest of your mush. A wonderful display of psychedelic colours can be found under the nose of a fainted airman. The thing was, we were forbidden to stop them falling or to assist in any way, shape or form; sway, sway, stagger and splat! Blood and snot everywhere.

~ Gas Chamber ~

One thing the DIs loved doing was making fun of our names, as they were usually read out in reverse – Novak R, Smith J, etc. – and so poor Andrew Pig was called 'Pig A', to which we would normally reply, 'Present, Corporal,' but in this instance the Corporal called out:

'A. Pig, A. Pig – who is A Pig?' and Andrew, bless him, replied:

'Me, Corporal,' as though he hadn't heard that one a thousand times at school; but the Corporal thought it was funny, and who were we to disagree? It had been rumoured that PMC (Personnel Management Centre) Insworth, where our service numbers were generated, did have a sense of humour.

Our service numbers consisted of an initial letter, followed by seven digits; this was our total identity. There were many Browns and many Smiths, so you could be identified by your name and service number; but Novak P. 1234567 is a bit of a mouthful, and so it was shortened to your name and 'last three' – Novak 567 etc. I pitied the poor twat whose name was Bond, with his last three as 007.

I wasn't sure what trade Andrew was going in for, but if it was the RAF Police he would have no fucking life at all. Drill and more drill, PT and classroom activities kept us busy for the most part, but the cleaning was demoralising.

I'd heard tales of people scratching the paint off their toothpaste tubes and 'bulling' (polishing) them to a high gleam, but that turned out to be total bollocks. The tiled floors in the ablutions, however, which were of the red, raised-and-grooved type, collected toe jam and excess skin with vigour; they had to be spotless. Hours and hours were spent with wire brushes, making sure that not a scrap of skin was found.

Sinks and toilet bowls had to be hair- and turd- free; even behind the U-bend was inspected, any faults would be recorded, passed to the senior man and we'd get another fucking 'bull night' (domestic evening) until it was right. Initially we had to polish the floors with 'hand buffers', a great weight with a piece of cloth underneath, on a broom handle.

There was much confab about how best to achieve a high polish – some said let the polish dry, put another coat on and keep doing that; others said polish it while it's still wet. It's too mundane to go into detail, but we achieved the required results.

After we had proved that we could get the desired shine with the hand buffers, we were eventually given an electric one with a rotating disc underneath. We actually had to buy the yellow dusters that went underneath the buffer, which was a real pisser, so I took my revenge by sitting on the buffer as someone else polished – that was until the motor burned out. Like all RAF equipment it was numbered and dated with a test sticker, so there was no way we could swap it for another flight's buffer.

We were threatened with a 'collective charge', which basically meant we'd all get done for the same offence and have to pay for it, but nothing came of it. But when the truth did come out and I got the biggest bollocking of my career to date, and was asked by my senior man, 'What have you learned from this, Novak'?

I replied, 'To sit on some other twat's buffer!'

Bed packs: if you've never done one or heard of them, think of a Bassett's liquorice allsorts and imagine it made up of neatly folded bed sheets, with white in the centre, two dark layers either side and then your bedspread wrapped around the outside. Crisp folds, square corners – and it had to be perfectly symmetrical, placed at the head of the bed in the centre with two pillows on top. This was definitely an art, and took up far too much time; we tried to cheat by using cardboard and safety pins, leaving it made up and sleeping in 'maggots' (sleeping bags), but the bastard inspecting always seemed to know. I tried in vain, only to have my masterpiece (which took over an hour to achieve) thrown out of the window by the Corporal several times; he even let me throw it out myself once, saying:

'Still shite, Novak – shall I? Or would you like the honour?'

I felt a strange and bizarre pleasure in throwing my own bed pack out of the window, only to have to walk around to the front of the block and bring it back and start all over again. At least it was one less time that Corporal Wild had done it, and I felt we really connected, just for a second.

It was still the first week and we were as full as farts with information, although no home visits for the first two weeks; I thought they must have lost too many on the first week after letting them go home. We had started to become 'a flight' now; we could march, drill and had the basic understandings of the rank structure and the difference between NCOs and officers, of which we were constantly reminded – as well as the fact that NCOs worked for a living and officers did not.

The natural order took hold in the barrack room and little cliques formed amongst the thirteen men and one boy. I latched onto two Scottish brothers – giants they were, from Glasgow, and was the only one in the flight that didn't keep asking them, 'What did you say?' I found that I had a flair for mimicking accents and was able to do just about everyone's by the end of the six weeks.

Still, things would go mysteriously missing and accusations would fly; occasionally it would end up in a brawl, but generally things sorted themselves out.

The constant moaning about who was getting which job on the next bull night was incessant; a couple of the 'I'm-allergic-to-dust' brigade tried it on, but were simply told that if they wanted to be on shit-pans the rest of their time here, they were welcome.

One of the more interesting times was definitely our trip to the MO (medical officer), to be inspected in just about every orifice you could imagine. Prodded, poked, having light shone in your eyes, your tongue pulled so that you gagged, and of course the dreaded 'dick inspection' –didn't bother me, though: not much dick to inspect and I knew it hadn't been anywhere!

Tales soon got out about Big Jock: that when the MO lifted up his 'tadger' with the pencil and said 'Cough,' Jock had given a little cough. 'Big one,' the MO had said. 'D'ye think so?' Jock had replied gleefully. Jabbed and sugar-cubed, we were then checked for nits, ticks, fleas and lice, and there was more than one who was squirted with the white powder, pants and all. It made me shiver, for I had a lot to learn about 'VD', as it was then called, and the RAF spared no expense in showing us detailed photographs of the most horrific cases of gonorrhoea and syphilis I'd ever seen. It was enough to put you off sex for life.

They did the same with the drugs and alcohol films, and I have to say it really worked on the drugs side – but they failed dismally on the drink!

The SGT policeman giving the lecture had a wooden case, the contents of which were closely guarded and contained all the drugs of the day – marijuana, cannabis, cocaine, acid: or LSD as he called it. As I looked around at the sea of familiar faces, there was a good deal of nudging and nodding going on, with the odd comment just out of earshot. It was then that I realised just how inexperienced I really was. I saw images of a man who had tried to hack his wife's head off with an axe, thinking she was a serpent; a man who had sanded his arm down to the bone believing he had creatures crawling beneath his skin; just awful, awful images.

I'd never even smelt grass or pot, never mind smoked it; I was as green as the proverbial herb itself. We were told, 'Under no circumstances will any illegal drugs be tolerated.' Anyone found smoking, buying, selling or even experimenting would be immediately 'dishonourably discharged'. That meant the corner of your 'blue book' (service record, similar to an NVQ file today, but passport-sized) would be clipped, thus rendering you unemployable after you left the service.

I suppose drug taking must have gone on, but if it did, they were doing a damn fine job of concealing it.

Many hours were spent in the cinema, where the information films were the standard of the day, even though I think those coal-powered, top-loading Betamax video recorders, the size of a fridge, were just emerging onto the market.

A cinema is a cinema, whether you're a civilian or in the service. When the lights go down the dead arms, slapping, flicking of ears and punching began, not forgetting the golf-ball-sized sweet wrappers that bounced off heads like hailstones. And on more than one occasion, Corporal Wild turned into an usherette, his torch scanning the sea of faces, head cocked to one side, looking along the length of his arm and over the top of the torch for the slightest indication of a chewing motion; the only thing missing was the obligatory tray of ice creams.

After we had been shocked, stunned, informed and partially brainwashed, the lights came up and we were told that the cinema would be inspected for 'debris'; but as no one had been eating there wouldn't be any, would there, Fifteen Flight? 'No, Corporal,' was the resounding answer, and to my horror, as I stood up I realised that I had amassed enough sweet wrappers to begin a recycling company. There was nothing else for it; I dropped my beret and shovelled as many papers into it as I could,

'Stand fucking still, Novak – what are you doing?'

'I dropped my beret, Corporal', I replied, knowing I would be passing a bin before we were back outside. The plan was simple: a rolled-up beret looks just the same full of sweet papers as it does empty; I would be able to tip it out before I had to put it back on. I was twisting and turning it so as to compress the papers, and I don't know to this day if that's what the Corporal spotted, or whether he just read my mind.

'Right, Novak, let's see if that beret still fits you – put it on.'

He was now only inches from my face and he could sense the fear. I felt a bit giddy; there was no time to get out of this one. I made a forward scooping motion to get the beret on my head whilst concealing the papers; it went on without losing a single wrapper, and for a brief second I thought I'd done it.

'Come on, lad, pull it down, pull it down' – and as I did, the lumps and bumps were clearly visible.

'Looks like there's something in there, Novak.'

What the fuck could I say? I could feel my sphincter loosening as he spoke; he lifted the beret and the cascade of wrappers tumbled out.

'Drop and give me twenty, you tubby little turd.'

I wouldn't have minded, but it wasn't even me who'd eaten them. I began the twenty press-ups as the lads filed past me; a couple playfully kicked me as they went past, trying to tip me over, and one stood on my fingers,

'I saw that, Smith – get down and join him.'

I couldn't work out who I was in the deeper shit with: the Corporal, or Smith for getting caught. Whenever the Corporal wasn't looking directly at us, we just grunted the numbers, 'Seventeen-uugh! Eighteen-uugh! Nineteen-uugh!' while remaining straight-armed. Without even turning around he said,

'You can both give me five more for cheating.'

Smithy and I just stared at each other and did five more perfect press-ups. I picked up the papers and deposited them in the bin on my way outside, reshaped my beret and 'fell in'.

On my way to the parade ground, I pondered the uses of the beret; they're really useful things – you can carry an awful lot in one, including water over a short distance. When rolled up, they could be used as a soft cosh to stop you talking, and if you kept on talking, they could be reversed so the end with the badge on came down on the back of your head, and that did hurt. It was at the parade ground I discovered that berets could have 'wee' in them too,

'What's that in your beret, Novak?'

'Nothing, Corporal,' I replied enthusiastically.

'Oh yes there is; it's got wee in it.'

He took it off my head and flung it across the parade ground like a Frisbee shouting 'Weeee!' It landed in a heap at the edge of the airfield, looking like 'road kill'. It was beginning to dawn on me that it wasn't going to be me who would put one over on the DIs. As the drill became more technical, we were introduced to Sergeant Lightfoot, a rather appropriate name for a drill instructor, I thought. He was much taller than the Corporal, but just as well turned out; the one main difference was his 'pace stick', a piece of highly polished dark wood with brass ends that was split up the middle – like a pair of compasses, for want of a better description. It also had a brass measuring piece, so the tips of the legs could be opened to exactly thirty inches, or whatever the required pace was, but generally it was thirty. He would then demonstrate the thirty-inch paced march by swivelling the pace stick from one leg to the other in a forward motion, like plotting a course on a ship's map.

He was able to do this with magical ease, and I thought, 'All he needs now is a washing-up bottle stuck on top, and he'd make a great jazz-band leader.' Sgt Lightfoot was from 'God's Country' – Edinburgh! And he took a shine to the two Scottish brothers – until he found out they were from Glasgow.

Then there were the usual put-downs of 'steers and queers' and every insult connected to being Scottish. The brothers were mountains, though, and there's something ironical about having to look up to a person whom you're insulting. The lads never 'flackered'; it all just bounced off them. The sergeant said he spoke 'the Queen's English', and I must admit there were times when his Edinburgh accent sounded almost regal – although if I closed my eyes, he was definitely Mr McKay without the 'tache from the TV series 'Porridge'. His voice was as loud as the Corporal's but had a much sharper sound to it, including some notes that actually went into 'falsetto'; I found this highly amusing and would do barrack-room impressions of him at every opportunity. Even recruits from the room opposite were amazed at the likeness and peered in, out of curiosity, to see me stood there in stockinged feet with a broom under my right arm, simulating a rifle.

We were coming to the end of our second week now, and would be allowed to go home; we had been paid twice, approximately £43 each time – it differed on age and marital status, but that's about what I got. It seemed like a fortune and I was bursting to spend it.

We were marched up to Station Headquarters and given our rail warrants to enable us to travel free of charge. For some of us this was heaven; for others more experienced and older it was shite! A similar coach arrived and collected us, bound for Newark once more, this time in our 'Number One' uniform, the type you see on parades and official ceremonies. Polished peak cap (not slashed), crisply creased jacket with silver buttons (metal-plated – gone were the days of the original brass buttons which had to be 'bulled' to perfection without staining the jacket), and trouser creases you could shave with, topped off with the shiniest shoes you've ever seen.

It seemed like an absolute age since we'd arrived; we had learned so much, we were smart, well behaved for the most part and on our way to becoming professionals. We were definitely bonding; our stories had a familiar air to them now, even from the other flights'; we had something in common, and I took the opportunity to use as many RAF abbreviations as was possible.

Once 'debussed' we made our way onto the platform, some going north, some going south, east and west. I took a moment to look at everyone and pondered: 'I wonder how many will be coming back?' The biggest carrot for some, and the greatest reason not to return for others, was the fact that on our return we would be introduced to rifle drill and weapons training!

Hurrah!!!

3. It's Not a Gun

After marching through my council estate in my 'Number One' uniform, I rounded the corner into the cul-de-sac. Decorated with shopping trolleys and bicycle frames with one wheel still attached, my house was now in view. I had accrued a number of small children on my short walk from the bus stop to the house, probably because nothing this smart had been seen on our estate unless it was on its way to court! I closed the garden gate behind me, barring the gaggle of urchins and their incessant questioning.

'Have you killed anyone?' 'Where's your gun?' ...and so on.

To inform them of the difference between the Royal Air Force and the Army would have been a wasted effort, so I didn't. After entering the house and being greeted by the 'Oh, let's have a look at you' crowd, I was pushed into the yard and photographed from every conceivable angle; even now there still survives one of me in a ridiculous, Winston Churchill-style victory pose.

The rest of the weekend was spent drinking in the local, even though I was still under age; my Dad adopted the 'If he's old enough to fight for his country, he's old enough to drink' attitude, and I wasn't going to disagree with him. He was 'pally' with the landlord and had done a couple of shifts behind the bar on occasion, for what was ironically called 'beer money'. I'd only been gone two weeks, but this feeling of being a big fish in a little pond was definitely a welcome change from being bawled at all day long. I told them of the names I was called and what I had been up to during my first weeks. I didn't know it, but my career as a storyteller had already begun and I held the floor for a good couple of hours, until the shandies had me reverting to the boyish giggles and laughter I'd known so well.

I felt great as we sang our way back to the house through the estate. Dad and I talked long into the early hours, as he relived his own time in the RAF through me. He was full of advice, some good, some not so good, and I fell asleep on the couch.

During my first two weeks in the RAF, I had gained so many things but lost one vital one: my girlfriend, Sandy. She had decided that two weeks was long enough to constitute a break-up and had gone off with a 'dwarf' (a boy who was even smaller than me and justifiably so for nicking my bird). I'd knocked on her door and gazed into her beautiful green eyes, cherub face and still nubile figure, only to be told.

'I'm not going out with you any more!'

I was gutted; she had been the image of my fantasies while trying not to get caught, if you remember. What was I going to do now? Well, I still had the memories of experimenting on her in my bedroom and in the coal shed – which was actually devoid of coal, now that even we in the North East had gas central heating. I would continue to rely on my memories for a good deal longer. Isn't it funny that whenever you played doctors and nurses, the girl always wanted to

~ 21 ~

bandage you arm or your head, or put a plaster on your knee? – yet when it was my turn to describe the injury I had, things were slightly different.

'Ah, Mr Novak,' she began, 'I believe you have a poorly leg.'

'No, nurse – I think you'll find it's me willy!'

Sandy was the unfortunate recipient of the regurgitated Pomagne and bottles of Snowball I mentioned in Chapter One; which may have had something to do with the reason why I was 'chucked'. But not before I'd gained those warm, heady memories of heavy petting, tit groping, and tracing her 'shape' through her jeans until I thought my knackers would explode.

Sandy was by no means 'easy' – far from it, and we had discussed 'doing it' and precautions long before we ever tried getting round to it.

I was, as I am still, 'a gentleman' when it comes to sex – considerate, and I placed my Mam's red chequered car rug under her bum to insulate her from the cold concrete floor of the coal house, while loosening her jeans in the blackness of the shed. By the time I had them around her ankles she was asleep in an alcohol-induced slumber. It didn't 'feel right' – and it wasn't. I wanted it to be 'memorable' my first time, not rushed. I had some romantic notion of how it would be, and this was definitely not it.

All said and done, though, if I'd have known it was going to be another four years before I would 'pop my cherry', things might have been very different. But I'm a great believer in fate and what will be, will be. I got her dressed, woke her up and walked her home; said goodbye and puked on her.

Back at Swinderby, it was about nine-thirty pm, Sunday evening, and the bragging was in full swing as I entered the room and threw my kitbag onto my bed. I followed it onto the mattress, staring up at the ceiling, listening to the impossible quantities of ale that had been quaffed, followed by the carnal conquests – which were described in some detail, I might add – and to round off a perfect evening, the obligatory battle which ensued after last orders.

I was both jealous and bored to death; the big Jocks were back, as was the senior man, but no 'Semper!' I wondered if he'd 'bottled it'? There was an air of excitement as time passed by. Who, if anyone, did we think was not coming back, and why? One by one the beds filled up as the night wore on, even 'Semper's', and I must admit that secretly I was a little disappointed that everyone had returned.

After all, there's nothing quite like watching someone else get 'in the shit' when you are OK.

We knew what would be expected of us in the morning and so were almost ready by the time Corporal Wild had finished his morning lament, 'Outside, Fifteen' – and so on to breakfast.

The Corporal had given his orders to the senior man about where we were going after breakfast. A couple of hours in the classroom would allow our breakfast to settle, while terrifying our minds with GDT (Ground Defence Training).

Up until now we had been square bashing and running around the forest, up hill and down dale until I thought I would collapse. We hadn't given any thought whatsoever to WAR – that very thing we were going to be so well trained in!

~ It's Not a Gun ~

While the men amongst us sat at the front, looking interested, I (still at school in my mind) took a seat at the back of the classroom: naive, yes; dumb, no!

I tilted my seat so that the back of it settled against the wall, the chair at forty-five degrees as I swished my legs backwards and forwards. I remembered a time at school, much like now, when the physics teacher, noticing my posture and seat position, dispatched his blackboard rubber in my direction at about Mach three as I daydreamed the day away. The rubber struck the back wall, two inches from my head, with such ferocity that the plume of chalk dust would have silenced McEnroe for a millennium.

The loud bang which accompanied this snapped me back into reality, where the sheer shock and 'startlement' had me saying the words:

'You missed, sir,' to which he replied,

'I aimed to miss, Novak!'

A cold shiver ran down my spine, not knowing if he really was that good a shot or I had just been exceedingly lucky, and so had he – not to blind one of his pupils! As this memory washed over me, I slowly returned my seat to its proper position, so as not to attract attention, learning from my earlier mistake. I might not be so lucky this time, and it might not be a blackboard rubber.

Anyone caught not paying attention, or in any way falling foul of the instructor – which was incredibly easy to do, even when we hadn't done anything – automatically volunteered themselves for whatever it was being demonstrated, usually painful and if not that, then certainly humiliating.

So the rest of the class would wholeheartedly agree with the Corporal, whatever it was we were supposed to have, or have not, done. But I myself have been in so many armlocks; headlocks and other types of holds that I might have done better to write a book about Origami, the ancient art of people folding!

The GDT involved NBC (Nuclear, Biological and Chemical) warfare.

This involved the instructors telling, showing and acting out scenarios in such detail that we wondered if we'd ever survive any type of attack at all! It must have been a dream job, to see so much fear on the faces of so many (not Winston Churchill); but for every terror they showed us, they also showed us how to avoid, be prepared for and or treat any eventuality – or at least that was the aim!

'N for nuclear': we'd seen many an OHP (overhead projector) slide about the distances from 'ground zero' (a term I think we're all familiar with now) at which you could expect to be 'vaporised' – nice. But the advice we were given was 'Place your head between your knees ...' (and I thought, 'Oh, hang on, that's OK for a plane crash, but ...') – '... and kiss your arse goodbye,' the Corporal carried on.

If you were outside that radius, you could expect to be at least impaled on something or other, have something of great mass hit you, or if you really hit the jackpot, become a missile yourself! Outside that zone – which incidentally was colour-coded, much like a traffic light – as to your expected rate of survival, you could expect 'THE RADIATION'. This came in three measures: alpha-particles, beta-particles and the dreaded gamma radiation, which is the one that actually does the most damage.

Alpha-particles, apparently (I say apparently because I have neither the equipment nor the expertise to find out if it is so), can be stopped by a sheet of paper.

Beta-particles will require approximately two feet of earth to protect you; and gamma radiation will 'X-ray' you if you do not have about your person at least six inches of good-quality lead.

One is bound to wonder whether those suspicious *Lederhosen* that the Germans wore were in fact lead pants; after all, once your testicles are irradiated, you will not be fathering any more children – but I digress!

If their intent was to scare, to teach by fear definitely worked; it certainly got your attention!

'B for biological': the film 'Outbreak' pretty much sums up what a weapon of this kind, or any other biological agent, is capable of (the more senior readers will remember the anthrax experiment), but it has one elementary drawback: its dichotomy as a weapon. Once released, it is unpredictable to a certain extent and cannot be controlled, whereas something ALL forces demand of their weapons is control.

Unlike nuclear and chemical, it is very difficult to detect and, as we have seen recently with the SARS virus, it cannot be contained within a 'battlefield' and/or country. Basically, you can't see it, touch it, taste it, smell, hear or feel it; by the time you get it; you're in deep shit!

Your best hope is that there is an antidote.

'C for chemical': and it doesn't take a genius to work out that what you have under your kitchen sink, if it is not properly used or is ingested accidentally, can cause a great deal of pain or indeed be fatal.

Ergo, it should come as no surprise that man has become extremely adept at devising potions that are a) extremely harmful, and b) not easily detectable – 'By the time you've sniffed it you're dead,' which is a direct quote from one of the instructors at Swinderby. So how the fuck are we meant to protect ourselves from such a weapon? I enquire in my mind before allowing some words to burble from my previously sealed lips:

'Preparation, airman – preparation and training.'

The two chemicals of the day in 1981 were 'blood agent' and 'nerve gas', the latter having been used in the Tokyo train-station attack. Blood agent I can remember little about, although it had something to do with drowning in your own body fluids and, quite frankly, I'm becoming nauseous just trying to remember anything more about it.

Just as our lesson was coming to a close, or so we thought, out came the 'Combo Pen' – a very, very big syringe with a pill in the top. It was an 'intramuscular' injection kit containing atropine, and the pill I think was morphine. The syringe was about four inches long and contained a needle inside of almost the same length; there were three of these in one's personal kit.

Lo and behold, a volunteer was required, and on this occasion it was Nassau. I don't know why he was picked; he just was.

'At the onset of a nerve-gas attack,' the Corporal began, 'you will experience the following symptoms' – and he went on to describe some pretty awful stuff.

'You will remove one of your combo pens –thus.'
Nassau was now on the floor in a semi-prone position,
'Flipping the top off the combo pen, you will ingest the tablet.' (He mimicked this with Nassau.)
'You will then thrust the pen into your thigh muscle.'

He mimicked this too, and Nassau's face contorted, as did ours, as we all leaned back in our seats and thought the four-inch needle had actually penetrated his leg; by the look on his face, so did he!

The instructors loved it, a roller coaster of emotion that could only exist in a training situation, where you are afraid of what you are being taught, but felt privy to information not on general release! That may save your life. It never occurred to me that when I eventually left the RAF, all this protective kit would be left behind; although obtainable through unapproved sources, walking around with an S6 respirator and a pack of combo pens strapped to my side would certainly draw unwanted attention.

In any case, in the event of a surprise attack, how long would it be before it was wrestled off my face by some thug who didn't know how to use it? 'Survival of the biggest.'

It was now time for our 'carrot'! Finally we would be getting our hands on the rifle – not 'gun': to call it this was a mortal sin. It is, and was, a weapon. Alas, these were not the ones we were to fire on the range; these were very old Lee Enfield .303 bolt-action rifles, made from wood, and modified, or just allowed to wear so much, that the metal cocking and firing parts would shake and rattle as the weapon was handled.

I gather this was the desired effect, and it made a fantastic 'cracking' sound when eventually we were able to 'Present' and 'Shoulder' arms as required. So it was off to the parade square, once more to learn how to march and salute, but this time with a rifle.

There was much throwing up, down, forwards and backwards of rifles, and when the Corporal wasn't looking, there was always one clever twat who thought he could do the American twirling display with his rifle – which inevitably ended with him dropping it. The Corporal might not have been able to see, but the sound of a dropped rifle is a very distinct one, not unlike someone dropping a tray of knives and forks followed eventually by the tray itself, and it was punishable by death (if you took the Corporal literally). These rifles had been dropped more times than Neil from the Young Ones.

'But not on my fucking parade ground,' Corporal Wild bellowed. 'I have eyes and ears like an eagle owl,' he continued.

'I can hear a rat fart at fifty yards – do I make myself clear?' The perpetrator was singled out and paraded in front of us,

'Drop and give me twenty, you numb c***.' From humour to terror in the blink of an eye; this was serious!

'This is not a toy, it is a weapon; this is your best friend. If you look after it, it will look after you. You will eat, sleep and even shit with it if need be; it may even save your life some day, although YOU don't deserve it!'

I'd never seen him like this before; he really meant it. I could see why, though; if we were complacent now with a wooden rifle, what would we be like when we had 'live' ammunition on the range? It was well and truly nipped in the bud, and we took rifle drill extremely seriously after that. We marched to the armoury and handed in our Lee Enfields through the two-foot-square, barred window for the last time. The next time we would be collecting the 7.62mm SLR (Self Loading Rifle).

I personally was looking forward to it; I had always had an air pistol, air rifle or catapult at home and was quite a good shot. I'd already stripped down my air rifle in an attempt to put washers behind the spring, so as to make it more powerful, but all I had succeeded in doing was putting so many in that the spring had become 'coil bound'; this is where the spring is compressed to such a degree that it becomes solid and you cannot cock the rifle.

No matter: removing one or two had the desired effect and I was back in business with my telescopic sights. Many a 'spuggy' (sparrow) had its wings clipped or was minus a few tail feathers as I stalked the bushes of the old mine works. But I will never forget the 'thwack' I heard when I actually killed one! It really upset me. One minute it was chirping in the trees; the next it was lying on the ground because of me – and this was something else that didn't feel right.

After that I assigned myself to shooting targets, bottles and cans; I had really become quite proficient with it as my targets got smaller and smaller. So as we collected our SLRs from the armoury, never a thought was given to the fact that I might be called upon to kill a man one day! The green metal hatch groaned as it opened outwards to reveal the two-foot window once more.

We lined up in alphabetical order, and would do so any time we collected weapons from or deposited them to the armoury; this was so you got the same rifle each time, and so any damage or misuse could be tracked down immediately. It was also because, for the duration of your stay at Swinderby, this was 'your' rifle.

We were encouraged to give them names and characters – obviously women's names, although it never ceased to amaze me just how diverse a group of men could be? Taffy's was 'The Widow Maker' – although his pronunciation of it somewhat took the edge off and had me pissing myself laughing.

'I'll fucking have you, Novak,' he said in his broad accent, but I was still laughing. That cost me an extra-tight headlock and a knuckle rub all over my face. I'm not sure if 'First Blood' with Sylvester Stallone as John Rambo had been shown yet, but Taffy had definitely seen too many war films.

Taff was a good deal older than the rest; loud, brash and very physical, he'd been a scrum half for some team or other and was constantly putting people in a headlock, asking them to 'Get out of that, boyo' – whereupon we would twist and turn as our heads turned purple, not wanting to be outdone by this stocky Welshman.

It was of course a method for seeing who was the strongest or toughest: the oldest natural urge, and he was up there with the big Jocks from Glasgow, who would open beer bottles with their teeth.

~ It's Not a Gun ~

We were handed our rifles 'butt first' for two reasons: so as not to be looking down the barrel, and because pointing a weapon, loaded or unloaded, at someone was unforgivable, right up there akin to dropping it. The advice went like this.

'Basically, the only time you will point a weapon at anyone is if you intend to kill them. Secondly, it is so you can see into the 'chamber' where the ammunition would normally be, thus ensuring the rifle is "safe" to handle and there is no chance of an ND (negligent discharge) where the rifle goes off accidentally.' (This never happens, according to the Corporal; rifles do not just go off, they are fired by means of the trigger.)

'Anyone having an ND on my shift will be picking his teeth out of the butt of his rifle! Am I clear?'

Once more we turned into the 'Churchill dog':

'Oh, YES!'

'On receiving your weapon' – and there was the usual mumble of 'knob gags' – 'you will check to see that the chamber is clear. On seeing it is clear, you will take hold of the cocking handle thus, pulling it smartly to the rear and then releasing it. The working parts will go forward; you will then place the safety catch here – are you getting this, Semper?' (he nods frantically) – 'to the "R" for round position. "S" is for safe; "R" is for round, which means firing. You will then squeeze the trigger, not pull; you do not "pull" the trigger, you squeeze. Are you a puller or a squeezer, Novak?'

'Squeezer, Corporal.'

'Very good. I do not want any "pullers" on my range! After firing off the action, you will hold the weapon at your side. You will not aim at low-flying aircraft, nor will you try to frighten the crows at the top of the hangar. Anyone caught in any other pose than I have described will "drop and give me twenty." What will you do, Fifteen?'

'Drop and give you twenty, Corporal,' accompanied by lots of nods.

We also collected two empty magazines (the thing that holds the bullets, to the uninitiated) and placed them in our pockets.

'As you can see, unlike the Lee Enfield this weapon has a "pistol grip", so it is slightly different to carry while marching.'

It was actually easier, as you could cup your hand around it, which bore the considerable weight whilst pulling it into the shoulder. Back in the classroom once more – only an open one, no chairs or tables this time; just mats on the floor.

We placed the rifle on the mat with the two magazines and gathered around the enlarged picture on the wall. The Corporal then explained how it worked, its weight, length and every other statistic connected with the SLR. Just as we were getting bored with all this: 'It will kill at approximately one mile' – and we were again interested. I was dying to get my hands on it, just to feel it, aim it and, if I was totally honest, 'play with it'.

'OK, back to your mats and familiarise yourself with your weapon' – again the knob gags etc., but I'd got my wish. I touched, felt and inspected every inch of that rifle, and this one was mine. It had three numbers on the butt and I was to

~ DROP AND GIVE ME TWENTY! ~

ingrain them into my memory so that I could always pick up 'my' rifle and not someone else's.

The rough-and-tumble trades, i.e., anything other than medic or clerk, got well stuck in as we were shown how to strip and reassemble it; while the aforementioned trades held the weapon at arm's length, as if it were about to go off at any moment.

'Get hold of it, ya great big Jessie; it won't bite you.'

It was time for another speech by the Corporal.

4. On the Range

Grasping the rifle with both hands, one on the stock and one on the pistol grip, holding it shoulder high, he began:

'This is a weapon or rifle; it is not a gun, gat, bang-stick, or any other childish fucking name you can come up with – believe me, we've heard them all. It is designed for one purpose and one purpose only – to kill, not to maim or wound. If you are in a situation where you have to fire this weapon against an enemy, rest assured it will do its job, providing you have done yours, i.e., kept it in clean working order and know how to use it correctly. This includes knowing what to do if the weapon jams. Another word you will not use is "bullets"; they are "rounds", OK?'

('YES!')

'If I hear of anyone putting "bullets" in their gun, I will personally rip off their arms and beat them to death with the soggy ends. Am I clear?'

'Yes, Corporal,' was the resounding reply.

We stripped, rebuilt and again stripped the weapons many times. It was quite tricky, and the less dextrous among us were all fingers and thumbs, the trickiest part being the 'gas plug' part of the automatic loading system, which was under some considerable spring pressure.

It was only about an inch long, the circumference of a thimble, and had to be inserted into the rifle towards the barrel end and turned ninety degrees to lock it into position. Many times 'Semper's' gas plug became airborne, launching itself across the room, swiftly followed by the dog-like patter as he pursued it on his hands and knees trying to retrieve it. Eventually we were all at a reasonable enough standard to progress to magazine filling. There is a definite technique required to do this and although we were shown the official RAF method, you were allowed to diversify slightly if it was more comfortable, or if you could do it more quickly.

Competitions were held to see who could fill a magazine of twenty rounds the quickest, but it didn't half make your fingers sore. After many, many lessons, we could strip and reassemble the weapon blindfolded (literally) and were ordered to stand on the bench on one leg and sing the national anthem when we had finished. Boing! – we could hear 'Semper's' gas plug ricocheting of the walls, while trying not to laugh. The Corporal got so fed up with him that he made him strip his weapon down and lay it out on the mat; still with his blindfold on, he kicked 'Semper's' parts all over the room and made him crawl around to find them and reassemble the rifle.

It was funny at first, but then not so much, as he struggled to put it back together. The DIs could be cruel at times, and it was a very fine line, which could easily be overstepped, from mockery to total humiliation in an instant.

Having perfected our rifle drills, we would soon be on the range itself, and I was almost beside myself wanting to demonstrate my shooting skills. There was one thing I didn't understand, and this is a perfect example of military logic.

'When the red flag is flying the range is safe,' the Corporal said, but this was a different Corporal, an RAF Regiment Corporal. The Regiment's main task was the defence of airfields; the simplest way of describing what they did was to say they were the army of the RAF, gung-ho and weapons-orientated. Surely red in most situations means danger? And when the flag is flying? I still think it should have been the other way around: if you can't see a flag, the range is safe, but if a red flag is flying it means the range is in use and live firing is under way. But no – it was the way it was! There was always the belief that if a simple task could be made more difficult, then just leave it to the military.

It was still March and still freezing. On the day of our live firing, and after a final stint in the classroom to make sure we were proficient in all our drills, we made our way to the live firing range – a twenty-five-metre range (about eighty feet in old money). This was the only time in my career when I was told that I could put my hands in my pockets to keep them warm, before entering the range; cold, slow hands and live ammunition do not mix.

The rifles were already on the range and were not our own; these were specially modified SLRs and only 0.22 calibre (5.56 mm) As we queued outside the range, some bristled with excitement, myself included, while others shook with trepidation. It was a heady time for me; I had been waiting to fire a real 'gun' for years. (There – I've said it.)

We queued in alphabetical order again, and we knew whom we were in front of and behind, providing the full complement was present; being an 'N' meant I was roughly in the middle. It was time for our final speech before entering the range.

'You are about to enter a "live firing" range; these are real ...' (for a second I thought he was going to say 'bullets', but no such luck) '... weapons with real live rounds. If there is anyone who has any doubts as to any of the drills or handling of the weapon, NOW is the time to speak up. DO NOT wait until you are in-fucking-side and lying down behind it!' (What a novel way of swearing, I thought – and there was more to come.) A hand went up and we all prayed it wouldn't be 'Semper's'. It wasn't.

'Will we be firing our own weapons today, Corporal?' someone said.

'Abso-fucking-lutely,' came the reply.

'Once you have successfully fired the small bore .22, ANYONE, AND I MEAN ANYONE, pointing a weapon at me or anything other than the target, will be immediately kicked to death by members of the range staff. Do I need to repeat myself? [shake, shake, shake] You will keep the weapon pointing down the range at ALL TIMES! Any other questions or doubts, SPEAK NOW!'

We all had doubts, lots of them, but we'd be here all day if we voiced them all. I wondered how many other people were worried that one of us was going to throw a 'wobbler' and shoot everyone else, because I was! As far as their behaviour with weapons was concerned, I didn't know them from Adam; it could be any one of us. The corporal knocked on the range door and we heard a heavy bolt slide across.

'OK, first five – in you go!'

The door closed and the bolt slammed across once more. We listened intently as the orders were given for real.

'Pick a mat and get down behind the weapon; next to you, you will find a magazine of ten rounds. Listen for the command, make sure your safety catch is at safe. ...' (a physical check was necessary, not just a look) 'If at any time you hear the command STOP – you will freeze. Suppose the man next to you has blood oozing from every orifice, you will not fucking move – am I clear?' [Definitely.] There were people with their ear pressed hard to the outside of the range door, and we jostled for a place to hear what was going on inside.

'Directly in front of you is a target. That is your target and no one else's; you will fire at that one only. You will not shoot at the man's next to you, or anything else for that matter. You will aim for the centre of the body, you are not Al Ca-fucking-pone; ...' (and he was off again) '... you will not wing, clip, shoot for the head or kneecap the target. Do you understand?' ... [Yes, hurry the fuck up!] '... Listen for the command: with a magazine of ten rounds – LOAD.'

A good deal of metallic clicking was heard – and then one extra one.

'STOP!!!'

And ten of us leapt in unison away from the door; something had definitely gone wrong! We did not need to have our ears to the door to hear this.

'Number 1, put that fucking weapon down and step away from the mat.'

There was a short silence that seemed like an eternity.

'Did I tell you to cock that weapon? Did I? At any time, did you hear me give the order for you to fire at that target?'

'No, Corporal.' He hadn't fired, but was only one step away from removing the safety catch and squeezing the trigger.

'GET OFF my fucking range; you are not safe to be on my range.'

The door flew open and an extremely harassed airman was ejected vigorously. Davies slid down the grass of the small incline outside the range, remaining on his feet whilst demonstrating the 'backward leg shuffle' perfected by many a 'Tex Avery' cartoon character. He was genuinely dazed as he stood there, not knowing what to do.

We flocked around him like a battery of hens, wanting to know what he'd done wrong, so as not to make the same mistake ourselves He just couldn't speak.

'Come on, ya twat, out with it,' someone said. 'What happened?'

'I don't know; one minute I was putting on the magazine – the next I was out here!'

Well, this had really unsettled the coop, but it wasn't long before the range door opened again and Davies was taken to one side. The last thing we really needed was scaring any more than we already were.

Davies was ushered to the end of the queue and, shall we say, given a quick refresher. At least he would have time to reflect on his minor indiscretion and talk to the lads who had already fired. On his way back into the range the

Corporal collected a wide-eyed airman at the front, to take Davies's place, the door slammed and they went through the same routine, without any problems this time.

'With a magazine of ten rounds – LOAD' [no extra click]. 'In your own time, at the target in front – GO ON.'

There was that silence again; who was going to be the first to fire? And then a 'pop' – the first shot was fired, and then several 'pops'; they were under way. A short time later the range fell silent, the door opened and five airmen emerged with grins from ear to ear and one saying, 'Piece of piss.' They were ten feet tall, weapons veterans – or at least you would have thought so. Tucking their thumbs into their imaginary braces – and they'd only fired a .22 rifle! The same bore as your peashooter rifle back home.

The recoil or 'kick' in the shoulder was equal to someone tapping you to get your attention. My turn now. Even though we were in alphabetical order outside the range, once inside we were to pick a mat and lay down behind the weapon on it, much as we had heard from the outside. 'Semper' was in my group of five and there was no fucking way I was going to be next to him; so as we were ushered through the door, I made a bolt for the mat furthest from it.

It seemed like a good ploy! And so it was, until later. We got down behind the weapon, with the magazine next to it, and went through the same drills as we'd heard.

'With a magazine of ten rounds – LOAD.'

The rifle had more in common with its showground counterpart than we were aware of; the sights were set up for Quasimodo and Marti Feldman. It was my opinion that the exercise 'real' was not to hit the target at all – just to introduce us to applying a magazine which contained live rounds and then releasing them without the proverbial duck shoot or the maiming of the range staff. Why do you think they were only 0.22 calibre? If mistakes were to be made, now was the time to be making them, and not with the 7.62mm ammunition which could kill at a mile distance.

It was a reasonable insurance policy by the range staff, I'm sure you'll agree. On we went, with little puffs of sand jumping up as the rounds buried themselves in the butts at the end of the range. One striking memory I still have is of the scorching smell of cordite (burnt gunpowder); it was akin to 'Castrol R' or 'Belray MC1', the two-stroke oil we used in our illegal scramble bikes at home. It was addictive, something that couldn't be copied anywhere else. It caught the back of your throat, but was lovely to boot! And this was just from the small-bore 'test firing'; I would practically cream my pants when it came to the 'big gun'.

Everyone else went through without any more major traumas; even Davies had composed himself enough to stop shaking and told us he felt pretty confident by the time the back of the queue had snaked its way through the green door. He emerged triumphant and we congratulated him 'en masse', because while it was funny to watch someone else get 'in the shit' we really didn't want anyone 'back-flighted' (sent to a flight usually one or two weeks behind us), for two reasons. One was that it meant we had failed to encourage and/or recognise that this individual had a particular problem with weapons; and secondly, there would be real human emotion at losing one of our group!

It did happen, but not with Davies and not with weapons. Before we could leave the range, we were lined up outside and required to give a solemn declaration thus:

'I have no live rounds or empty cases in my possession, Corporal.'

While it sounds like the simplest thing to say, you would be amazed at just how many variations could be heard as the range staff started at the 'A' end of the queue and worked their way towards the other.

'I HAVE live rounds,' one began.

'You'd better fucking not have,' the Corporal replied, and he began again.

'I have no cases of live rounds,' someone else said, and it began to deteriorate quickly.

'Just how fucking dumb are you? Can you not remember a short sentence? I'm sure if it were a girl's telephone number or address, you would abso-fucking-lutely be able to remember that.'

The laughter trickled its way to the end and the Corporal got his declaration from everyone concerned. It dawned on me that someone must have actually stolen live rounds or empty cases for it to be necessary.

The chickens that had flocked around Davies had now become roosters, clucking and strutting as we marched towards the airmen's mess for lunch.

Little thought was given to what was on offer, and much thought was given to our first 'live fire' and to drawing our own weapons from the armoury after lunch for 'the big one' – the 7.62 mm live fire. During lunch Davies was seen as both donkey and hero of the morning; no one wanted to go first but we all wanted to know what had gone wrong, and he came through it all still smiling, 'Top bloke', the 'piece-of-piss' merchant from the first firing group, however, was full of disparaging remarks about Davies, and how he'd 'let the side down'. The fact that there wasn't yet a side to let down (as far as shooting went) and the only person he'd disappointed was himself, came as no surprise.

We were only three weeks into our training, and as quickly as bonds could be made, they could be broken even more quickly! What a 'knobhead'.

There was much talk over lunch about acquiring one's 'marksman's badge' – although I wondered what exactly would be required of us to get this badge, which was a small piece of material baring the image of a pair of crossed rifles and was to be sewn onto the left arm of one's uniform and worn with pride. Still, it was something to 'aim' for (if you'll forgive the pun); while the RAF did its best to drag us down to the same level, and then build us up as required, we did our best to remain individuals, or at least have something the rest did not, and in my case it was a marksman's badge.

Back outside and into our line of threes as we made our way to the armoury, collected our 7.62mm SLRs and then we were onto the range once more. We had absolutely no concept as to the difference between the 0.22 that we had already fired and the 7.62 (ask anyone who has fired one, except the RAF Regiment, who would call you a big poof if you even spoke about the recoil of an SLR). Into our alphabetical line we went again, and Davies was in his correct place and looking OK.

The main difference this time was that the range staff arrived with a cardboard box full of 'ear defenders'. We looked at each other as we dipped in and picked a pair, wondering why we needed them now but hadn't this morning. We would soon find out! The familiar green door swung open and the first five were lifted into the range, same as before; down behind the weapon and:

'With a magazine of twenty rounds – LOAD.'

Much clicking, as some of us had our ear defenders tilted at ninety degrees, so that the 'muffs' rested on our temples and not over our ears.

'We are now going to "zero" your weapon – that is, to adjust the iron sight so that it enables you to hit the target accurately and constantly' [if only].

'You will fire five, not four or six, but five shots at the target in front, aiming at the same spot each time – which will be the centre of the body. Am I clear?'

'Yes, Corporal.'

'Listen for the command. At the target in front for grouping – GO ON.'

The same short silence and I assumed that the first person that fired last time would do the same now! BANG!!! The first shot rang out; anyone leaning with their back against the wall snapped forward to an angle of ninety degrees so that their arses pushed them away from the wall. That's why we needed the ear defenders.

The noise was incredible. 'Fuck me,' said one of the big jocks, followed by as many expletives as one could imagine from the rest of the flight.

And suddenly we were not so keen to 'Get it on!' The range door opened and five very sullen airmen emerged with their rifles, rubbing their right shoulders.

'How'd it go? What's it like?'

We gawped before being dragged inside again. I bolted for the mat furthest from the door, the last to the right; 'Semper' was at position one or two.

'We will now "zero" your weapon.'

As we'd heard from outside, I placed my rifle on the mat and lay down behind it.

'With a magazine of twenty rounds – LOAD.'

I picked up the rifle and tilted it to forty-five degrees, looked into the magazine to make sure the rounds were the correct way round and clicked it into place, giving it a little shake to make sure it wasn't going to come off once we started firing (this was part of our standard drill).

'You will now fire five shots for grouping; once you have finished you will apply the safety catch, place the weapon on the mat and stand up behind it. Does everyone understand?'

'Yes, Corporal'. Still wearing our ear defenders meant we had to listen that much harder.

'At the target in front – GO ON.'

I'd started to concentrate in my own little world now and forgot that the Corporal was talking to four others; in my mind he was talking only to me.

~ On the Range ~

I squeezed the trigger and the little fat orange man from the Tango advert got a sledgehammer from somewhere and rang the bell on my shoulder!!! Fuck, that hurt! The Corporal could see some of the rifles dancing forward.

'STOP!' he cried.

We applied the safety catches and craned our necks around to see what was up.

'Pull the weapon into the shoulder. The harder you pull it in, the less it will move and the more accurate you will be.'

Nothing about the pain we were experiencing.

'At the target in front – CARRY ON.'

I finished my shots and stood up, with one or two others, while we waited for the rest. All standing now, we were to follow the Corporal down to the target and gloat at our expertise (as if ...). We stood in front of our respective targets and listened to the humorous commentary.

I kept looking back towards my rifle to make sure that some unsuspecting twat hadn't got down behind it and was going to make us all dance! (I too had been watching too many gangster films.)

'Foster, well done; you have succeeded in removing one testicle from this man, rearranging his hair and putting a couple of holes through his FUCKING umbrella IF HE WAS CARRYING ONE!'

The Corporal had a piece of chalk which he would twist in any visible holes in the target, thus making them stand out – different colours for each batch of five rounds.

'Ah, Semper – which target were you firing at? It clearly can't have been this one, AS THERE IS NOT A SINGLE FUCKING HOLE IN IT!'

'It must be the gun, Corporal,' Semper exclaimed! And that was a case of 'Light the blue touch paper and stand well back!' The Regiment Corporal flew into a rage the kind of which I had never seen, nor ever want to witness again.

'GUN! – FUCKING "GUN" – YOU ARE NOTHING MORE THAN THE DEVIL'S OWN DOO DOO!'

And that was it, I was floored – there was no way I could hold this in. I turned my back and lost the plot.

'OH, FUCKING FUNNY IS IT, NOVAK?'

That only made it worse.

'I'm sorry, Corporal; it was just ...'

'IT WAS JUST WHAT?'

'Just what you said, Corporal'.

'DO YOU THINK I'M A FUCKING COMEDIAN, NOVAK?' (He was about six inches from my face now and I was doing my best to look worried; I would have loved to say 'yes').

'While I'm here, let's see what you've managed to do.'

He took his chalk and drilled the five holes in the target, albeit not together; that took some of the wind out of his sails.

'Not bad at all; you must have one of the weapons we've previously used.'

You never got a compliment from an RAF Regiment Corporal, but it was as close as I was gonna get and I languished in its candidness.

He checked the other two targets and we returned to the firing point and got down behind our weapons. The Corporal went along the line tweaking the sights with some sort of special tool to correct any offset the firer was experiencing, hence just five shots. He paused at 'Semper's' rifle and just did a magic wave of his hands, saying:

'Until you hit the fucking thing, I can't tell which way to adjust it.'

'At the target in front: five more rounds for grouping – GO ON.'

I squeezed my trigger and the orange man returned five more times. I was determined to get better; having had my sights adjusted, the rounds and consequently the holes were getting closer together and I was well chuffed. To get your marksman's badge, you had to get a certain amount of rounds within a four-inch grouping; I forget the exact amount, but it would be equivalent to about eighty per cent.

We repeated the exercise another two times until the rounds were going where we wanted them to. Even 'Semper's' were now striking the target, although not necessarily into the picture of the charging solider. Magazines empty, we completed the unload drill and placed our weapons on the mat for the final time, walked down to our targets and had them marked.

'Foster: a good improvement from the beginning.' Pause for effect.

'Semper, I dare not tell Her Majesty where her rounds are going; needless to say it is not into the oncoming enemy. The best thing that you can do is take the rounds out of the magazine and throw them at the enemy; while that distracts him, you can run the twenty-five metres and beat him to death with the butt of your rifle. WHAT THE FUCK WERE YOU SHOOTING AT, MAN?

'It looks like you've had Michael Jackson down here! What were you doing? – trying to dance him to death? The enemy is not going to stand still while you decide where you are going to shoot him.'

The whole group was now in hysterics; the Corporal really had the 'gift' of comedy timing, vocabulary and delivery. The one thing I failed to mention was my selected position inside the range: the mat furthest from the door collected the most empty shell cases. Notwithstanding that, a good deal of them bounced around my head while I was actually firing, and they were bloody hot! They all had to be picked up at the end of the shoot – another very good example of what the beret could be used for – every last one of them, hence the aforementioned declaration. With lots of airmen, lots of weapons and lots of ammunition, the range staff could not be sure that every round had been fired at its intended target; therefore a declaration must be buried deep in 'QRs' (Queen's Regulations) somewhere, so that the emphasis is placed on the retaining of the unspent round and not the range staff! (Another fine example of military passing the buck.)

I remember seeing someone wearing a T-shirt that said 'The buck stops here,' and wondered whether it actually did? Queen's Regulations (or as I'm sure our more senior readers will remember, 'King's Regulations') covered not only a multitude of sins, but every conceivable indiscretion that one could imagine, think of and create in one's own mind after having given it a great deal of thought.

Rumours abounded that one could place his left hand in his pocket at any time, and if questioned why so, could reply, 'I am concealing my erection, sir.' This natural assumption that everyone 'dresses' to the left was surely a welcome loophole? I would love to have been a fly on the wall at that 'charge' (being punished in accordance with QRs).

Another rumour was that you could not be held accountable for your immediate actions (in the first sixty seconds or so) after being awoken abruptly; this was therefore the perfect time to 'twat' someone – even an officer, but to this day I have not heard of anyone actually using it, even less making a defence out of it.

Basically if you'd 'fucked up' enough to bring something to the attention of your superiors, then the RAF would find a suitable way to punish you, whether you were guilty or not; message being sent: DON'T GET CAUGHT! Or if you did, blame it on someone else – and there was a good deal of that with those 'career boys'.

I'd adopted the attitude of 'If I can cover for someone, I would,' but I would never take 'the full tumble' for anyone (explained later at Cranwell). We were approaching our fourth week now and had reached the expected standard; the only way to determine this was the fact that life at Swinderby was becoming not only easier, but much more tolerable and – dare I say it? – enjoyable, as we began to accept that 'this was the way it was' and had always been!

'Bucking the system' (going against the RAF and all that it stood for) was futile; flights previous, present and I'm sure in the future might try to change things, but it was all to no avail. We were now well versed in appearance and the level expected of us, depending on the situation: drill, weapons handling and parades, marching, first aid, NBC, cleanliness and the ability to distinguish between officers and non-commissioned officers; whom to salute, why, where and when.

❖ ❖ ❖

5.   M.F.T.

It was time for MFT (Military Field Training) and my memories of this are, to say the least, sketchy. I have contacted several colleagues, including by becoming a member of 'Forces Reunited', which I have found extremely useful. But this was one single week, out of a ten-year career that ended over thirteen years ago, so I'm doing extremely well to remember anything at all, as the amount of alcohol I consumed, and its effect on my brain during that period, are directly proportional to the amount of information it can now hold.

I must have killed off the majority of my brain cells, except for those that are actually required for motor skills, i.e. the movement of one's limbs – hence the ability to drink was always present.

MFT was basically a week spent camping out in some godforsaken, forgotten hole in the middle of nowhere, where we had to survive on the minimalist 'rat packs' (ration packs) and one 'field kitchen meal' (a frying tray and a pan of boiling water to keep the fried stuff lukewarm) a day. If the RAF cooks couldn't get it right back at camp, we were dreading the gastronomical efforts of a pissed-off cook with a field kitchen.

But after eating 'compo biscuits' (extremely high fibre), glucose tablets and boiled sweets, we were bloody grateful for it. The compo biscuits, far from making you regular, tended to bung you up. That was a welcome side effect, because no one liked shitting over an open, freezing metal bucket, which would spit 'Racasan' onto your bare arse if you hadn't put paper down first – and all this in the blackness of night, surrounded only by a sheet of canvas.

Much enjoyment was heard coming from the bog, as individuals did their best to evacuate the stubborn stools. Care was also required that one took note of the level in the bucket, so as not to be the one to have to empty it out. My claim to fame? – not having to do it once, in the whole week I was there!

Now we were garbed in our DPM (Disruptive Pattern Material – oh, how the military loves initials) camouflage clothing and wearing our full webbing, complete with full water bottles: and woe betide anyone whose bottle was full of anything other than Adam's Ale, although many before us had tried. The DIs told us of the attempts to conceal all manner of liquids, and as a result bottle inspections where carried out at regular intervals, but always when we least expected them.

The DIs would stand us in one continuous line and empty out every bottle, then sniff it, practically keeling over when they got to Taffy's.

'What did I fucking say was to go in these bottles, airman?'

'Water, Corporal,' Taff replied sheepishly.

'Drop and give me twenty, boyo.'

Whatever he'd put in there, it certainly wasn't water. So, along with the other half-dozen culprits whose bottles contained coke, diluted juice, and one idiot who actually had milk in his, he began his press-ups.

'Water bottles is for water, otherwise they would be called lemonade bottles, or coke bottles, and in this dumb bastard's case MILK bottles. The reason they is for water is that when it gets hot, either from your body temperature or direct sunlight, you can still fucking wash or drink with it. How the fuck are you going to quench your thirst after a four-mile run in full battle kit with a fucking YOGHURT?'

Taff was none too pleased at this, being older and more experienced than the rest of us. I seem to remember he'd been in another service for a few weeks before coming over to the RAF. We were never sure if he'd been chucked out of the other one, or just didn't like it. He swore he would get his revenge and, true to his 'Welsh' word, he did.

The end of March was upon us and the thought of being here for April 1st had the 'rumour control machine' belting out 'would be' scenarios at a phenomenal rate. Tales of capture and torture during the night exercise were rife and quite frightening. Being hooded and made to stand on your tiptoes and fingertips, while at forty-five degrees to the wall, was one technique described; this was known as the 'stress' position – as was having the living crap beaten out of you. After all, many a crime has been committed under the cover of darkness, where the identity of the assailant would remain unknown.

'I 'eard that someone of 14 Flight got smashed in the face with a rifle butt last week,' a voice said, out of the darkness.

'Bollocks: you're making the c*** up,' said another.

'No, that lad that was back-flighted; he told me,' the first began again.

Our eight-man tent had ten of us in it, rotating guard duties of two hours on and one off. Our flight had been split into two groups on opposing sides, a blue team and a red team. Each team had a territory to defend and a lamp, which had to be guarded twenty-four hours a day.

The object was to attack the opposing team and either snuff out the lamp or capture it altogether, along with as many prisoners as possible. As well as that, we had to cope with sneak attacks from the DI staff, who knew every weak point and trick in the book, from simulated gas attacks at three o'clock in the morning to thunderflashes being left at the rear of your tent – and believe me, if you hadn't had a trip to the freezing bucket, a change of underwear would be required when they went off.

It was on one such assault that Taffy had spotted and challenged an intruder inside our camp, who was making his way towards the lamp. The intruder turned to run.

'STAND TO!' Taff shouted, which was the signal to call out the guard. As we fell over ourselves, trying to worm our way out of our sleeping bags, grab our kit and find the tent doorway, Taff had launched himself full length and in midair towards the intruder. He wrapped himself around the waist of the assailant, dragging him to the ground with a sickening thump; there was a good deal of pushing and shoving and a few choice words, some in English and some in Welsh.

The intruder managed to squirm forward, but Taff was having none of it and held on for dear life. Taff dragged the assailant's trousers around his ankles and felled him in a ridiculous pose, where the cheeks of his arse had fallen out of the huge white underpants he was wearing, which now shone like a moon in the torchlight of the called-out guards.

'All right, ya Welsh bastard, ya got me. It's Corporal Smith – now get the fuck off.'

Taff relinquished his hold on the DI and –wouldn't ya know it? – it was the one who'd given him the press-ups. Oh yes, there is a God! Taff was our hero, and the tale travelled far and wide and was exaggerated a little more at each telling.

In the morning light, there was a tingle of excitement and we knew we would be seeing the felled intruder as we were shepherded to the field kitchen for breakfast. Like a gaggle of schoolgirls we giggled and pointed at the Corporal (obviously when his back was turned) – but oh boy, were we going to pay for last night!

After finishing our breakfast we would queue to use the washing area; the first vat was for actually washing our mess tins, and the second to scald them sterile. The fact that there was as much food floating, bobbing or partially sunk in the second as in the first made no difference; they were to be spotless.

The Corporal inspected them after washing and at least seventy-five per cent of the tins were thrown in varying directions as far as the Corporal could manage, once taking the time to scoop up some mud from a nearby puddle. Even the ones that were clean got flung, and some landed on the roofs of nearby huts.

'How am I going to get it down, Corporal?' a saddened airman questioned.

'Not my problem,' came the reply. We did manage to recover them eventually with a little teamwork, and washed them all again.

They were flung a second and sometimes third time; it wasn't funny any more.

'Now that you have made yourselves late with your dirty mess tins – you have FIVE FUCKING MINUTES to get back to camp: by the left, double march!'

With me in full battle kit, my two sausages, one egg and scoop of beans washed down with a beaker of tea were now at the back of my throat fighting for an exit; it wasn't long before a couple of the lads were blowing airborne chunks for England, tea still dripping from their noses. I wished I had been sick and then I wouldn't have felt so bad all day.

We broke up into smaller groups and were taught the art of giving and receiving 'Firing Orders' as we attacked a brick building on the airfield. We crawled through the still-wet grass, glistening with morning dew, and gave instructions like:

'Target: brick building two hundred yards in front – watch and shoot – watch and shoot.'

The DI staff were inside the building, taking pot shots at us with blanks. I crawled forward on my elbows, keeping as low as I could, my breakfast still swishing from side to side. For the last hundred yards we were to stand up and charge the building, firing as we ran; a DI's SLR appeared at the windows and a burst of automatic fire was heard. We dropped like ninepins instead of running past the building.

The automatic fire is a trick only the RAF Regiment and the armourers are privy to, and is achieved by placing a matchstick underneath the safety sear of the trigger mechanism; the only downside is that once fired it will expend the rest of the magazine without stopping. No matter – we were all dead and a bunch of poufs and pansies, according to the Corporal.

The rest of the day was spent running around in gas masks, panting like bloodhounds and generally knackering ourselves out to the point of exhaustion. The whole exercise was geared around sleep deprivation, stress, teamwork and stamina. The constant interruptions of what little sleep we were allowed began to take their toll as tempers frayed. The last thing you needed was to have some clumsy bastard's size nines tramping over your shins in the early hours of the morning, while you're trying to sleep in your gas mask – which was actually possible if you're tired enough. That is, unless some other devious bastard (namely me) has stuck a piece of 'clingfilm' over the intake of your respirator so it sucks down onto the contours of your face until you awake gasping for air and realise something is desperately wrong.

We were awoken hour after hour, if not on guard duty then on 'fire picket'. This duty required two people to walk around the interior of the camp with a pickaxe handle, checking that the fire buckets full of sand were still in place and that the fire extinguishers, which had a habit of 'discharging themselves!' were still full. I was mystified, as I am to this day, as to what we were meant to do with the pickaxe handle if we discovered a fire.

The remainder of the week was spent rehearsing what we'd already learned, with some night raids, although no one managed to extinguish the other's lamp. A few prisoners were captured, on both sides, but not tortured and generally we were getting more tired and ratty as the week wore on. When I later contacted a lifelong colleague, his memories of that week were not dissimilar to mine. We spent the entire week being cold, wet, hungry and tired and were extremely glad when it was over. It is the only time I have ever been on an RAF coach when the occupants have not been singing or getting even more pissed than they were when they got on; the coach was almost silent and the low hum of the tyres on the tarmac, coupled with the noise from the engine, gearbox, prop shaft and rear axle, only helped us towards the three-hour ride back to RAF Swinderby and into our catatonic state.

Back at Swinderby, after unloading all the kit, most of us headed for the showers or baths, as the best you could manage in 'the field' was a strip wash. 'The field' was the term used to describe any activity that took place away from your normal base or 'parent unit', but usually it meant camping out in some form or another. The lad lying on his pit was preliminarily questioned:

'You not having a shower?'

'Yeah, I'm just waiting till the queue dies down,' he replied.

Later someone else commented:

'I hope you're getting washed, ya fucking minger!'

But it was only one of the big Jocks saying, 'Every c*** else has had a shower; you'd better not be the only thing stinking up this room in the morning or you're fucking dead!' that seemed to have the desired effect where others had failed.

Hurrah for diplomatic leadership skills – and they both were going on to train for the RAF Police.

The six weeks we had thought were going to be the worst were just that in some people's minds, while I bathed in the glory of my Dad's advice prior to coming to Swinderby:

'NEVER volunteer for anything – you'll be volunteered soon enough. Keep your head down, your mouth shut and your ears open [I managed two outta three] and the time will just fly by!'

The truth was that I had learned more in the previous five weeks than I had in my entire life before then – about living with men and their rudimentary habits, about compromise and confrontation, teamwork and trust, and how to make friends as well as lose them. Fifteen Flight had one week left to do now, and we looked down in contempt at the new recruits getting off the bus, as we had done forty-two days ago.

It felt great, but of course it was ridiculous for us to feel this way; the Corporal wanted us to be the best flight Swinderby had ever seen and by that time so did we. Little encouragement was needed now; as our own self-pride took over, we were earlier, smarter, sharper than ever before. I will never forget the day Corporal Wild said he was proud of Fifteen Flight.

I could have cried; it was like a Friday-afternoon black-and-white 'weepy'. The only thing that snapped me back to reality was the realisation that this was almost like a script, and we, as humans, would react for the most part in the same way as every entry before us who had heard the same thing; on the day we passed out, the cheeky old bastard would have smoked more fags and drunk more free pints than the commandant himself. 'Fag for the Corporal; drink for the Corporal?' – and we would be falling over ourselves to get him whatever he wanted. It was a win–win situation; he, Bill Wild, had taken sixteen civilians of diverse classes, experience and ages and turned almost all of them into the beginnings of Royal Air Force professionals.

❖ ❖ ❖

6. Pass-Out Parade

Our last week was spent practising and perfecting our drill ready for our 'Pass Out' parade (official completion ceremony), when our parents would be invited to watch us perform to the best of our abilities. As smart as carrots and puffed up like courting cocks, the final days were spent on the parade ground, with the highest-polished everything. During this week we were issued with our 'white webbing belts' with brass couplings; the belt was made from a nylon-type material and only needed washing, while the brasses would be 'bulled' along with everything else to a standard nothing short of perfect.

As we put the finishing touches to our Number One uniform, Nassau discovered an unwanted crease in the sleeve of his jacket, near the shoulder. While still wearing it, he picked up the iron and proceeded to iron it out; the only thing was that he'd forgotten to turn off the steam and managed to badly scald himself through the material, leaving an iron-shaped blob of skin dripping from his arm.

I have never heard a man scream in so much pain in my entire life. He was carted off to the medical centre forthwith, where he apparently bawled the place down as though giving birth. There was talk of him being 'back-flighted', as he obviously found rifle drill excruciatingly painful. The mere mention of being 'back-flighted' made our hearts sink; to have come so far and then have to stay for another week or two was soul-destroying.

This was, however; a serious injury and we lost one of our own with just two days to go. He would be placed on the 'general duties' flight, which meant that you were basically a 'gofer' for whichever office needed you most.

He ceremoniously removed the red disc from behind his beret badge, which had denoted him as Fifteen Flight for the previous five and a half weeks, and handed it to the Corporal. He was almost in tears, and would have to wait until Sixteen Flight was ready to pass out and join them. He bade us farewell and headed off for the guardroom to receive his instructions. We often saw him wandering around the camp with an important-looking envelope as we marched to and from the parade ground.

If it hadn't been for those couple of seconds with the iron, he would still have been with us, but it was the steam that had caused the real damage. Still, he wanted to be an RAF policeman, and so it served him fucking right!

The big day arrived; we were up at the crack of dawn, about five-thirty-ish, checking and rechecking our uniforms, webbing-belt brasses and shoes. People were still putting more and more creases into their jackets and trousers, trying to eliminate the accidental 'tramlines' that had crept in; it was like a Chinese laundry – steam irons galore, people 'bagsying' the iron next, squabbling over who had asked for it when, and who was actually using it was taking too long, etc.

'Yis 'r' like a bunch o' fuckin' lassies,' Big Jock said, and the level of tension in the room was now rapidly rising. A squabble had turned into a punch-up between a prospective MT (mechanical transport) driver from London village and someone else.

'For fuck's sake – you're going to be on parade in a few hours; do you want to be stood there with cauliflower ears and black eyes?' said the senior man, getting in between them. It was all over in a flash and no damage was done. This was the day that we would all remove the red discs behind our cap badges; no longer Fifteen Flight but 'real' airmen, about to embark to our respective 'trade' training camps all over the country. Mine, and anyone else's in MT, was to be 4S of TT (4th School of Technical Training), Royal Air Force Saint Athan in Wales.

On the way to breakfast I spared a thought for my parents, who would be travelling the hundred and fifty miles or so from County Durham to Swinderby, which would take about three and a half to four hours in my Dad's dark blue, Mk 1 Escort, 1100cc – when petrol was creeping up to sixty pence per gallon.

My Dad would be in his absolute element, hobnobbing with the NCOs and having a few brief words with the 'hofficer', while my mother, having modelled herself on Hyacinth Bucket, tilted her head quizzically like a puzzled dog, trying to keep up with the 'RAF-speak'. Dad had left the same service himself in 1976 (only 5 years previously), his last station having been RAF Scampton, just fifteen miles from Swinderby. So the RAF was still very much 'fresh' in his mind; he had never wanted to leave the service, but my mother, 'sick and tired' of dragging the children from camp to camp, had other ideas.

The RAF was my Dad's life and he was never the same after leaving; it was utter purgatory to watch any kind of military film with him, as he named every aircraft that appeared on the screen, even if just for a fleeting moment. He would rush outside and stare into the sky at the sound of ANY aircraft, commenting on whether it was multi-engine or single prop on his way out of the door, before even seeing it.

'Ya see that, boy? That's a … [whatever it was],' and he would give a full running commentary as to its origins, age, markings and any other miscellaneous fact that Father carried around in his head connected with said aircraft. He would stare until it was just a blip, slipping into the cumulo-nimbus as its engine note faded.

I could see on his face that he regretted every single day that he was no longer an airman; and being a Cumbrian, used to the rolling hills of his beloved Lake District and the village of Cummersdale, he hated the life he now had in 'Geordie land', away from the nature and meandering rivers that supported the beautiful kingfisher and the aircraft he loved so much.

The parade was scheduled for 11am and we had one final rehearsal until we were 'perfect'; then it was back to the blocks and into our Number One uniform for the final time at Swinderby, home of Recruit Training. Corporal Wild 'collected' us from the block as we used the 'buddy' system to make sure each of us was like 'a new pin' – straightening hats, a sharp tug of a tie, and a general spin round to see all was in order. We marched to the armoury and collected our weapons, ready for the 'real' parade. There was some concern that the white gloves we had been issued with, for today only, that complemented the webbing belt, were now getting dirty from the oil of the serviced weapons.

No matter – they were only dirty on the parts you couldn't see when we were actually carrying the weapons, and we would just be marching with them today and not firing them. The butterflies in my stomach must have landed only on dandelions (Pittley Beds in the North of England), because I was bursting for a piss; it was of course just nerves, but the fact that I was getting this feeling every five minutes was completely unexpected. The thought of actually pissing myself on parade, in front of my parents, the parents of another forty blokes and the camp commandant, was too terrifying to contemplate.

Now that I come to think of it, there was a good deal of fiddling of the bollocks going on, and I was glad it wasn't just me. For those who have been lucky enough not to experience the 'fear' we were now experiencing, allow me to enlighten the gentlemen amongst us about it and its effects. The 'fight or flight' reaction will have been experienced by every male at some point or other during his life; this is when the 'rational' part of the brain has collected its P45 and is now signing in box 1 at the jobcentre, while the 'instinct' part of the brain is now supplying you with copious amounts of adrenaline to perform such tasks as lifting cars off old ladies, jumping unbelievable obstacles and running distances only ever heard of at the Olympics.

The reason the body can do this is because it withdraws blood from every 'non-essential' organ and redirects it to where it is needed most – and in this situation that does not include your 'willy'. To summarise, then, your penis not only retracts but practically turns itself inside out, and where once used to hang our gladiatorial tackle, it now bears some resemblance to a one-eyed chick looking out of its nest, in fear of falling below onto a couple of shrivelled nuts!

This was the level of fear we were experiencing: the fear of 'fucking up', the fear of letting down Corporal Wild, Fifteen Flight, our parents, the commandant – and, most importantly of all, ourselves! Much as I would later take great literary delight in both remembering and writing that someone had fainted in the April sunshine or dropped a rifle, faced the wrong way in an 'about turn' or just spoilt it, they, we and all concerned didn't at the time. It was as the Corporal had asked for – perfect! The nerves had gone moments into the drill as we, I assumed, went onto 'autopilot' and did what we had been trained to do, although not in front of a crowd or the commandant. A flypast of ever-ageing propeller-driven aircraft was the icing on the cake for most of us, although my father was extremely disappointed that it wasn't the Red Arrows, or the Hastings he had worked on at Scampton. Nevertheless, I still retain a picture-card memory of the scene as our parade closed and we stacked our weapons in a 'tepee' configuration and were allowed to greet our parents. I marched smartly up to them, coming to attention and cracking a crisp salute, before shaking my father's hand and kissing my mother on the cheek, returning to attention, then 'at ease', and finally taking my hat off and getting the biggest hug I had ever had in my life.

It didn't get much better than this. For the first time since my Dad had left the forces, and I had joined, we forgot we 'hated' each other in the way most parents will have experienced during the teenage years. I had respect! – from the one I revered most, although I wouldn't let him know it. It couldn't have had anything to do with his taunting me with that, 'You'll never last a week,' could it? Mmm: I wonder.

After returning our rifles to the armoury and agreeing a place to meet up with my parents, we headed off towards the airmen's mess for what was essentially a 'Sunday lunch'. Even on the day of our passing out the standard of cooking was disgraceful, and many comments on the quality and presentation of the meal were made by both parents and airmen alike. Some parents chose to avoid the experience altogether, and it did put a 'dampener' on an otherwise perfect day. To make up for it, we all gravitated to the 'Halfway House', a pub/restaurant at the end of the road out of Swinderby, and incidentally halfway between Lincoln and Newark. It was here that we plied Bill with drinks, cigarettes and cigars, congratulating him on a job well done, until he reminded me of Sgt Bilko.

Alas, the time had come to say our goodbyes, and we walked the short distance back to Dad's car; a final handshake and a hug from Mam, and they were on their way. I walked back to the block and put my white gloves and webbing belt in their respective boxes ready for collection. Most of the GDT kit had already been returned – respirator, webbing, etc., along with our bedding – and so we readied ourselves to move to the next step: 'trade training'. We had arrived with just a suitcase or two six weeks earlier and were leaving with one extra: the blue RAF holdall that contained our working uniforms.

We took one last look around 'Hansen block' and left for the coach park through the front door, scuffing the floor shamelessly with shoes and suitcases alike to give the new recruits something extra to do. I shook hands with all the people I had bonded with, and poured scorn on the ones I hadn't; it was par for the course. The RAF Police cadets, of whom there were far too many in my opinion, were off to RAF Newton, near Nottingham, about half an hour's ride away; little did I realise then that I would be meeting some of them later in my career, in the 'professional' sense.

The RAF Regiment trainees were going up the A1 to RAF Catterick, North Yorkshire, a good two- to three-hour ride; and I and my MT mates were going to RAF St Athan in deepest Wales – five bastard hours away! Some of the scenery as we crossed into Wales was magnificent, and then we happened across a row of pink cottages set back on a hillside; I couldn't quite see where all this fitted in with the rough, mining image we had been given by Taff.

He had also warned us of the 'Valley Commandos', and in my naivety I thought they were an elite force to protect Wales. In fact he described them as '… sex-hungry women, but looking as though they had fallen out of the ugly tree, hitting every branch on the way down. I 'ad to be pissed before I could make my mind up whether I wanted to fuck 'em or fight 'em,' he said in his strong Welsh accent.

❖ ❖ ❖

7. Jock and Pat

By the time our coach had swung through the gates of RAF St Athan and around to the Guardroom, it was about seven thirty pm and we were tired and travel-weary; it had been an awfully long day. But I still remember commenting to the driver about how flat Lincolnshire was in comparison to the steep turns and climbs we had made to get here.

He looked at me disparagingly and 'shooed' me off the bus. Whenever you arrive at a station out of normal working hours and require somewhere to sleep, the only place usually available is 'Transit Accommodation' (a shambolic room which contained a number of broken-down beds and wardrobes in dire need of repair). As its name implies, it is a short-term stopover before being allocated a block and room number the next day – unless it was your misfortune to arrive on a Friday evening, in which case it would be Monday morning before anything happened.

We collected our blankets and a pillow from the guardroom and hopped back on the coach for a short ride to the transit block; grabbed our suitcases and bags, shoved them into a lockable locker and headed for the NAFFI. One thing we always had about our person in the early days was a good set of padlocks, as it was an 'offence' to leave your bedside locker/wardrobe unlocked.

There were a few beds already made up, as people from other camps had arrived before us and from the 'holding flight' (where people waiting to join a new course were kept milling around the station until the course had a sufficiently large number to justify its existence). St Athan was basically an RAF technical college, and the main subjects taught were MT (mechanical transport) Mechanics and Technicians; Driver Training, both basic and HGV; Workshops GSE (ground support equipment), who were allegedly so skilled that they could weld shit to chocolate; and aircraft painters and finishers.

It may also have had a photographic section, which was housed in the mysterious wooden huts on stilts we marched past on a daily basis. The camp had an 'active' runway, which I believe was an emergency relief airfield for Cardiff International Airport, but I can't be sure. It certainly had its fair number of noisy visits from fast jet aircraft from RAF Valley and surrounding stations.

As we entered the NAAFI, almost every head in the lounge bar turned towards us and we hesitated slightly, feeling we were somewhere we shouldn't be; this was indication enough to let everyone else know we were brand-new 'sprogs', as we had been referred to. Many of the people present were permanent staff, from varying camps, who were just here to pass their driving test – a short attachment of anywhere from two to six weeks, depending on the standard of driving of the individual concerned. The interested looks from the others were probably because it was a training camp, with a constant turnover of staff, so you never knew who you would bump into next.

The club, like the camp, was massive compared to Swinderby and had every convenience imaginable: video, vending and fruit machines, pool tables, a 'hot' serving hatch where you could get chips and burgers up until about nine pm, TV rooms upstairs – and the *pièce de résistance* was the snooker hall, which contained four full-sized tables with bridges, rests and a good selection of cues. I was going to like it here. After giving the place the 'once over' we made our way back down to the lounge, where the level of noise from the many individual conversations was remarkably low; it was decidedly pleasant.

We, the four of us, picked a seat close to the window and watched the endless stream of vehicles to-ing and fro-ing as permanent staff and trainees moved around the station, well into late evening.

Still under age and looking as though I wasn't old enough to buy condoms, let alone a pint of beer, I got one of the other lads to get me one – which turned into three – and by ten thirty I was 'goosed'. I left the other three in the NAAFI and wobbled my way back in the cool evening air; pausing for a minute, I was surrounded by blocks all facing in different directions. Disorientated and dizzy, I hadn't a fucking clue where I was; not wanting to look a complete twat, I walked and walked, hoping I would happen across it and remember. No such luck and not a soul in sight to ask – just the reassuring lights of the guardroom that burned constantly and brightly throughout the night.

I had two choices: I could retrace my steps to the NAAFI, which was now quite some distance away, or risk the guardroom and, I thought, a possible charge. My fresh and highly flushed face entered the guardroom at about ten-fifty pm.

'Can you tell me where the transit block is, please, Corporal?' A sea of inquisitive faces appeared from out of the woodwork to see what was going on.

'I can't even tell you the time until you tell me who you are, airman.'

'AC Novak, sir,' and for the life of me I cannot think why I called him 'sir'. The faces had got the gist of what was happening, and stayed for the entertainment value and the relief from the boredom of a night shift in the guardroom.

'I'm no' sir. Do I look like a sir to you?'

'No, Corporal,' I replied, and the faces were tittering like a bunch of schoolgirls.

'Where's your ID?' he barked, and I nearly shat myself, fumbling for my wallet and dropping it as I tried to get the 'RAF Form 1250' out. This is your service identification card and carried a mandatory 252 (charge) and fifty-pound fine if lost or, God forbid, stolen, given its security implications. A request for its production usually meant you had done something wrong, so the other person could check your true details; many an intoxicated airman has given a false name and 'last three' after giving someone in authority some 'lip', usually a guard or at best the RAF Police – but not at this stage of my career and not at this camp: that was all to come later.

'Aircraftsman Novak – last three?' he inquired.

'567, Corporal.'

'Date of birth?'

'19-2-64, Corporal.'

'That would make you ... that would make you ... under age!'

I must have turned ashen; my heart was pounding in my chest.

'Ah, we're only fucking with ya – hoy, Jones, take this airman to the transit block and get me some fags out the vending machine while you're at it.' He returned my '1250' and I couldn't wait to get out of the 'circus arena' I had so foolishly entered.

As Jones escorted me back to the block, I was thinking about the number 1250. RAF form 1250: that would automatically necessitate that there must be another 1249 forms below that; the RAF loved form numbers and abbreviations and I was surprised there wasn't a course on that as well. For instance, RAF Form 252 was the one used to officially discipline you after a breach of 'Queen's Regulations'; when you came up in front of your OC (officer commanding) and the charge had been read out, your previous conduct taken into consideration and you had been offered the chance to speak for yourself, the CO would ask, 'Will you accept my punishment?' For the two times I had to go through this procedure I was dying to say, 'No-go, blow it out your arse' – but that would have been professional suicide and probably a court-martial.

So you reluctantly agree, cringing slightly as you await the dastardly thing about to be bestowed on you. In my two cases, which were both for 'sleeping in', it was a ten- and twenty-pound fine with seven days' 'jankers' (extra duties); the Army know this as 'ROPS' (restriction of privileges), which is basically what it is.

First you must parade at the guardroom in your Number One uniform at 7am to be inspected by the orderly officer, before returning to the block and getting changed for your normal day's work. You parade again in the same immaculate uniform later that evening – and the standard had better be good or the duties would just keep piling up.

After being inspected a second time, you return and get changed, then report back to the guardroom, where you would be given instructions as to where you would be working until about ten o'clock that evening. All this 'bullshit' should have had the desired rehabilitation effect; but you would be surprised and amazed just how many times the same people were there, on the same charge, week after week, trying to get an 'admin' discharge. Basically there were a number of ways to get out of the RAF, if you had arrived at a point where it had become so unpleasant the only thing to do was leave, and it happened to many.

There was PVR (premature voluntary release) – which was a contradiction in terms, as it usually involved a substantial sum payable by the person wanting to leave, calculated by how much time you had left to serve and, I gather, how much the RAF had spent on you in terms of training, along with a consideration of its current manning levels in that particular trade.

This was by far the most popular route, the one possible exception being 'natural wastage': people completing their agreed term of contract and deciding not to 'sign on' (apply to extend the length of their service contract).

Then there was medical discharge, where one has become permanently unfit to serve or is 'barking mad' – extremely difficult to fake and I hadn't come across anyone who had successfully got away with it, although I encountered many who had tried. Keeping up this façade for any length of time is extremely difficult, and there were occasions when someone who had professed to being 'mad as a hatter', or had started the 'rumour' machine to reflect that, were observed at weekends behaving 'abnormally normally'.

The 'admin' (administrative) discharge was having your service contract nullified by the RAF without any disciplinary procedure, and was an acquired art. I know of only a few, who became such a thorn in the side of the service that they had become more trouble than they were worth. It would involve the perpetrator committing 'minor offences' with such regularity that the paperwork and manpower hours lost became uneconomical. You can see where the danger lies; the definition of a 'minor offence' could be reconstructed in such a way as to become 'major' and necessitate a substantial stopover at Her Majesty's most feared service correctional facility, 'Colchester', where the combined services guards would eat your liver with a nice bottle of Chianti and some fava beans, if you believed the 'hype'. Nevertheless, its deterrent value worked on all but a few; it was rumoured to be like Swinderby, only a hundred times worse!

Most of its inhabitants would be 'DD-ed' after serving their sentence, depending on its length in relation to the crime; that meant 'dishonourably discharged' and having their 'Blue Book' (service record to take to civilian life) 'clipped' – cutting off the corner to show a 'DD' had occurred. Trying to get a job with one of these 'clipped books' would be practically impossible – or so we were led to believe. The reality was that no one even asked to see my book while I was applying for a vast number of jobs after leaving the RAF, when I couldn't make my mind up which line of work to go into; and in any case mine was not clipped, but a glowing report to any prospective employer.

The numbers of the forms ran past my eyes each time the room span around my head as I lay on my itchy blanket. I placed a leg on the floor to try and stop this happening, but it didn't work and I had that distinct, familiar feeling. I sat up, lay down and sat up again; went to the toilets and performed the inevitable. The next thing I knew it was morning, as I was automatically awake at 0600 waiting for 'reveille', and I was glad the alcohol had gone down the toilet and not worked its way through my body, resulting in the traditional hangover which the other three I had left in the NAAFI were now so obviously displaying.

A corporal from the 'GD' flight (general duties/guardroom staff) arrived with a 'Welcome to St Athan' booklet, and some more coloured discs to go behind our badges. It would appear that whenever you go on a training course, the RAF likes to be able to distinguish you from the 'permanent' staff so that they can 'bollock' you as and when they please; I mean they always did, but recruits seemed to bear the brunt of most of it. The booklet contained a map and information as to the amenities 'us recruits' could use and orders as to what was 'out of bounds', i.e. married quarters! It didn't occur to me why at first, until Pat, the oldest member of the group, smiled with glee, saying:

'I wonder how many of their husbands are away?'

Pat was our 'senior man'; he was well over six feet in height and reminded me of Blakey from 'On the Buses'. Tall and slenderly built, with the moustache to boot, his dry wit and the fact that he didn't give a shit only served to make our time at St Athan that much more enjoyable. Pat viewed all this training as

~ JOCK AND PAT ~

'unnecessary'; he was already a qualified and very experienced diesel mechanic in 'Civvy Street'.

He flew through the initial mechanical tests we were given to assess our level of knowledge. His cohort, drinking partner and incidentally our 'Deputy Senior Man', was a short Scottish terrier whose temper was as short as he was. His 'lived-in' face told many a tale and the furrows that lined his brow were from scowling at all who encountered him. Like many a Scotsman he had the disposition to drink copious quantities of whatever was lying around, but had a particular penchant for whisky. Pat and Jock would spend the next twelve weeks rolling in at all hours of the morning, waking everyone as they toured the room, tipping people out of bed, pulling off blankets and generally annoying all concerned.

The Senior and his deputy had their own single rooms, small though they were, at the entrance to the main room, so there was no actual need to come into ours at all; it just seemed like a fun thing to do. On one boozy occasion, Pat was walking up the centre of the room and had got about halfway up when Jock bounded in, kangarooed onto one of the beds, leapt onto the next one and then launched himself at Pat, catching him around the neck and swinging around him like a child at the bus stop. The pair crashed to the ground and sustained some slight injuries; the quality of their evening excursions was judged by the amount of bruises and gashes they had acquired.

Mornings were no less exciting and one of us had been tasked to make sure Pat was awoken at the appropriate time; this was a task filled with trepidation and carried with it a risk to one's own personal safety if within hitting distance. Jock, on the other hand, was just a 'no go' area and we left it up to Pat to approach that challenge, which could go on for at least half an hour. The pair of them snored like thunder, and I recall putting in earplugs before they got back from the pub. If I pretended to be asleep I might avoid the bed being either turned over or stripped: how naive!

I was spun out of my bed and my mattress confiscated for 'bed diving'. The lights went on in the room, although it was after midnight. The last two beds at the top end of the room were unused – just metal frames; my mattress, along with several others, was placed on the floor and against the back wall at the top of the room. One metal bed frame was placed in the centre of the 'runway', about a metre from the mattresses.

Pat took off his shoes, then snorted like a bull while reversing away from the metal bed frame until he had a decent run-up; and he was off. His lanky legs flailed recklessly, his socks polishing the lino, while they slipped down his toes as he tried to gain enough speed to clear the bed frame and land on the mattresses. With just a couple of feet to go, he took off skyward, his gangly physique contorting in the air as he prepared for landing. CRUNCH! He landed head first into the mattresses, his feet overtaking his head, heels slamming down onto the windowsill at the far end of the room. 'Hurray!' everyone cheered – secretly wishing he'd permanently crippled himself.

'Beat that, ya Jock bastard.'

This was something you should never do! Never dare a drunken Scotsman to do anything.

'Put another bed in front of that one, ya English pouf.'

So there were now two beds, side by side in front of the mattresses. Jock lined himself up.

'Ah, ah, ah – get ya shoes off, ya poisonous little dwarf,' Pat said.

'Away tee fuck, ya lanky streak of Sassenach pish – I'm jumping two beds,' Jock replied.

'No socks – no dare,' Pat taunted the 'wee' Scotsman. Jock took off his shoes – and incidentally had the stinkiest feet I'd encountered to date; that, combined with the drinking and snoring, burping and farting, made it no wonder he was divorced. Once more on the 'runway', Jock reversed further than Pat, thinking he would need a longer run-up; further and further back he went, until he disappeared from view and had gone through our entrance door and out into the main foyer, leaving wet footprints which changed the colour of the dark brown lino to even darker. The thundering of feet could be heard long before we saw him, which added to the comedic effect, and the 'Flying Scotsman' hurtled towards the two beds at breakneck speed. Something went wrong, though; one of his socks had come off just enough to provide his bare foot some friction with the lino and he was off balance and heading for disaster. He careered shin height into the two beds, toppling him onto the bare metal springs and finally into the mattresses; he just lay there in a heap moaning, while the rest of us pissed ourselves laughing. This was high entertainment and divine retribution for waking us all up.

The next morning, Pat had poked Jock with a broom handle enough times to bring him into the land of the living, commenting on his injuries. Jock looked like he'd been in a car crash: two beautiful purple, blue and green bruises on his shins at the same height, scratches and cuts on his arms and face. I couldn't wait to hear the reason he gave for the shin bruises when we would eventually get to PT (physical training)

Like Swinderby, we formed up on the road outside the block and would be marched to the mess for breakfast, the correct order being 'By the left – quick march.' This was Pat's version: 'Squad – squad, 'shun. For those that can be fucked – quick march!' We laughed all the way to the mess; Pat was as dry as sticks. He and Jock would verbally abuse each other constantly, with ever more imaginative names and insults; it truly was a joy to behold and we were often picked up by the permanent staff for talking in the ranks. The ever-present danger of being given another 'bull night' was very real; on more than one occasion we had to do this and the one caught talking would get the toilets to clean.

The food was of a better standard than at Swinderby, although the rubber eggs seemed to be a feature of every camp I've ever been to! That and the strange-tasting tea, which we still believed contained 'bromide'.

After breakfast, which Jock consumed with vigour – it never ceased to amaze me that no matter how much beer and spirits had been drunk, or how rough he looked, he could always manage a full, in every sense of the word, English breakfast – Pat took the opportunity to remind the 'Scotch c***' that it was an *English*

~ JOCK AND PAT ~

breakfast and not a Scottish one! Jock replied with a flick of a small spoonful of beans at Pat's head; most went over the top, but a couple made their mark, leaving the juice and then sliding down his face.

Pat's retort was to deposit the entire contents of the salt-cellar on what remained of Jock's breakfast. This was how it was for the next twelve weeks – the two supposed to be the most adult, behaving like children.

All fed and watered and back outside, we marched to the 'admin' block for our first day of form filling; the RAF clerks lived to collate! At mid-morning, with writer's cramp, we would get a fifteen- to twenty-minute break, mostly taken at 'Sandy's'. For want of a better description, that was akin to a massive transport café, run by some kind of religious faculty; the women were butch and the men were camp, and we would come to give them different names and characteristics the more we frequented the place.

Pat was particularly good at 'mincing around' after collecting his cream puff and coffee; Jock was having none of it, being the hard-drinking Scotsman. Pat would wind him up something shocking by saying that the one with the beard fancied him, and it was true that Jock seemed to get served before most others. The prices were extremely competitive: 10p for tea and 15p for coffee, I seem to remember; and it had many amenities such as video games, pool tables and pay-phones. It was also a place where you could talk to other 'flights' and trades, and where insults were flung around like sowing seeds – but 'Sandy's' staff always curtailed the language. Hence it was rechristened 'Snidies'.

The break over, it was back to form filling before dinner, and then onto the classroom that would be our home for the duration. The building, as large as an aircraft hangar, with its 'up and over' steel roller doors and one normal, opening door within the shutter, was impressive; I gasped in awe as I stepped through it. Before my very eyes was every mechanical aid to teaching I could think of: engines on stands – which we would later tinker with and make run; brake circuits laid out on display boards; work benches; tool boards; air-brake set-ups; fuel-injection displays – oh yes, this, for me, was mechanical utopia. We were given a guided tour and my head was bursting with questions; you know the kid always with his hand up? I just couldn't help myself; here were the answers to all my prior frustrations. I had been riding and stripping down motorbikes for the last two or three years, but had never progressed onto vehicles.

I had a good understanding of how an engine worked, but only on single- or double-cylinder machines, which were usually 'two-stroke' while the engine in your car is 'four-stroke'. It would take too long to explain the difference, and to the non-technical person it wouldn't change the way they used their car, but I'll go so far as to explain that a two-stroke engine requires oil to be mixed with the petrol before being burned in the engine, but a four-stroke doesn't.

Can anyone remember those dreadful 'Wartburg' cars from the Eastern bloc of Germany? An aerodynamic brick that sounded like a hairdryer, with plumes of blue smoke jetting out of the exhaust – they were two-stroke, and along with any fuel put into the vehicle, the corresponding amount of two-stroke oil had to be measured out and put into the fuel tank at the same time. Once I even witnessed a bloke shaking his car, so the petrol and oil would mix. This was all too technical for most lady drivers and their attitude to the amount of oil was akin to cooking, where a 'splodge' or 'you can never have enough oil' either had them leaving smoke-screens behind them or seizing the engine owing to too little oil. It was an ecological disaster waiting to happen, and I think the government 'outlawed' them soon after.

The tour completed, we entered the classroom and I picked a seat at the front; I was keen to get as much information as possible and wasn't interested in lounging around at the back. For once in my short life, I actually *wanted* to learn.

The classroom was smaller than I was used to, and had one of those roll-around continuous blackboards and a wooden podium. We were given book after book; these were broken down into categories, such as 'the engine', and then further broken down into large sections on the carburettor, transmission, steering, suspension, brakes, chassis and finally the wheels and tyres. We would only touch lightly on diesels; it was explained that new mechanics would not be working on vehicles with diesel engines.

After getting to my first 'operational' posting, as opposed to a training one, the only vehicles I can remember having diesels were aircraft-refuelling vehicles and the MK9 fire truck. I seem to remember having an exam – sometimes two – each week, and it was a very steep learning curve, as all RAF training is; we were absolutely swamped with information all the time. If not in the classroom then we would be doing practical work, such as being shown a braking system and then having to re-create one and diagnose faults. This was an area in which I would become extremely proficient in later years. A few pertinent questions as to how and when the fault occurred – Was the engine hot or cold? Was it wet or left standing for any length of time? etc., –could cut the work in half and eliminate needless stripping down of components to find the fault.

Little did I realise that once out in the big, bad world, although we knew how it worked and could draw it with our eyes closed, we would rarely get to strip down major components; an engine or gearbox would simply be replaced, crated up and sent to the REME (Royal Electrical and Mechanical Engineers) workshops, where it would have an in-depth repair. Although I would find my job extremely interesting most of the time, there was a level of monotony at being a 'component changer', however.

When our first day was over, heads numb with information, I can't even remember marching to the mess, or what I had to eat. I do remember lying on my bed trying to take it all in.

Our flight of about ten men soon fell into a routine of marching and learning, learning and marching and, just to shake the cobwebs out of our heads, some PT – which inevitably involved a five-mile run around the airfield or up some God-forsaken hill. I absolutely hated running; it was the dullest of all exercises and aside from all that, my legs were too bloody short! And I was always last.

It was much more fun to watch Jock and Pat tear lumps out of each other during 'British bulldogs' in the gym. I loved basketball and despite my small stature I was, and always have been, a 'good dribbler'. The showers afterwards were always a time for fun, much as I've described before, with extra shampoo being poured onto someone's head, as in the advert, black-face soap, the confiscating

~ JOCK AND PAT ~

and hiding of towels, deodorants being replaced with hair sprays, and generally making everyone's life an absolute misery at every opportunity. I'd even purchased an 'electric-shock lighter' from Cardiff on one of my excursions into town, and took great delight in leaving it lying around in conspicuous places and watching the thieving bastards try it out before deciding whether to nick it or not (as ya do!) It was flung, dropped and hurled in many directions, although the greatest joy came from watching Pat try and try again after thinking that 'jiggling it' would cure the fault!

'What's up with it?' I asked innocently.

'Fuck knows – it keeps electrocuting me.'

Never a thought given to putting it back and leaving well alone. It wasn't long before the glee washed over his face, as his thoughts turned to his adversary.

'Let's put it by the Jock twat's bed; it's the first thing he does every morning.'

The plan was set. The heavy front doors of our block squeaked slowly open at about eleven-thirty pm – a rare occasion when Jock had been out on his own. He was never any trouble when he'd been out on his own and shot like a pinball up the short corridor and into the room; even if all the lights were out, we still heard the salutary greeting, 'What're you looking at?'

He had a habit of arguing with himself, and on many occasions it was the highlight of the week as I cowered beneath my blankets, shoulders rolling with silent laughter until my sides hurt, listening to him stabbing the door in a vain attempt to hit the lock to his private room.

'C'mon, ya bastard'; yis is doin' this on purpose to me, 'cos ah had a wee extra one.'

He would hold the key up to his face and waving it around like a magic wand.

'I'll sleep on the floor, I don't care.'

Still talking to himself, he was now on his knees with his eye an inch from the keyhole, sliding the key across his nose and amazingly into the lock, I gather this ploy must have worked previously or we would have found him on the floor, or one of the beds with just the metal springs on.

'Ah ha! Ya ...' frrrump! The door opened and Jock followed it in, face first.

'Oh, there's nae need for that, eh?'

A few more groans and mumbles and finally, that unmistakeable sound of an RAF single bed when it's first occupied – like the creak of an ancient trampoline. He had left his door ajar and the snores oozed from behind it as cartoon 'Zzzz's; someone was going to have to close it. Pat had already crashed out earlier and I said, 'I'll do it,' complaining all the way for maximum effect.

I padded my way towards the door, pushed it open slightly, removed his shiny 'Zippo' lighter and replaced it with my squarer zapping machine. I pulled the door to, deciding not to close it completely but leave a small gap, so as to hear the morning's noises. Only a select few were in on the joke; after all, it would be as funny to watch those who didn't know what Jock was up to as it would be to hear Jock himself. We awaited the morning with anticipation. When it came, people were milling around as usual, to and from the bathrooms and showers; Jock was always last up anyway, and the suspense was killing me. Pat nonchalantly poked his head from around his door.

~ 57 ~

'He found it yet?' He nodded towards Jock's pit.

'Not yet; you'll have to give him a prod,' I said.

Pat produced the required broom-shank from his room and slid it through the gap in the door, poking Jock relentlessly from behind the wall – not wanting to risk actually opening the door for fear of low-flying shoes and keys that he'd encountered on previous occasions. Jock moaned, and there was a good deal of thrashing of blankets as he turned away from Pat and towards his wall in attempt to protect his 'jewels'.

Pat was not averse to poking him in the bollocks or the arse, and to this end Jock would spin around like a top to avoid the broom handle.

'Away tae fuck, ya bastard!'

'Get up, ya Scotch twat,' Pat said, knowing the correct terms was 'Scots' – but it wound him up something chronic.

'Scots – Scots! Ya lanky streak o' pish!'

Jock had started to wake now, and, true to his nature, the first thing he reached for was his 'fags'.

'Oh c*** – ah've nay fags left,' was the exclamation.

'Hey, pish – geeze a fag, eh?'

A small blue-and-white packet whizzed from one room to the other. Jock's door was now open enough for us to see that he was sitting on the edge of his bed with his head in his hands while clutching the cigarette box with his left hand, so it rested against his cheek.

Everything about this little man was comical to me; he was still partially clothed from the night before and his socks had slid at least half their length off his feet, making him look like 'Wee Willy Winkie'. He opened the cigarette packet.

'Only the wan, ya tight bastard.'

Pat barged into Jock's room and attempted to wrestle the fag back off him.

'Ya can give the fucker back, you ungrateful Celtic troll.'

Jock rolled away from Pat and into the foetal position, protecting the fag; Pat would have scrunched it up in front of him if he'd managed to get hold of it. Jock flicked the prized cigarette triumphantly into his mouth, like Brando, and reached over for the lighter. Still grinning at Pat, he cupped both his hands to his face and:

'Aaaarrrrgh! – What the fuck?!!'

The lighter and the fag fell to the floor as Jock opened his big gob, contorting his face in the process and shaking his hands in shock.

'Ya fucking miserable shower o' shite! Can ah no have a fag without yus ripping the pish this early in the morning?'

He picked up the cigarette, which had become 'kinked' in the incident, and replaced it in his mouth, then stood up and announced to all and sundry that he was away for a shite, as it was the only place he would get any peace. The extra pieces of sock folded themselves underneath his feet as he shuffled off to the lav, with his wonky cigarette still unlit.

I reclaimed my lighter, putting it in my pocket ready for its next outing. I would have to get as many people as I could quickly, as once the gag was 'out' I would no longer be able to use it.

Once more into the breach, dear friends, as we braved breakfast. I left the lighter lying around the table and had 'got' most of the flight by the time we left for class. Once in the classroom and seated, I was dared to put the lighter on the instructor's podium, but I was unsure.

'Go on: it's just a bit of fun,' someone said, backed up by another soon after.

'Keep a look out then,' I said and scampered up to the podium, placing it on the rest at the bottom. Ron entered the room a few minutes later; he was a silver-haired gentleman who looked as though he wasn't too far from retiring. His stocky build and brown 'overall', which inevitably had a grubby hand placed in one of its pockets as if fiddling with something, was a cause for concern as I wondered what it was he was actually fiddling with.

All that was missing was the stutter, and he could have been Ronnie Barker at Arkwright's store any day of the week. He bade us 'Good morning', opened his leather carrying case, took out some papers and placed them on the podium. Noting the lighter but not doing anything about it, he cast an inquisitive eye around the room. Still nothing: he wasn't going to be drawn in so quickly. Once more the suspense was killing me; 'Go on – go on,' I thought to myself; this would be a major triumph if I could electrocute the instructor.

He handed out some booklets on the carburettor, and while we flicked through them I could see that curiosity was getting the better of him. He pushed and flicked the lighter around the podium, as though not sure if it was going to explode or something. He must have 'seen it all' in his time and was indeed extremely wary; finally he picked it up, admiring its highly polished finish like a magpie.

'Does this belong to anyone?' he said, holding it between his thumb and forefinger, end on, like a matchbox, avoiding the trigger. The class looked around aimlessly and shrugged its shoulders.

'OK then; turn to page one and begin reading the first chapter.'

As we did; he lowered the lighter from view and placed it in his left pocket. I thought, 'The cheeky bastard's going to pinch it, and all without being electrocuted;' this was devastating. I thought how he would take it back to the staff room at break time and show the rest of the instructors what I had tried to do, and then I would never see it again.

After reading the first chapter and having a question-and-answer session, Ron rolled the blackboard around and revealed an enlarged diagram of a simple carburettor. He dived his hand into his pocket many times, bringing out different-coloured chalks to represent air, fuel and then a mixture of both, as would be found in a running engine; it was during an explanation of how the 'cold start' or 'choke' mechanism worked that he inevitably fiddled with the lighter with his left hand while colouring the blackboard with his right. A scattering of coloured chalks bounced off the walls, ceiling and desks as he pressed the trigger unknowingly, while doing some sort of Irish jig.

The class jumped, as we had all forgotten about it by now. Ron stood there, staring at the multicoloured fingers of his left hand; not sure of what had caused the shock, he gingerly pulled at the flap of his pocket, peering inside in case it was something living that had caused the pain. All that was left was the remains of chalk sticks and a dusty lighter. Not wanting to touch it again, or in case he had missed a tiny creature with huge teeth, Ron turned his pocket inside out onto the desk in front of us. The lighter clonked out as it tumbled from his pocket and the whole class erupted with laughter.

'OK, whose is it?' he inquired, relieved that he hadn't been punctured by some kind of miniature Tasmanian devil. I sort of half put my hand up, not knowing what to expect; it was a mixture of excitement and trepidation, but above all else it was fucking funny!

By the time we had settled again it was break time, and Ron asked if he could borrow the lighter for the staff room. How could I refuse? After all, he had been such a good sport and I didn't even get a bollocking. We returned from our break and continued being instructed on the working of the carburettor. One thing I do remember is that during the time Ron had to 'baby-sit' our flight, he never once lost his temper or raised his voice: a 'top bloke'.

He told us of the Welsh exclamations as the lighter was passed around the staff room. Ron wasn't Welsh and it gave him as much pleasure to hear these obscenities as he had given us.

We collected handout after handout on different parts of the carburettor, different types and makes; essentially they all did the same thing, which was to mix the correct amount of fuel and air before going into the engine for burning, which is what gives you your power. We were given homework almost every night and our 'best book' had to be up to date. The best book was a plain ruled A4 book, into which selected passages of what we had learned during the day had to be copied, along with detailed drawings. This had the effect of reinforcing the learning, and we would test each other constantly.

The end of the week approached and our first exam proper, aside from the initial tests we were given to assess our mechanical and electrical knowledge. I had stripped motorcycle carburettors down many, many times, but was unaware of the correct names for the parts disassembled; this was the hardest thing for me, remembering all the different names and moreover, what their function was and how they did it.

On the day of the exam, I had jets, accelerator pumps, variable venturis, mixture- and volume-control screws, diaphragms and float chambers coming out of my arse; I was as full as a 'seaside shithouse' on a bank-holiday Monday. The only thing in our favour was the fact that all the questions were multiple-choice, so the correct answer would be in front of us; all we had to do was pick the correct one. Out of the four possible answers, one was so ridiculous that your granny could eliminate it; the second would be a little more tricky; and the two remaining would be so similar you had to take semantics and punctuation into account. Exam rules applied: no talking, chewing, cheating and copying – although of course it all went on, from tiny pieces of paper filled with 'keywords' and inserted into the hollow 'Biro' pens, or rulers with the same etched into them, to writing between the fingers and the brazen piece-of-paper-in-the-pocket scam.

After you had finished you were to hand in your exam sheet at the front and leave the room to the waiting area, just to the rear of the staff room. The examiner would place a 'Master' grid over the exam papers enabling him to have an instant marking system.

The pass mark, I seem to remember, was between seventy and eighty per cent, depending on the subject; and if we did incur a couple of forties on the first exam, they would have to be resat. I seem to remember getting sixty-eight per cent on carburettors – and failing; I would have to resit too. 'If only' and 'Just that one question': I was furious with myself, but had expected to fail – so I did. I made sure I passed the resit, though, and with flying colours; all the ones I had had doubts about were much clearer now and I had got over my first exam nerves.

The waiting room was akin to a gannet colony in full voice,

'What did you put for question ...?' – etc., etc.

Pat, being a qualified mechanic before arriving at St Athan, flew through all the exams with confident ease, with Jock coming a close second. They were always the first to leave, and it unnerved me when I was only halfway through my paper.

No one wanted to be last out of the room, but on a couple of occasions, I was. I thought it better to pass and be last out, than leave early and have to resit. By any standards, for a new mechanic the carburettor is the most technical and intricate part of any petrol engine, and would require a great deal of experience to set up correctly and fault-diagnose.

The weekend was almost here and it was POETS day (Piss Off Early, Tomorrow's Saturday). The teaching staff were great; if they could let us go early, they would. Pat had his own car and gave Jock a lift somewhere or other; the rest of us would trot up to station HQ to pick up our rail warrants for the journey home. Chuffed that I'd passed my resit so well, I was in high spirits, rushing back to our accommodation and packing my kitbag to the gunnels for a weekend away.

Four of us shared a taxi to Cardiff Central station, which was an adventure in itself, with the taxis – mostly Ladas – held together with 'bodge' tape, sporting racing slicks and driven by 'Stavros' (from the Harry Enfield television programme). With a Welsh accent, 'Cardiff, is it you want, boys?' would propel us at breakneck speed, so as to be back at camp before the endless stream of paying airmen ran out. This was a journey from hell; four lads and four full kitbags made the Ladas handle like the proverbial blancmange. Several times the rear wheels lost traction and the back end of the car 'stepped out', forcing the driver to do a rally-style 'crossover' during the fifteen terrifying miles from camp to the train station – and we had it all to do again on the way back.

'It all adds to the excitement, isn't it?' said 'Stavros'.

We squashed, leant on and elbowed each other like a row of budgerigars on a perch as we were hurled from side to side around the winding and twisting roads of St Athan. I have never been so glad to get out of a taxi in all my life; I knew the others felt the same, as hardly a word was spoken during the journey.

~ Drop and Give Me Twenty! ~

'What about my tip, you wankers?' Stavros called after us.
'Drive fucking slower, boyo, and take a shower,' said the tallest of our group. 'Stavros' gestured as if he was going to give chase and we flew into the station like men possessed, merging into the crowd. God, that was scary! And I offered many prayers up to the Lord that we weren't going to get the same driver on our return. We would remain in our group of four until Birmingham, where two of the lads were going in different directions; we said our goodbyes and wished them a good weekend.

❖ ❖ ❖

8. Train Mischief

I was going to Durham and Darren was changing at York for somewhere else. Darren wasn't from my course; he was somewhat ahead of me and I think he got tired of my incessant questioning,

'For fuck's sake, Bob – give it a rest; my ears are drooping at the corners.'

I was just so excited – smart in my uniform, money in my pocket, free education and travel: surely you'd have to go a long way to get better than this?

I wanted to keep talking, but he just slid back in his seat and nodded off. I stared out of the window, watching the scenery rush by, occasionally catching my own reflection when entering a short tunnel. It was an old-style train with a compartment of about six to eight seats and a corridor to the left of it, accessed by a sliding door.

I would go for a short walk, sticking my head out of the window just enough to inflate my cheeks, only to be practically sucked through it by a train passing in the opposite direction. I thought of the 'Young Ones', when Vivian reads the sign telling him not to put his head out of the window and wonders 'Why?' – then ignores it anyway. I had walked up and down the carriages, been to the toilet several times, using up the last of the toilet paper and hiding the replacement roll, so the next person, if they needed 'a sit down', wouldn't have any. I even stood on the carriage joint, so that my feet moved up and down and in different directions at the same time, making up a little dance to the rhythm of the train as it crossed points and rounded corners, which would expand and contract the ageing concertina between the two carriages and allow faint whiffs of diesel fumes to irritate my nose. In short, I was bored, and when I get bored mischief is never far away!

A bloke excused himself as he pushed past me and into the toilet of 'no paper'; he was in there a good while and I kept smiling to myself, knowing he'd have been out by now if it was just a wee. We never think to check for paper before sitting down, do we? 'Bastard!' was the cry from the little room, followed by a flush and then a face emerged from behind the bog door.

'Can you see if there's any paper in the loo across the way, please?' the face said.

'Yeah, sure,' I replied and popped into the adjacent bog.

'No, mate – none left,' I said, wearing my 'butter-wouldn't-melt' face.

There was – loads of it; but that would have been too easy. The face slid back behind the door, muttering something about 'fucking British Rail' as it went; there was a good deal of running water and I thought I'd better make myself scarce in case he did check the other lav. I returned to my carriage and sat down. A man kept opening and closing his brief case, the type with the rolling combination lock; every time he put the case down next to me, I would roll one of the wheels around so that it would be locked when he picked it back up. After a couple of times he became suspicious, but it was entertaining nonetheless. Looking around the carriage for more mischief, I glanced into the corridor, to see the man from the toilet going past doing a kind of 'duck waddle'. I laughed towards the window, causing the rest of the carriage to look up with curiosity, wondering what I'd seen.

Darren was still asleep and we were approaching York; I toyed with the idea of leaving him asleep, waking him as the train was pulling out, but then I thought how pissed off I'd be if someone ruined my weekend, so I didn't.

'Hey – Darren, Darren: this is your stop, isn't it?' I shook him gently.

'What – where are we?'

He scrunched his fists into his eye sockets, rotating them concentrically. Still sitting, he stretched his arms and legs out, like a waking cat, groaning as his muscles lengthened.

'Right, Bob – have a good 'un. Might see ya on the way back?' he said, while reaching above for his RAF holdall. 'Yeah,' I thought, 'thanks for the scintillating conversation; I can barely contain my excitement.' I waved as he passed outside the window, wondering what would have happened if I hadn't awakened him!

I grabbed the two small handles of the aluminium windows, pulling them apart smartly, sticking my head through the gap and shouted:

'Ay up, duck – get thee sen darn chip oil; an 'ev' whale 'n' sack 'o' chips for me. Tha knows – in't it 'ot? Sup wi' thee?'

It was an inexperienced and crude attempt at a Yorkshire accent. Someone once told me that you could always spot a Yorkshireman in a crowd, as they all have sticking-out ears and bald heads. On lowering my normally raised guard, I asked, 'Go on then,' expecting some sort or sarcasm or ridicule to be poured on me. He cupped both hands behind his ears, forcing them forward, and said:

'HOW MUCH?', swiftly followed by a pressed palm sliding over his dome towards the back of his head, going 'F-U-U-U-CK ME!'

I watched the Cadbury's chocolate machines on the station wall glide by as our train 'hokey-cokeyed' into life once more. I've always fancied one of those thick bars, but never dared darting onto the platform to get one in case I was left behind, and in any case some bastard would always pinch your seat!

With just an hour to go, my thoughts turned to my Dad, who would be picking me up from Durham train station in whatever 'piece of shit' he could afford at the time; lately it was a 1500cc VW ('deerstalker') Beetle in darkest green. Considering he had been a mechanic in the RAF himself, albeit an aircraft mechanic, he had an aptitude for buying cars that looked nice initially, but fell apart within the next six months, never again to qualify for an MOT. We actually had one with 'grass' growing out of one of the wings; I think it was a Mk 1 Escort. The 'deerstalker' Beetle had been purchased for, no doubt, an exorbitant fee just a few days earlier, but when Dad was driving it to work on the notorious A19 towards Peterlee in the early hours of the morning, a deer jumped out in front of the German 'people's wagon' and was duly struck 'full force', leaving a huge crater in the 'snot green' bonnet and wing of said car and a dying carcass at the side of the road.

I imagine the incident would have been over in seconds but would have been quite frightening at the time. Nevertheless, in time Dad would be chastised by his mates for not stopping and collecting the carcass, which we were assured would have covered the costs of repair many times over; but Dad loved nature and embraced its wild animal life. I doubt he would have the stomach for such callousness, having taken the life of one of nature's gifts. Meeting Dad was both exciting and fearful; I never knew what 'mood' he would be in and there would be a period of time when I would have to walk on eggshells until I either remained silent for the rest of the journey home, or told him of my exploits with my new comrades. The reason for the eggshells was that Dad was a drinker, and coming to collect me from Durham train station would have interfered with his weekend 'slurp' – not that he didn't have a midweek slurp, or indeed a Monday, Tuesday and Thursday one to complement the weekend. I could never work out if he was coming down from Sunday night, or building up to the following Friday.

Anyway, he soon tired of picking me up and after a short time the task of being collected from the station on a Friday night would fall to Mam. This was great for me as I was in possession of my provisional licence, and on occasion she would let me drive the 'snotmobile' back home. It was the following Saturday morning, when Dad had gone to the pub and Mam wanted to go shopping, that I volunteered to drive her, as I did at every available opportunity to get in as much practice as possible. While she was shopping I lifted the boot lid and began tinkering with the German carburettor, thinking I knew what I was doing.

I had never even seen this make of carburettor before, never mind tampered with one – and why would it need tampering with? It was running as well as could be expected for a car of this age, albeit a tad heavy on fuel for a 1500cc. Still, tinker and tamper I did, pulling and pushing at linkages, imagining what was going on inside the carburettor, now that I was fully versed in all aspects of the intricacies of fuel management. Mam appeared as 'Shirley Valentine', weighed down with numerous colourful carrier bags from different shops, bulging to breaking point so that the handles turned her fingers and wrists white. I hurriedly closed the lid, hoping she hadn't seen me; she hadn't, and I opened the driver's door, tilting the seat forward so as to make way for the shopping to fill up the back seat – which it did.

We climbed in, dragged the heavy seatbelts around us and locked them into place with that reassuring, over-engineered 'Clunk'. I turned the key to the start position and the engine began turning ... and turning ... and turning, I'd flooded it, with all my tampering with the linkages. 'Bloody German crap,' I said, now that I was allowed to swear – being in the Air force.

'What d'ya think's the matter with it?' Mam enquired.

'I'm not sure; I'll have a look,' I said, climbing out and lifting the boot lid once more, pretending to do something knowledgeable, getting my hands dirty and allowing a couple of minutes to pass. I turned the key once more, leaning through the open window, and the German 'Snots-Wagen' spluttered into life.

'Aren't you clever?' Mam said, and I was flushed with false pride. On the way home I explained in simpler terms what the carburettor was for and what it did, including the accelerator pump, which, for a want of a better description give you an extra squirt of fuel (before the advent of fuel injection) when needed, say for overtaking or pulling away. 'Allow me to demonstrate,' I said, taking my foot completely off the accelerator. The 'Love Bug's' nose dived into deceleration and the contents of the back seat slid onto the floor, including the eggs, milk and the small box of sticky buns that Mam loved so much and were to have been our Saturday teatime treat. Mam, too, lunged forward, only to be thrust backwards as I stamped on the accelerator pedal once more.

'Well, I didn't think it would be that severe,' I bleated. Needless to say, I went without a sticky bun that Saturday.

Not content with that misdemeanour, to keep fit I ran alongside the Beetle, Miami Vice-style, as Mam was driving it out of our cul-de-sac. One day I leapt onto the passenger-side running board with both feet, like a gangster, grasping the door handle as I went into a semi-crouched position. The running board came completely away from the car and I skidded to an abrupt halt as Mam sailed out of the street, totally oblivious to the incident. I looked down at the rubber-coated runner, which was now lying at my feet and thought. 'OH, FUCK!' Boy, was I gonna get it when Dad found out! I picked it up and skulked back into the garden, finding a suitable hiding place where I could either dispose of it altogether or attempt to reattach it at a later date.

It never got reattached. I just placed it on the grass in the dead of night, directly below where it should have been on the car; of course when Dad came to drive to work the next morning, reversing off the grass and onto the road, he noticed the long, slug-like shape nestling in the short grass. He got out, cigarette sloping out of his mouth like a gunslinger, walked over to it, kicked it and then the car, got back in shaking his head and drove off. The Beetle deteriorated rapidly after that, with things going wrong on a regular basis and him having to get lifts into work etc. Parts were both expensive and difficult to obtain and the death knell sounded for the green people's wagon.

The next time I came home, I had been studying Ignition systems and decided to give Dad's 'new' garden-centre Ford Escort (with the grassy wings) a well-deserved service. I bought new plugs, points (older readers will remember these with relish, especially if you owned a Mini), distributor cap, rotor arm and leads and replaced them all with an 'air of confidence', much more than before now that we had moved on with our studies. But if it hadn't been for the bloke next door, the Escort would have never run again!

I got the 'HT' leads mixed up, so that it backfired, farted and tried to run backwards as I turned over the engine. Deciding it couldn't have been anything I'd done but it must be the 'points', I took out the old ones – which looked in remarkable condition, I have to say – and replaced them with the new ones. After that it didn't even backfire! After I had almost flattened the battery Dave, our next-door neighbour, had seen enough; with a fiddle here, and a 'plop' there as the plug leads were put onto the correct plugs, the little Ford purred into life as it had once before.

I was as grateful as any man could be. Dave smiled and I promised him the Earth before he went back into his house, pressing a taut finger against his lips and winking a secret wink.

However! – the wink wasn't as secret as I had thought and after a night in the pub, Dad threatened to hide whatever car he had when I returned after studying the braking system.

On one of my long train journeys back to St Athan, I met up with some 'matelots' (Navy personnel) after York; they were in the party mood, necking bottles of Newcastle Brown Ale as if it would be their last for a very long time. It may have been: I never found out. I put my kit bag in the overhead storage rack next to their 'sausage bags'.

'Ah, crab fat,' one of them said.

'Ah, fish heads,' I replied, noting that one of the address labels had HMS something-or-other on it. 'Crab Fat' was what the Navy called the Air Force; I'm told it has something to do with the colour of our uniforms. We called them 'matelots'; I know not why, although I'm sure the answer will be on the internet somewhere – but then again so is the answer to 'life, the universe and everything, which is 42', if you believe 'The Hitchhikers' Guide To The Galaxy'. If I looked up every little curiosity that scampered across my inquisitive mind, I'd never get off the damn' thing!

'Want one?' a voice said, holding out a bottle of brown in an offering gesture.

'Sure,' I replied. 'Thanks.'

I listened intently to the unfamiliar 'Navy speak' and tried to guess what it meant. We swapped questions and consumed much ale; when theirs ran out I offered some money for one of the lads to go to the buffet car and buy more cans. He did, and we proceeded to get 'hammered'. All I can remember is the low mumble of the lads as I slid into an alcohol-induced slumber.

When I awoke, the train was just pulling out of Cheltenham Spa. I knew I could change at two places, Cheltenham Spa and Birmingham New Street; unaware of the order in which we would pass them, I inquired of a guard.

'What time do we get into Birmingham?'

He twisted his wrist and jerked his sleeve to uncover his watch.

'About an hour and a half ago.'

He grinned one of those very special British Rail grins that only a guard above any riposte can give. His grin turned into a fully fledged smile that was inversely proportional to my saddening frown.

'I've got to get to Cardiff,' I said.

'Not tonight you're not, mate,' he replied. 'No more trains to Cardiff on a Sunday night now; next stop Bristol Temple Meads.'

'Can't I get one from there?' I asked.

'Not tonight,' he repeated. 'Earliest one'll be about six am.'

'Shit! I'll never get to camp before eight o'clock,' I muttered. 'I'll get charged!'

My childish face must have looked as if it was going to burst into tears at any moment. I was still dazed from all the Newcastle Brown and could feel myself welling up. He must have detected a real fear, because his attitude changed to that of a concerned individual.

'Come on, stand with me in the guard's van, and I'll make sure you get off at the right time and see what I can do for ya.'

~ Drop and Give Me Twenty! ~

I never left the bloke's side in fear of missing the Bristol stop. As we pulled into Bristol he pointed to a little room at the end of the platform, where the door was slightly ajar and a warm, welcoming, yellowish light shone out.

'Go in there, tell them you've spoken to me and explain the situation.'

I thanked him; he turned, waved a flag, blew his whistle and climbed back into his van; the solid wooden door and that distinctive carriage 'slam' announced his departure. I watched the red lights of the guard's van disappear into the cold night; it had gone midnight and I stood alone on the platform, not another soul in sight. What if the little room was just a waiting room, with no one there? How cruel would that be?

As I walked towards the shaft of light like a transfixed moth my spirits lifted, as I could hear the clanging of a spoon against the side of a tea mug. I knocked on the door, pushing it open at the same time; a bearded old man sat in a moth-eaten armchair, with the padding missing from its arms, at the back of the room. He continued to stir his tea while glancing up from his newspaper and over the top of his half-moon glasses.

'What can I do fur you, young feller?' he said in his strong Bristol accent.

I thought, 'That's all I need! Wisdom and guidance from the Wurzel fucking Gummidge appreciation society.'

'Erm – the guard on the last train said you would be able to help me get to Cardiff,' I began.

'Oh did ee now? Might be so, might be not – you got any fags?'

'No, sorry, I don't smoke.'

The nicotine-stained finger took the spoon out and placed it on the wooden table, but not before tapping it twice on the rim of the mug. There was something very ritualistic about this man; if he got any more laid back he'd be lying down.

'I'll just go and look at the timetable,' I said.

'No need; I been 'ere afore the war and can even tell you the names of the rats that run on these lines – and what time 'im comin',' he boasted.

He looked as if he'd been in that fucking chair since before the war! The first one.

'Nuthin comin' thru 'ere 'sept a cattle truck at 4 am, an' he's stopping fur sum mail,' he continued.

'Where's it going?' I asked eagerly.

'You got any chocolate?' he asked.

'No, I haven't.'

'There's plenty in them vending machines on the wall outside,' he gestured with his head.

'Would you like one?' I asked expectantly.

'I might,' he replied.

And the penny dropped, or rather the fifty pence dropped for a bar of chunky chocolate from off the station wall. This chap was my only hope of getting back to camp before I was missed, and he knew it.

''Em cows be bound fur Swansea,' and the conversation was 'back on track', if you'll forgive the pun.

~ 68 ~

''Im's stopping at Cardiff fur more post as well.'
All I had to do now was get on the fucking thing.
'D'ya suppose I could ride in the guard's van?'
'Unauthorised passengers in the guards van – unheard of,' he said, snapping a finger of chocolate off the bar.
'I'm gonna be in real trouble if I don't get back to camp in time.'
'Camp – what camp?' he questioned.
'St Athan,' I said.
'Oh, you be one of them pilots; I 'ad a cousin was a pilot in the war – he used to fly ...'

He looked up to the ceiling, trying to remember the name of the aircraft, his right hand straining the bristle of his unkempt beard, while small pieces of chocolate fell into his lap. He went off on a nostalgic rant; I thought of snatching my chocolate back and stuffing the remaining fingers into my mouth: surely that would bring him back to reality?

'No, it's gone,' he said. 'Can't remember.'
'Sopwith Camel – Tiger Moth?' I said sarcastically.
'No, they's long ago, them 'uns is.' He looked at me in a 'second take', as if he'd just cottoned on I was taking the piss.
'You young 'uns – don't know nuthin!'

I was thinking I might tell him that what he had just said was a double negative, as I recall from my schooldays when the Physics teacher asked me what I was doing. 'I'm not doing nothing, sir,' I replied eagerly.

'Then you must be doing something,' he beamed.

His white teeth looked lost in all the black facial hair – he too had a full beard and used to stroke it almost sexually; I often wondered what he was thinking about while doing this. While everyone else's head was in a book, mine was watching everyone else and the teacher. Maybe that's what reminded me of the double negative? I don't know when I started comparing teachers to characters I'd seen on television or read about, but the Physics teacher was 'Oddbod Junior' from the 'Carry On' films, where he was regenerated from a finger that had fallen off his father's hand. It still makes me laugh today.

Our French teacher was the 'Wicked Witch' from the 'Wizard of Oz', always having nervous breakdowns outside the headmaster's office. The Technical Drawing teacher was akin to Patrick Moore from 'The Sky at Night'; he had a passion for 'Bakelite' and was locked in his paper cupboard by one of his pupils. He had plenty of time to find his Bakelite in there, looking for the light switch.

The Metalwork teacher was definitely Mr Rigsby, but he had a speech impediment that meant anyone within three feet of him was showered with spit. He also had the worst-fitting dentures that anyone could have; on several occasions they made a bid for freedom, flying out of his mouth, but were immaculately caught by a perfected encircling, swooping motion by his right hand before they could get very far. A couple of times it led to a swift, frantic, midair juggle as the slippery 'gnashers' took on a life of their own, but they never made it to the floor all the time I was there! Good on ya, sir!

By this time I was sitting with my back to the wall on top of my RAF holdall, my head sinking into my hands, which were supported by my elbows on top of my knees. Partly due to tiredness, partly frustration and mostly wishing I hadn't met the 'matelots'' fucking Newcastle Brown! I must have dozed off, because the next thing I remember is being shoved sideways and doing one of those 'pig snuffles' that you do when you've just woken up.

'C'mon, lad – your train's 'ere.'

Picking my bag up I walked towards the train, now standing at the platform nearest us.

'This is 'im,' the stationmaster said.

He pushed me towards the guard's van; it was still pitch black – Lord knows what time it was. All I could see as I looked along the length of the train were wisps of chilled breath coming from the carriages and the occasional 'Moo'.

I felt as though I was in a Mel Brooks film, waiting for something ridiculous to happen, but it didn't. Once on board I was soon sitting down again; the train's air brakes hissed, a door slammed and that romantic rocking motion pushed me over to sleep once more. I hadn't even said thanks to my rescuer; had he not awoken me, I'd have missed this one as well.

My eyes had been closed for what seemed like thirty seconds, when a firm grip took hold of my shoulder.

''Ere we are, boy – Cardiff, this is Cardiff; mind the cows as they get off.'

Of course the cows weren't getting off and his humour fell on stony ground. I made sure he would pass on my thanks to 'Catweazle' at Bristol and thanked him a great deal also. It was six-thirty; I had an hour to get back to camp, get changed and try for some breakfast before being in the classroom and seated by eight o'clock. I felt as rough as a badger's arse: unwashed and unshaven, sweaty and stiff as a board.

The station was mostly empty; I made my way towards the taxi rank, yawning as I went – one of those yawns that forces you to close your eyes, tilt your head back and put out a cautionary hand in case you miss your step. I knew I would have to pay for the whole journey myself, as opposed to sharing the cost with a few others; basically on a Sunday night we would hang around the entrance to the station looking for kitbags or very short haircuts and ask if they were going to St Athan and if they wanted to share, all the time scanning the cars to make sure we didn't get 'Stavros', the maniac who brought us here only a few weeks earlier. I looked into the car at the front of the rank; it wasn't 'Stavros'.

'How much to St Athan, mate?' I inquired.

'You leaving it a bit late, isn't it?'

'Yeah, I know – how much?'

'Tenner – tenner it is to St Athan.'

'OK.' I threw my bag on the back seat and strapped myself in.

'Quick as you like, mate,' I said, trying not to look too desperate.

'Morning traffic can be quite busy, you see,' the driver said.

~ Train Mischief ~

I got the distinct impression he would be fishing for some extra cash. He was, and talked about the night he had just had: a Sunday night in Cardiff City, lively by all accounts,

'I 'ad this one woman rubbing my knackers with her bare feet from the back seat,' he began, I smiled.

'Her and her two mates was well pissed – "I hope I'm getting this for nothing," she said. With trotters that smell like that – I'm charging you double, you hacky mare!'

I rolled with laughter.

'What was the outcome, then?' I humoured him.

'They was all over me like a rash – I 'ad to fight em off with a shitty stick.'

He was nothing to look at, but I laughed again anyway. We arrived at the camp gates at about ten past seven; taxis were not allowed on camp, so I still had to walk to my block. By the time I got there the lads had already left for breakfast, so I knew it had gone seven-thirty. I grabbed my washing and shaving kit and made for the ablutions: a quick cat-lick and a 'rasp' with the razor, putting on Friday's crumpled uniform that had been in the bottom of the bag since Sunday night, and I was off!

Looking and feeling as though I had been dragged through a hedge backwards, I made it to the large green door of the training section just in time. I went straight to the classroom and sat in my normal seat, while the lads had a fag in the rest area. I was well chuffed: I had come out of this adventure unscathed and uncharged, which was my major concern.

The rest of the class filed in and took their seats as normal, picked up their folders and opened their books at 'Transmissions'. FUCK! In all the rush, I had come out without my folder or books, pens or pencils. Well, nearly a perfect escape; it just meant that I would have it all to copy at the end of the day – a small penance considering what could have happened.

The next two months at St Athan would be pretty much the same as before, studying for exams and continuing to pass them with ever-increasing grades. I had really grasped the RAF's way of teaching and the fact that in 'multiple choice' exams the answer was right there in front of you; you just had to pick the correct one. Three months had now passed and we faced our final exam, a combination of all that we had learned previously. We all passed, but with grades considerably lower than in the individual modules – but pass we did. Our reward was an LAC badge (Leading Aircraftsman), consisting of two horizontally opposed propellers, to be sewn onto the shoulder of our uniforms by the camp tailor, ready for another 'Pass Out' parade.

For those of us who couldn't wait for the tailor, this was a rudimentary introduction to sewing. I tacked my badge on as best I could; it was rough, but it stayed on, unlike some others that had gaps big enough for the wind to get behind and cause them to flap and eventually come off. The parade ground was cleared of traffic cones that the driving school used to instruct its recruits, and a time was set for our final parade.

Done and dusted, we were marched up to Station Headquarters to receive our certificates for completing the course, 112 MT Mech. Our City and Guilds

~ Drop and Give Me Twenty! ~

Certificates would be posted on to us at a later date. We were also told the name of our first 'operational posting'; mine was to be RAF College Cranwell in rural Lincolnshire. A good deal of 'rumour control' was in play as to what the various camps were like, even though none of us had ever been to any of them. For some it was the concern of how far they would be from home – and I do declare that the RAF did its utmost to put as much distance as possible between one's home town and one's first posting; I could see why. After spending all this time, money and effort training us, they wouldn't want us running home to mummy every weekend.

When the time came for an overseas posting they wouldn't tolerate 'apron string' girlfriends or even fiancées, but if you were married, that was a different kettle of fish.

❖ ❖ ❖

9. Buffoon Apprentice

Royal Air Force College Cranwell, beautiful and picturesque: set in rural Lincolnshire and the home of IOT (Initial Officer Training) and BFTS (Basic Flying Training School). With its central thoroughfare lined with mature oak and chestnut trees, and the odd cherry and apple blossom thrown in for good measure, it was in summer a beauty to behold – and in winter an absolute nightmare, because of the amount of leaves and petals that had to be constantly cleaned away. The small left-hand-drive Bedford road sweeper was always in demand.

The 'Orange' was a large, grassed oval in front of the magnificent College Hall, where the sound of leather on willow could be heard on rare occasions on a warm summer's evening. The Hall was as grand as the White House; it was on a slightly smaller scale, but performed the same function. This was where the highest of the high went about their duties of running the station, waited on hand and foot by the 'coffee jockeys' or 'plate slingers' – stewards was their official title.

It was also the place where visiting dignitaries would be paraded so the camp photographer could get their 'best side' with this magnificent backdrop. He, incidentally, was the only person permitted to be in full 'Number One' uniform but still wearing a beret; this always struck me as odd, and looked completely out of place among the medals and 'spaghetti' of the 'top brass'. Inquiring of one of the corporals, who later became a good friend – almost a surrogate father – I was asked, 'Have you ever tried to take a photograph with a peaked cap on?' I had one of those 'oh yeah' moments. So grand was this place that us 'erks' were not allowed to enter, except on official business and via the 'tradesman's entrance', i.e. round the back, or when on an escorted and guided tour, of which I chose to partake a little later on.

If we did have call to be there on official business, we had to make sure that our uniforms were perfect, berets correctly positioned with the badge over the left eye, etc.: the RAF Regiment had a passion for shaping and contorting berets into shapes and styles one could only imagine. They would tear out the protective plastic square on the inside, because it allegedly made your head sweat and could cause premature baldness; then they soaked the beret in water and let it shrink-fit onto their 'noggin', so that when they took it off it left a Frankenstein-type ring around the forehead, complete with little pleat marks: just perfect.

Swinderby and St Athan were both presentable camps as far as training goes, but this was 'Hofficer training' – where they would read *The Times*, *Guardian* and other huge papers that required the knack of folding them up in such a way as to be left with a neat square, with the story you were interested in at its centre. There would be the reading, and then the unfolding – so much so that the paper was rarely still; it sounded like kindling burning, with the inevitable 'crack' as it was shaken out to its full size while a page was turned, then the whole process started again. It all seemed a bit much for me, and on the very rare occasions I had recourse to be in the Officers' Mess I would mimic the 'big read', trying to cross my legs like a gentleman – only they were too short and fat, and one leg would inevitably slide over the other's knee. I could never get the paper to 'crack', either; it usually ended in my inadvertently losing my grip on the back page, causing the whole thing to disintegrate into a shambles.

Cranwell's flora and fauna, pristine lawns and whispering trees would be my home and grounding for the next four and a half years. I would hone my skills in my chosen craft, fall in love, get married and, while on honeymoon, be told I was going to the Falklands for four months. I would become estranged, separated and finally divorced two years later.

But first I needed somewhere to stay; on this occasion the transit accommodation was a converted married quarter, where the two upstairs bedrooms and one living room had been fitted with Yale locks and made into 'bedsits', for want of a better description, the kitchen and bathroom being on a shared basis.

My front bedroom looked out onto the 'main drag', as it was referred to; it was the civilian road that split the camp, with the operational part on one side and the married quarters, NAAFI and post office on the other. I remember dropping my kitbag, with a resounding but comforting 'thump', and thinking: 'This is it; I've made it!'

I remember it was raining, too; I knelt on my bed, placed my elbows on the windowsill and watched the rain join up into mini-rivers as it drummed on my window. I decided to have a hot soak in the bath, followed by the complementary wank to celebrate my new surroundings and send me off to the land of slumber, ready for my first day at my first operational station. As I lay in bed, with my crisp sheets (from the laundry, not from me) I heard a key in the front door, at some time approaching midnight. The voice was singing AC/DC while negotiating the stairs.

''Cos I'm back-back in black', followed by vocal air guitar; it was one of those situations where you cannot be sure whether you're awake or dreaming. Anyway, I was far too warm and comfy to do anything about it now, although I do recall feeling a little reassured that I wasn't in the house on my own.

'GOOD MORNING, CAMPERS!' No reveille here; it was up to little old me to be 'shit shaved, showered and shampooed' in time for my 'Welcome to Cranwell' speech. Only there wasn't a shower and last night's bath was still in force. I was as smart as a carrot, with highly polished shoes, razor-sharp creases and light-blue shirt and tie; I was proud of my appearance, and although it was terribly time-consuming, I had decided I would keep up this standard always. If only you could have seen me 'morph' into a 'sack of shit' within six months: I wouldn't have believed it. The 'White Crane Club' and the influence of my fellow work colleagues took their toll almost immediately, My introduction to frequenting the 'Pigs' Bar' was to see two lads at opposite ends of the bar dipping pickled eggs into their beer, putting them whole into their mouths and blowing them simultaneously across the room with a 'PAH' sound; his corresponding mate would catch it whole in his mouth!!! An almighty cheer went up as the eggs were displayed, unchewed.

I don't know who started the craze, but I practically became addicted to pickled eggs and ready-salted crisps. You put the egg or eggs into the crisp packet and shook vigorously; some vinegar went into the crisps and some salt onto the eggs – perfect. However! – if there's one thing I learned during my ten years in the RAF, it is that almost ALL, bar a chosen few, could make Le Petomane (the Frenchman who made a stage career from farting at will) look and sound like an absolute amateur! – and that included women.

The small changing room at MTMS (Mechanical Transport Maintenance Section) on a Monday morning required the nostrils of a camel and the constitution of a rhino if one wasn't to blow chunks. Ten pints of John Smith's and a vindaloo, rounded off with a couple of pickled eggs, took their toll on the digestive system, and marks out of ten were awarded for duration, character, pitch, aroma and sound; it was always a lively time. I distinctly remember one particular character whose purple farts left a lingering haze that would take several minutes to dissipate. The locker-room door would open, but no one entered. Then a familiar arse reversed just its cheeks into the doorway and deposited a massive guff; a quick pat of the pants and the door was firmly slammed and locked from the outside, leaving us to put berets over our noses (another great use for the beret) and open the tiny window in a desperate gasp for clean air.

The Saturday-morning 'duty fitter' had usually been up to some mischief in the locker room, ready for Monday morning; this would include sewing up the legs of some overalls. There is nothing more entertaining than watching a person hopping around the locker room, in the vain hope that the leg of his overall will unfold at any second, bringing the improvised 'River Dance' to an abrupt end. Swapping the contents of lockers around, so you had ALL of someone else's gear and vice versa, was another ploy.

Then there was placing countless porn mags into a married guy's locker and – the 'grand finale' – actually climbing into the locker itself, awaiting the owner to open the door and be pounced on. I have seen this done on several occasions and, believe me, it lost none of its originality each time it was performed, probably due to the unsuspecting, hung-over airman who opened the locker – 'Good Show'!

So my first day began with the usual paperwork bollocks at the guardroom and then onto SHQ (Station Headquarters) for some more. It was then time for lunch. I was constantly trying to take in what was where in relation to my accommodation, but in fact the camp was very compact – unlike St Athan, where a good fifteen-minute Land Rover ride was required to get from one side of the camp to the other. Most places, or 'sections' as they were called, were within walking distance, albeit at a brisk walk; it wouldn't take you long to visit all the major places – the Mess, Guardroom, Accommodation, Stores, SHQ, the medical and dental centres – which, incidentally, were staffed by relatives of the Fuehrer himself.

You had to be at death's door to get a day off; even then you were chastised for being a 'pouf' or a 'lightweight'. I once spent four days in Cranwell's medical centre with food poisoning, being allowed only 'clear liquids' – which the nurse took to be water only. After being declared fit for duty, I was told that clear liquids included the likes of Ribena and diluted orange juice – bastards!

The dentists, unlike civilian dentists, were not dependent on the number of patients treated to dictate their income; they could torture you for as long as they wanted, without reprisal – and they did. I still have a morbid fear of dentists, even to this day, and I have to be prised off the sides of the chair to get me to lie down.

It's the only place where you have to pay for pain, unless of course you're a masochist. The Airmen's Mess (I often wondered why it was called a 'mess': I must look into that) was pretty much as before but a little grander, with paintings of Lawrence of Arabia, astride a motorcycle, on the wall. A selection of exotic-looking plants sat wearily in the alcoves in the wall, begging for a drink. But now I knew I had really made it – we had carpet on the floor, and not tiles! I remember thinking that the quality of the food had reached its ceiling for an airman; unless I was going to dine in the sergeants' or officers' mess, this was as good as it was gonna get – apart from those fucking rubber eggs, that is.

I am utterly convinced that this is no accident, and that all RAF cooks have to go on a special course to achieve that very individual consistency. The cold bacon and 'raw on one side and cremated on the other' sausages were as common as the cold. It appeared that no one liked cooking breakfast, wherever I was. The endless scorn poured over the cooks was relentless, but even though they had pretty much heard it all, occasionally someone would come up with a new, relevant and original insult, which would cheer us all up no end.

After the formalities I was given a tour around 'the section' (MTMS), which was originally called MTSS (Mechanical Transport Servicing Section) until some 'knob-head' decided that workplaces on camps in Germany might have had an 'SS' in their title and we couldn't have that now could we? This was, to me anyway, political correctness gone mad; I've always spoken my mind, which is probably why I have ended up in so much trouble. The tour started in the Tyre and Bicycle bay at the bottom right-hand corner of the large yard, which contained many vehicles in various states of disrepair.

As the name implies, it was where tyres were repaired, replaced and balanced and where the camp's huge fleet of bicycles, some three hundred in fact, was serviced and repaired.

There was a rumour that my predecessor had been caught sniffing a WRAF officer's seat when she returned to get something from the saddlebag, after dropping the bike off for servicing; apparently he didn't know where to put his face. Given a little more thought, it wouldn't have been where it was when he was caught; she allegedly fled in purple embarrassment, and the culprit had an agonising wait to find out if she was going to report it.

I would have loved to be a fly on the wall at that reporting. Needless to say, the chap was posted off the unit soon after, but he wasn't charged.

The next bay to the left of the tyre bay was for specialist refueller servicing, where the tools were made from an antistatic and anti-spark material. Only very experienced mechanics and technicians would be allowed to work on these vehicles, and it would usually be a corporal or sergeant. It was 'dirty' work; the vehicles would be covered in a fine silt of dust and paraffin that would ingrain itself in your skin if you opted out of the 'barrier cream' provided. Once when one of the fitters from the refueller bay brought his sandwiches into the tea bar and left black finger-marks, where he had been holding them in between bites, a fly landed on one of his sandwiches. He leapt up, shooing the fly away, and taking the Dalmatian-spotted bread, threw it into the bin.

'What've ya done that for? The fucking fly's cleaner than you!' someone said. The room erupted with laughter, and for the very first time I had seen the power of humour in full flight. I laughed too, but the fitter glared at me, so I stopped and put my head down. The new kid always gets the shit and I was no different. You had to 'get some in' – meaning time, of course – before you were allowed to take part in any ridicule. I was to make this mistake on more than one occasion, and I paid the price heavily. I was incredibly immature, naive, impetuous, inexperienced – but eager to please. I would do anything I was told; after all, that was all I'd ever known. All I ever wanted was to be accepted as 'one of the lads', and it seemed to be taking forever.

During the tour I was summoned to the 'Gruppenfuehrer's' office – a Flight Sergeant, which is one rank down from 'top dog' in our trade, with the top being Warrant Officer. This was like having an appointment with God; I was petrified and couldn't imagine what I had done to warrant an audience with 'the man' so soon. It was time for another speech. I entered his office, which was extremely orderly, like a company director's office. I was still wearing my beret.

'Hat off, lad – no woodpeckers in here. Shut the door.' I did as I was told and stood to attention, rigid as at Swinderby.

'Sit.' He gestured, a pointing-down motion with his finger.

I did, although 'Shit' would have been a more appropriate order. He interlocked his fingers across his chest and, leaning back in his chair slightly, he began:

'I consider myself to be a fair man-a good boss-if you have a problem-my door is always open-I expect a lot from my staff and will be watching you like a hawk for improvement-I know everything that happens in this section-there are no secrets-no places to hide-I know them all.'

I could feel my sphincter chewing on the gusset of my underpants; I thought I was going to faint. 'As I have said-I am a fair man," he continued, "all I ask is a little respect.' He shot forward, thumping the desk, fist clenched except for the one loaded finger that pointed directly at me. 'But if you ever cross me I will rain shit, fire and brimstone down on you so hard you will wish you had died as a child-am I clear?'

Well, to say that he had my undivided attention would be the understatement of the century. He reached into his right-hand drawer and produced an official-looking letter marked 'Top Secret' and 'Eyes Only'.

'I have to know if I can trust you-I want you to take this letter to stores. Do you know where they are?'

'Yes, sir,' I nodded.

'I'm not a "sir", I work for a living' (which seemed to be the stock answer whenever this happened).

'You will address me as Flight Sergeant or Flight; you have signed the Official Secrets Act, so you know what this means.'

He pointed to the red 'Top Secret' stamp on the envelope.

'"Eyes only" means you will ONLY give it to the addressee – no one else – do you understand?'

'Yes, Flight Sergeant.'

He wrote a name and rank on the envelope and handed it to me.

'No one – and I mean NO ONE must see the contents of this letter other than the person named – OK off you go and wait for any further instructions.'

I took the letter, memorising the name and rank of the person on it. I gripped it so tightly my finger went into a cramp and I had to keep swapping from hand to hand, making my way swiftly to stores, not stopping for anything; I knew this was a test and I was eager to please my new boss. I pushed the squeaky wooden door open to stores and was greeted by the pungent odour of mothballs, as always happened.

An SAC (senior aircraftsman), a rank above myself, looked up from his work. 'Yeah, can I help ya?'

'I've got a letter for Sergeant Smith,' I said, holding the letter close to my chest.

'Hand it over and I'll see that he gets it,' he replied.

I moved a little close to the counter.

'I have to give it to him personally,' I said turning the letter around so he could see the 'Top Secret'.

'I've got clearance; just give it here.'

He reached out towards the letter, but I snatched it away from his grasp, leaning towards him at a slight angle like something from ''Allo, 'Allo' I whispered, 'It's eyes only.' The lad leant back a bit, raising his head slightly then dropping it with a knowing wink.

'I'll just go and get him,' the SAC said, and disappeared into an office.

A concerned-looking sergeant appeared moments later.

'You got something for me, airman?'

'Yes, if you are Sergeant Smith.'

He pointed to his arm and said 'What are these, then?'

'Sergeant's stripes, Sergeant,' I replied.

'Well, then?'

'But you might not be Sergeant Smith,' I choked, feeling both trepidation and excitement. He reached into his arse pocket and produced his ID card (1250); I put my hand up to look, but he lifted it out of my reach as I had done with the SAC.

'Satisfied?' he scowled.

I felt fantastic that I had used my initiative to check his ID before handing over the letter.

'I had to check, Sergeant; it's "eyes only" you see...'

The sergeant and the SAC looked at each other questioningly. The SAC shrugged his shoulders and the sergeant disappeared back into his office with the letter.

'You need anything else while you're here?'
'No: I've just got to wait for any further instructions.'

The SAC went back to what he was doing before I came in, while I twiddled my thumbs for what seemed like an eternity. The sergeant eventually reappeared with another letter marked as before but with a different name and rank on it.

'You must take this to the medical centre,' he said – which, incidentally was at the other fucking end of the camp.

'You were right to check my ID; it is vital you observe the same protocol.'

He handed me the letter and I was on my way, gripping the new letter as before, although I have to admit a certain curiosity was stirring in my soul; if it was so important, why trust a 'sprog' with its secure delivery? I gazed at the letter, but dismissed any wonderings and pressed on to the medical centre. As before, I entered and requested the named person; there were many more people here than in Stores and I couldn't help feeling they knew something I didn't – maybe it was something to do with the contents of the letter. The person arrived with a name badge on, but I still insisted on seeing his ID card.

Once more I found myself standing around, although in a much more enjoyable setting as the pretty nurses to'd and fro'd around me, looking and smiling; I thought they were just being polite.

The person I handed the letter to returned and inquired whether I was aware of the contents of the letter.

'No,' I replied, 'it's "top secret".'

'Well, there's another one for you, but this has only been classified as "secret". It's for the guardroom,' he said in his slightly effeminate voice.

So I was on my way again and any curiosities I thought I had were sent to oblivion, because this was for the guardroom. If you remember, I had already encountered this at St Athan and there was no way I was having a repeat performance of that charade.

I called at the guardroom window and told the corporal my mission; he told me to go to the door where he would let me in, exactly the same as before – except the person was less than co-operative at the request to see his ID card, but I wasn't backing down just because they were guardroom staff, and I refused to give him the letter until I had confirmed his identity.

'Well done, young man-you did well, standing your ground like that,' the old fart said, although I felt like a peacock in full fan.

'OK, take this one to POL (Petrol, Oils and Lubricants); it's been classified as "confidential".'

So the level of security was coming down the more people that saw the letter; it seemed completely plausible to me that the more people who knew what was in the letter, the less secret it would be. POL was an offshoot of stores and was in the same vicinity at the lower end of the camp; I was beginning to get pissed off at all this wandering around and began muttering to myself on the way – it would have been so much easier if I'd had one of those station bikes.

The new letter wasn't stuck down, just tucked inside the envelope; curiosity had now become a burning desire to know – but what if someone saw me? What if what I read had life-changing consequences? FUCK IT – I just had to know! I called into the White Crane Club, made out like I needed the toilet, locked myself in a cubicle and teased the envelope open. It read: 'THIS IS A NEW TWAT – SEND HIM SOMEWHERE ELSE!'

I was fucking furious! What a set of bastards! Traipsing around all day: just wait, just you fucking wait! But then it dawned on me! – I couldn't let on or they'd know I had looked at the letter. So I spent the best part of the afternoon wandering from place to place, thinking how many other people had done this before, and did they look at the letter sooner than I did? Eventually they must have gathered that I had cottoned on to what was happening, but I had the sinking feeling that my journey was a record of places visited. I returned to the section and was greeted by a sea of smiling faces and a round of applause. I still couldn't say anything, or they would know I was playing a double bluff.

'Novak! My office,' the Flight Sergeant bellowed. Oh, sweet holy mother of God – he knows! He knows I looked!

'Where's the letter?'

'There wasn't any more, Flight Sergeant; I took the last one to the Padre!'

He asked how many letters I'd delivered; I told him eight or nine, I wasn't sure. The padre had kept the last one and sent me back here.

There was a long, long silence as he bored holes in me with those experienced, beady eyes, sat back in his chair, and in the calmest voice said.

'Did you look at the letter?'

'Oh, fuckety fuck, bums, tits and willies,' I thought; what was I going to say? My mind was a raging torrent of adventure and innuendo; I'd better make my mind up what I was going to say, and soon.

'No, Flight Sergeant,' I tried, confidently.

'Are you sure? You wouldn't lie to me, Novak, would you?' he said, sounding like Shere Khan the tiger from Rudyard Kipling's 'Jungle Book'.

'No, Flight – but one of the last ones was just on a folded piece of paper marked "Private" and I dropped it; it opened and I ... I ...'

The chief technician (one rank down from flight sergeant) put his head around the door and said, 'Are you still torturing this poor sod, Eric?'

'No, you can have him back now. I get so little fun these days.'

I was as relieved as a very relieved thingy could be. I had been rescued by the shop foreman, to resume my tour of the section.

We started where I'd finished (forgive the pun). Adjacent to the refueller bay was the lubrication and pre-servicing inspection bay, which had a built-in 'pit': a purpose-built hole in the ground that vehicles could be driven over so the mechanic could walk down some steps to view the underside of the vehicle – a hoist in reverse, if you like. As its name implies, it was where the vehicles – mainly cars, some vans, and very rarely an HGV – would go to have their oil and filters changed, and a comprehensive inspection would be made as to what parts would be required when they returned for their routine servicing some three thousand miles or three months later, whichever occurred the sooner.

Obviously, the 'airfield caravan' (part of air traffic control) or 'ice-cream van', from its red-and-white-chequered appearance, would barely turn a wheel between servicings and would return with every exposed surface in a state of seizure; whereas the 'Hofficers" vehicles would amass more unnecessary miles than a sales rep on 'speed', hence they appeared at MTMS more often with things worn out – rarely an engine, a little more frequently a gearbox, and more often than not the rear axle.

I recall my very first engine change was on a Hillman 'Hunter'; that should give older readers some indication of the time that's passed since then. I would never see one again, as they were replaced with the Mk 3 Ford 'Cortina', a blancmange of a vehicle – a tad experimental, I thought, and the engine certainly was. It was the first overhead-cam 1.6-litre we had seen in a passenger vehicle, developed from Ford's racing 'Pinto' engine. Bedford had been using a 2.3-litre overhead-camshaft engine in its CF vans and Vauxhall 'Victors' for some time, albeit tilted at sixty degrees from the vertical and an absolute bastard to work on. It was still only a four-cylinder engine, but its pistons were like buckets and it would snap your head back under acceleration – quite scary in a small, matt-green removal van.

The Ford 'Pinto' had the performance of a racing slug; the variable venturi (VV) carburettor and automatic choke never seemed to do what they were designed for. They either wouldn't start in summer, owing to flooding, or were still 'hunting' when the engine had reached operating temperature. The rubber diaphragms perished quicker than a moth-eaten sock and were impossible to set up; but in defence of Ford, of whom I later became a worshipper, it must be said that a certain amount of 'driver error' had to be taken into account.

There was a knack to starting an engine with a VV carb. I believe Ford suggested that you press the accelerator ONCE all the way down to the floor, which engaged the automatic choke mechanism; then you should release the accelerator, turn the key and the vehicle should start in any conditions, hot or cold. As long as the ignition leads weren't damp, the distributor cap wasn't cracked and the spark plugs were not 'coked' up to the arse, indeed it would start.

Enter the 'driver error' portion of the equation: upon hearing the faintest inkling that the engine was about to burst into life, the driver would river dance all over the accelerator, drowning the spark plugs, washing all the oil from the cylinder walls and flooding it. Many a Roadside Assist has gone to an early Ford, lifted up the bonnet and sniffed, leant in through the driver's window and just turned the key until it cleared itself and started – assuming that the driver hadn't flattened the battery, of course.

The next bay was the 'spray bay', where everything from bicycles to buses, trucks to fire engines and the ever-present matt-green Land Rovers, covered in brown paper and masking tape, were given the once over prior to being primed with 'red lead'. The bay was staffed by the two Stans, who were painters and finishers – an 'aircraft trade' that paid a bit more than the others. One was a tall, slender guy with light brown hair and a 'tache, and the other a rather stockier tall guy with dark hair and 'tache. One was a career-driven person who would drop the other in the shit as soon as look at him, while the other was the kindest, most helpful and unselfish person I had ever come across. He had a curiosity for things unusual, but had a habit of making mistakes of a proportion that would get him noticed on a regular basis. The two things you do not want to do in the military are: 1. Make mistakes on a regular basis, and 2. Get noticed, unless you're doing it for promotion.

I will elaborate on each bay more fully later. The only other building between the spray bay and the main hangar was the tiny changing room I touched on earlier.

I spent some time in all the bays except the spray bay, which was after all another trade altogether – oh, and the refueller bay, for reasons I've already mentioned. This is the way it has always been, and always will be: if you're gonna fuck up, better to do it on bicycles, tyres and oil changes than by dropping a gearbox or an engine on someone's head. I would become more experienced while working my way through the bays and towards the hangar, but not without being threatened with the SIB (Service Investigation Branch – the equivalent of the CID) and being bollocked for just being what I considered to be 'adventurous'.

I was lucky to make it to the hangar at all, or so I was told; it was the Holy Grail for baby mechanics.

The main hangar was a garage – granted, a fucking big one, but nonetheless a garage! Unlike any other garage I'd ever been in, its ceiling was about twenty-five to thirty feet in the air; this puzzled me initially, until I thought: 'Hangar – aircraft.' OK, it wasn't a purpose-built garage, more an inherited space; and because it was so large it always felt cold. It was the kind of cold you feel at home when you daren't turn the radiators up any more, when you put an extra pair of socks on and lift your feet up onto the couch, when the coat you recently took off, is now under your chin and covering your legs, and – God forbid – the quilt is required! That's when you know it's cold.

Yet my four-month tour in the Falklands would introduce me to temperatures in which piss freezes on its way out; if any part of you was wet it would weld itself to any metal object, either removing your skin or badly 'burning' you. Allegedly two inebriated people had frozen to death when seeking shelter in a bus.

I'd been in the hangar before, but it was when I was beckoned to the boss's office and wasn't paying much attention to anything else. This time I had time; the 'chief's' voice kept on rambling, like a train fading into the distance. It had become an inaudible mumble; I gazed at the vehicles, heard the sounds of hammers, spanners, grinders, hydraulic lifts and –

'Ya fucking will go in, ya fucking piece of Land Rover shite.'

It was one of the mechanics trying to get a gearbox to line up with the clutch; anyone who has ever tried to fit one will know just how heavy they are; only a master can get a four-wheel-drive's gearbox to 'line up' first time.

'That's your assembly point,' he gestured.

'Eh?' I replied.

'In the car park – that's the fire assembly point.'

'Yeah – yeah.'

I hadn't heard a word of it: I was mesmerised. Just as I'd had to beat Swinderby and St Athan, I had to make it to the main hangar and become 'one of the lads'! It had been a long, long day. I'd been shown my ladder of expected ascent; had met my fellow comrades briefly; had the shit ripped out of me on such a scale that I vowed to have my revenge on each, double-fold; had been terrified by my new boss so that I had to do an unplanned wash; and had been so excited at being in the 'main hangar' I would have probably burned to death, because I didn't know where the fire assembly point was! Once again, I was 'full as fart' – but because I wanted to be, not because I had been told to be.

I couldn't take the information in quickly enough, and surprised even myself at my ability to recall most of what had happened; it was fantastic. I was bursting with information once again, and I loved it. I dragged my beret from my head wearily, like a person clocking out, rolled it up and stuffed it in my trouser pocket as I entered the airman's mess for tea; my head was so full of the hangar that I had forgotten about the 'secret letter'.

As I pulled the heavy wooden door open and made my way down the few steps into the foyer, which was used as a smoking room and after-dinner chat area, the whole place began singing or humming the James Bond theme. Who were these people? I didn't recognise a single one! – but they all seemed to know me. I blushed enthusiastically, turning my head from side to side to avert any lengthy eye contact. There were another couple of steps down towards the serving area, and I dared to look back a little in case it was someone else they were making fun of.

Nope, it was definitely me. A rush of paranoia now enveloped me: my chest tightened, and my blush vanished as my heart palpitated and my voice disappeared.

I picked up the empty wooden tray and placed it on the serving rails. It slid effortlessly towards my first server; I gestured toward the chips and tried to say 'Chips, please', but whatever came out, it wasn't that. I tried to clear my throat, but it was dry. A shovelful of chips landed on my plate, and I moved to the next dish.

'Peppard's shy, please,' I said.

'What?' the bloke questioned.

'Er, er – that.' I pointed, they all laughed – and suddenly my first glorious day was turning into a fucking nightmare.

I didn't bother with a sweet; I walked straight into the room with the carpet on the floor and the plants still wanting a drink in the alcoves in the wall and sat on my own. A few of the lads from my section were there, but I didn't dare approach them for fear of rejection. I'd had the piss taken out of me before at Swinderby and St Athan, but this seemed to be the whole camp. Of course it wasn't – only the eight or nine places I had visited that day with an 'Eyes Only – Top Secret Letter'. On my very first day I had learned a very valuable lesson, one that would influence the rest of my career: the services 'grapevine' is faster, more elaborate, more scandalous and furious than any tabloid newspaper could ever hope to be!

My bubble of expectation had been so cruelly burst by people I barely knew. I did know that the new kid always 'gets it', but this was beyond a fucking joke. I have always been of the belief, even in school, that if you give it you've got be able to take it – and believe me, I've taken more than I've ever given! But this wasn't school. It was a massive disappointment; I'd had plans to go to the White Crane Club to end off an otherwise perfect day, but I didn't; I slunk back to my bedsit, had a bath and reflected on the day's events. I kept thinking that if I let it get to me, I'd be giving in – giving them what they wanted, crumbling under the pressure. I was extremely timid, but decided to be silent, not rising to anything: just looking at people in a strange way, sometimes pausing to look at someone a little longer than was comfortably acceptable.

I was an 'unknown'; the more I said nothing to anyone, the more they strived to categorise me; the more intriguing I was, the more interested they were. I hadn't a fucking clue what I was doing; all I knew was the longer I held out, the less interested they became, and that suited me just fine. I finished my tea and cleared away the plate and cutlery, hoping that the gaggle of 'Bond' fans would have left by now; if they hadn't I would get a sweet from the servery and take my time to eat it very slowly.

Most of them had gone; only the smokers still lazed around at various angles of posture. Occasionally people would fall asleep here after a particularly hectic weekend of wine, women and song – usually on a Monday, when a good deal of personnel had travelled back to camp from a weekend at home very early the same morning, arriving just in time for work or, if the traffic had been kind, in time for some breakfast first. Falling asleep here was particularly dangerous, as the never-ending pranksters were always on patrol and would dare each other to perform dastardly deeds on the unfortunate sleeper. Ever more adventurous they became, and I have seen a couple of people lose an eyebrow or two to 'Immac' or some other fast-acting hair remover. Sticky buns would be hidden in berets, cigarettes put out in people's coffee . . . life just being made less tolerable for the fool who fell asleep.

I headed off towards my digs, wondering how long it would be before I got a room of my own in one of the many 'blocks'. As it turned out, it would be almost six months; it was very unusual to spend so much time in 'transit accommodation', but it was warm and dry, I didn't have to pay for the electricity, and so I was reasonably content.

Danny, the vocal air guitarist was just arriving at the house on his 250cc Sakakaki in blood-red. He was short, about the same height as me, but wore glasses and had dark hair. He worked in Air Traffic Control, although I wasn't sure exactly what he did there; he might have driven the 'bird scarer' Land Rover on the airfield for all I knew. For anyone not having encountered this phenomenon, it was a four-wheel-drive vehicle with large public address speakers on its roof and an antiquated tape machine in between the passenger's and driver's seats. The Land Rover would be driven up and down the grass parallel to the runway, with the hideous recorded noise of various birds in different states of distress, so as to keep them away from the aircraft. The sound was ear-piercingly loud and uncomfortable, even for humans. If you could imagine all the seagulls and crows from Hitchcock's 'The Birds' rounded up into one room, and then a street-smart, raggedy-eared ginger tomcat being thrown into it, you'd be pretty close. I said 'hello' and complimented him on his bike, hoping secretly to get a go on it sooner or later; I was bike-mad before joining up and knew quite a bit, so the conversation flowed easily.

Danny was an SAC and had arrived from another camp, not straight out of training like me. He was into 'heavy' music and played it quite loud; I didn't mind though, as I had no TV or radio of my own, nor had I experienced 'heavy' music. We would leave our doors open and wander in and out of each other's rooms except when some privacy was required.

I took the opportunity to question Danny about the other camps he had been to, and what it was like to be an SAC.

'No different from you,' he said. "Cept I get paid a bit more.'

This has been, and always will be, I think, the biggest bone of contention within the forces: people would constantly ram down your throat how much they got paid. Aircraft trades and technical trades were the best-paid; it was a standing joke at the end of the month when the pay slips arrived, usually opened at tea break. The varying exclamations ranged from whoops of excitement as they got their back pay from a promotion, or had received a travel claim after being on leave, to 'Look at the state of that shite; how am I supposed to live on that? Wankers!'

Often SHQ would make mistakes, omitting to reimburse us our 'food and accommodation' costs that we were entitled to after a period of leave; if you hadn't received it on your pay slip this time, it would be another month before they got it right, and if it happened near Christmas it could be a real pisser.

Danny used to let me sit in his room and watch his television until I could afford one of my own. At weekends when he went away or home, he would lend me his records and tapes of rock and heavy music, along with his 'novel' record player/radio and tape deck, which was housed in an innocuous-looking briefcase. I had certainly never seen anything like this before; the record player I had at home had been a hand-me-down from an uncle. It played 33s, 45s and 78s and had that automatic arm system, which enabled you to stack about three or four records on top of each other, the next record dropping down onto the turntable after the previous one had finished.

I was fascinated, playing the Kinks' song 'You really got me' at 33 and 78 rpm, sounding like John Wayne and Pinky and Perky respectively.

So that brought my first day, at my first operational station, to a close. Tomorrow I would be back at stores, collecting the rest of my station kit, GDT (ground defence training) gas mask, webbing belt and camouflage uniform, overalls and steel-toe capped work boots – initially these were black, but because people were so lazy and wore them to work instead of the correct shoes for the uniform, the suppliers were asked to change the colour to diarrhoea-brown. That did the trick; no one would be seen dead with them on outside work after that.

❖ ❖ ❖

10. Tyres, Bikes and Bollockings

'Good morning, campers: up one-two, down one-two, then the other sock!' Today I would be given my own little domain to look after: the bicycle and tyre bay – a tiny building that was as far away from the main hangar as you could get without falling into the Royal Air Force College Band's car park. I wasn't best pleased; after all, my entire goal was still to get my sticky little paws on anything remotely mechanical, and in my book bicycles didn't count, as they were void of one vital magical ingredient – an engine!

Still, I had been assembling – or more accurately, disassembling – bikes and motorbikes for the past couple of years and took to it like a duck to water. I had amassed a large collection of frames, shock absorbers and engine parts by the time I left school; they littered our backyard and annoyed the hell out of my father, who was becoming more like Steptoe every day, which was fine by me as I thought he deserved it for being a miserable, grumpy, obnoxious old pig – or was it me, with my delayed puberty? Mmm! It's true that I could be argumentative, cantankerous – and spotty.

Cranwell had a fleet of over three hundred station bicycles, some being the old 'sit up and beg' style with cantilever brakes, which were an absolute bastard to set up correctly. They reminded me of Douglas Bader cycling around RAF Scampton (about twenty miles away along the A15) with his dog Blackie, without a care in the world, while the Luftwaffe rained bombs down on them like confetti. 'Jolly good show!'

I seem to remember that most of the bikes were glossy black for the 'Hofficers', although there were a few in that disgusting 'snot' (matt) green colour the military seemed to be so fond of; fair enough, I suppose, if you are going to hide most of your 'kit' in the trees. Quite why anyone would go to the trouble of targeting a thirty-year-old dog-eared bike was beyond me, though – unless of course the Camp Commandant's arse was firmly in the saddle at the time.

Each bike had its own unique number emblazoned on the back mudguard, so I could make a list of all the ones that were due for a routine servicing. I had a list of who was supposed to be responsible for each of the said bi-pedalled modes of transport, but it never turned out that way as the 'Rodney's' (officers) would lend or give them to their colleagues while on leave, or when posted off the unit, without notifying me; hence when the list of bicycles required for servicing appeared in SROs (station routine orders), either the right number with the wrong name or vice versa was the usual outcome and a game of cat and mouse ensued.

After all, this was my domain and I was not going to be outdone by some snotty officer with a plum in his mouth. Consequently, I loved phoning them up and demanding they give up their bike for servicing; on the rare occasions when the culprit avoided bringing it in for too long – and six months overdue was not an uncommon occurrence – I would reallocate the bike to someone else, usually a higher rank than the one I'd taken it from; that way I didn't get in the shit for it. Fnar fnar! That's one in the eye for you 'Rodders'.

Along with the routine servicing I kept a reasonably well-stocked cupboard of replacement parts and consumables (oh, I love that word!); it meant that on odd occasions when the need arose I could borrow a part to keep my own bike in tiptop condition, and it was. Brand-new tyres, brakes, cables and a ready supply of inner tubes for when I'd been a tad overzealous through the woods and had come a cropper.

It didn't take long before those 'in the know' were asking me for this, that and the other, and if I could help them out without depleting my stock or making it too obvious, I would. It was advantageous for the 'hands on' lads to repair their own bikes, as they didn't lose them for three days while I soaked them with an oilcan and blew the tyres up, and it made less work for me.

But the all-seeing eye of the Flight Sergeant was, as he had promised, watching me like a hawk; I couldn't seem to fart without him knowing, given the geographical distance from his office to my bike bay (some thirty yards). I was totally bemused by how closely he was able to keep an eye on me. I was convinced the room was bugged, or at least there was a rat in the camp. For instance, when there wasn't much to do – which wasn't very often – I would get bored and invent games to keep myself occupied.

One particular favourite was to attach a piece of rubber tube to the 200 psi (pounds per square inch) tyre inflator and fire ball bearings at targets I'd drawn on the back of job cards. I got quite good at it, but it made a hell of a racket: the high-powered hiss of the airline, accompanied by the 'thwack' of the ball bearing burying itself in the wooden door at the other end of the bay was a dead giveaway – and let me tell you, they went in with some force.

One day I was asked by a visiting colleague how I would like the notion of blinding someone on my conscience, so early on in my career. Yes, I thought, that's sound advice: and heeded it forthwith (cheeky smile).

I wasn't quite sure what eventually made the boss call in the SIB (Service Investigation Branch – feared throughout the services), although it could have been something to do with the amount of spares I was requesting on a regular basis, which had to be countersigned by him. Christmas was the busiest time, understandably – when everyone wanted their bikes in good working order so they could get 'hammered' and still get around the station. (Ooh look! Pigs flying past the window.)

Summertime was the quietest, when people were out cycling to the local boozer or down into the village to frequent the club (oh, those long, lazy, summer evenings – what a joy). It was one frosty December morning, just before tea break (10am and 3pm), when several brightly coloured frames of my own creation where attracting shiny parts at an astonishing rate. A colleague came bursting into the cycle bay and told me that SIB were on their way to inspect the dubious bikes. My hands were in a flurry like bee's wings, and I can honestly say I have never, to this day, ever disassembled anything so quickly in all my life, forgoing my tea break and returning said shiny objects to their rightful places.

~ Tyres, Bikes and Bollockings ~

The boss strolled through the door with eloquent ease, ducking his six-foot-plus frame through the open door and blocking out the daylight. I swallowed hard, trying to look as though butter wouldn't melt in my mouth.

'No tea break today, Novak?' he enquired innocently.

'I just thought I'd get these couple finished for the weekend, Flight,' I tried, pointing at an upturned bicycle with a wheel removed, while twiddling an inner tube through my mucky fingers.

'Ooh, these are nice colours: whose are they?'

He pointed to the now naked, brightly painted frames hanging up.

'Oh, just a couple of scrap frames I've sprayed – bit of a hobby,' I said; and I knew the crafty bastard was onto me.

'What ya gonna do with them?'

'Oh, you know when the lads gets posted they often leave knackered bikes behind the block? If no one claims them I try and make one good one out of a couple of scrappers, that's all.'

I was avoiding eye contact and trying to continue with the puncture.

'You wouldn't put any of my bits on them, would you, Novak?' He was glowering at me as a golden eagle might when surveying its prey.

'Absolutely not, Flight Sergeant; that would be stealing.'

I could feel my guts tying themselves in knots, and nearly fainted wondering what was to come. A cold ache settled in the pit of my stomach.

'Thought not,' he said, spinning on his heels and heading back through the door from whence he'd come, without so much as a by-your-leave. I was perplexed; I spent the rest of the day shitting myself waiting for the SIB to come. They didn't.

I wandered around the bike bay thinking, '*my* bits,' he said, 'you wouldn't put *my* bits on there, would you?' Does he own the fucking Air Force? I wasn't trying to be clever; it was just sheer, unadulterated, undiluted relief.

So I suppose you could call this lesson number one, and I couldn't believe I didn't even get a bollocking. I was expecting at least that, and at worst getting 'done'; but no, his approach left me to stew in my own juices long enough to not want to get caught ever again. The 'Chief Tech' came to gloat a little later on at my misdemeanour and I will never forget his words as long as I live; with a 'loaded' finger pointing directly at me, he sneered and said:

'Just you remember! You need me – I don't need you!'

I can honestly say that I have never been made to feel so utterly inconsequential as I was at that exact moment in time.

The cycle bay was also used to repair and replace vehicle tyres of all shapes and sizes and could become extremely cramped at times, with its dilapidated and antiquated wheel-balancing machine, which required the operator to smear a white paste onto a circular rotating disc that would indicate the point at which the lead weight needed to be placed to counteract any imbalance of the wheel. The larger the 'apple' shape drawn in the indicator window, the larger the weight required. It was crude, but it worked. Also contained in the bay was a large selection of hammers and tyre levers of the large variety – and I mean 'large'. Considering that all I had had to use at home were a couple of my mother's finest dessert spoons – which looked as though Uri Geller had been performing with them by the time I had finished – these were huge, about three feet long, and purpose-built for almost any eventuality you might encounter.

Some of the fire-truck and refueller tyres were almost as tall as me and definitely as 'thick'! To give you an idea of just how big they were, it was a two-man job to change some of them, as I was not strong enough to turn over the tyre myself; on the occasions when I tried to, I would almost give myself a hernia attempting it. I would inevitably lose control of the huge tyre, overbalancing and practically ripping my spine clean out as I tried to stop it toppling over and snapping off the valve extension on the opposite side of the wheel, and often rupturing the inner tube.

I couldn't afford to keep making mistakes on this scale, so eventually I gave in and asked for help which, after a bit of moaning and groaning, duly arrived.

Directly outside the tyre-bay door was a large tyre bath, a black plastic circular container about a foot and a half deep filled with water, akin to a child's paddling pool. Partially inflated inner tubes would be immersed in it, showing a steady stream of bubbles if there was a 'slow' puncture. In the summer months partially inflated airmen frequented the tyre bath for any number of reasons, but usually as a punishment, being immersed head or arse first and held still until the underpants had fully saturated and lowering the water level by a good couple of inches. I, as the smallest and newest recruit to arrive at Cranwell, would have done better to secure myself a pair of sturdy water-wings given the number of times I found myself spluttering 'Bastards!' as I sunk to the bottom like the proverbial stone, followed by that very distinctive 'I've shit myself' waddle as I headed off to the changing room for a dry pair of overalls.

Now knickerless, with the air swirling around my collection of soft, dangly bits inside my new overalls, I felt a kind of freedom that I imagine women must feel with just a skirt on – quite uninhibiting, and it made it look a bit bigger: something that the following definitely didn't do!

In the winter months, an inch of ice would have to be smashed from the tyre bath before it could be used. A sharp eye was always required when using the bath in the winter. Like a drinking gazelle at the water's edge, wary of crocodiles, my eyes darted left and right. No matter: the 'two-pronged' approach was nearly always successful.

Someone would engage you in conversation from the front, while another crafty twat would encircle you stealthily from behind. It was purely a matter of teamwork; before I knew it my ankles were grabbed and 'hoicked' skyward, tipping my 'noggin' into the icy pool.

As if that wasn't enough, the first pair would summon reinforcements, who miraculously appeared from nowhere to grab a limb each, stretching me out like a starfish. I stretched and recoiled, kicking out viciously and causing a kind of 'hokey-cokey' push-me–pull-you effect, but it was explained in no uncertain terms that the more I struggled, the longer I would stay in. I accepted the inevitable and calmed slightly, but this bunch of poufs didn't want to get wet or cold themselves, so instead of the 'full dunk' they just suspended my arse and bollocks into the water, causing me to take sharp inward breaths as the shock set in. It seemed to take for ever, but I gather it was over in minutes and I swore blind vengeance against every perpetrator – double, treble and quadruple-fold.

They released me simultaneously, running away like girls, and the best I could manage was to do a kind of gymnastic 'crab' to prevent the rest of me sliding into the bath. Oh boy, were they ever gonna fucking get it? And soon.

Having donned another pair of dry overalls I returned to work, muttering to myself and planning my dastardly deeds, with the odd giggle as I complimented myself on the sheer devilment of my revenge – but not as soon as I would have liked, as they were all expecting it.

During my first year never a week seemed to pass without me getting some kind of a ducking, usually for being cheeky; my two spare pairs of overalls were constantly hanging over the radiator in various states of dampness. I was ecstatic when a new boy was posted in and some of the attention turned to him.

Another piece of safety equipment in the bay was the 'tyre cage', a heavily constructed steel box made from two-inch angle iron and painted red for danger. It stood about four feet square and about a foot and a half wide and was of lattice construction. Tyres that needed to be inflated to extremely high pressures would be rolled inside the cage – no easy task, I can assure you.

It was difficult enough to roll an inflated tyre of that size into a narrow gap, let alone a flat one, which tended to take on the random guidance of a shopping trolley.

Once inside, the inflator would be connected and it could take an absolute age while the inner tube pushed the massive tyre onto the rim seats. I would often drift off into a daydream, only to be snapped back to reality when a hundred and eighty pounds of pressure 'banged' as a stubborn part of the tyre finally slammed home. You can hear this sound in any tyre-fitting shop, only reduced, as the pressures in a car tyre are some five times less.

Countless times I would be covered in rubber dust, debris and any excess tyre lubricant, which is just a soapy liquid designed to allow the bead of the tyre to slip easily onto the rims.

The RAF was somewhat less than subtle when it came to explaining safety issues to do with high pressures and tyres. Dotted around the walls were photographs and stories of people who had paid the price for getting it wrong, culminating in a picture of an exploded tyre that allegedly killed an airman when he failed to put it into the cage before trying to inflate it. As he stood over it the locking ring, which secures the removable rim of a 'three-part' wheel, had not seated properly and he was blasted into the air and crushed against the ceiling by the rim and locking ring. It made horrific reading – and the picture didn't do anything to instil confidence in our working practices, either.

'Had the tyre been in the cage,' it said, 'yes, it still would have exploded, but the rim and locking ring would have been contained within the cage.' The unfortunate airman might have been deafened by the blast for a while, but he would still be walking around to tell, and more importantly learn from, the tale.

One story that was bandied around was of an inexperienced tyre fitter being reminded to use the cage when reassembling and inflating the large truck tyre he was working on, left to get on with the task, and then reminded again and again to use the cage.

Not wanting to look a tit and keen to impress, he assured his overseer that he knew exactly what he was doing (oh, how many times has *that* been used as a defence?) and that he would use the cage. When his superior returned to check on the airman, the free-standing tyre was almost at its maximum pressure and the airman was inside the cage! Yes, he was safe, and yes he was using the cage, if in rather an unconventional manner. The tyre was deflated immediately and the unfortunate, highly flushed and harried airman was given a speedy refresher in the use of the safety cage.

I always had the feeling that Forces people tended to overreact to situations and exaggerate them to gigantic proportions, so that the individual concerned could never live down the misdemeanour until he was posted to another unit; believe me, there have been several occasions when the intimate grapevine has provided embarrassing and piss-take-worthy information in abundance, long before the cause of it had even arrived.

The bay became so cramped with the endless Land Rover tyres awaiting replacement, or with punctures, that it became a safety hazard and was eventually extended into two separate bays.

Working here was more enjoyable than I first realised; the tyre bay was the warmest of places and in the winter people would often drop in for a sly fag, a chat or a 'warm' if working outside in the yard. I had to conceal the dog-ends, as smoking around flammable liquids (vulcanising glue and tyre solvent used for degreasing the rubber before it was glued) was strictly forbidden; then again, so was shagging officers' wives, but that went on as well, and I didn't even smoke!

After the bay was enlarged, new pieces of equipment began to appear, such as a new wheel-balancing machine that was a damn' site easier to use and much more accurate. Many a time I've had to balance a wheel over and over again using the old machine, or have hammered on so many weights that it went completely off the scale, vibrating itself into an early grave. Still it was fantastic for putting your 'knackers' up against – and I did. 'O-o-o-oh! Yea-ea-ea-eah!'

The bay had a terrific smell to it; as soon as you walked through the door you would be greeted with a pungent, rich aroma of rubber, intermingled with glue and evaporating cleaner –not that I'm kinky, you understand, but it was a heady mix and could be overpowering at times. I would often get surplus glue on my fingers, which would solidify after a time, leaving little rubber strands that needed picking off, taking with them any ingrained dirt. The sensation was not unpleasant either – akin to picking off a scab– and on more than one occasion I remember gluing my fingers together quite deliberately, stretching them apart just as the glue 'went off' and making tiny 'cat's cradles'.

But I'm beginning to sound a bit weird – so that's enough of that.

Before we put this chapter to bed, a final mention of bicycles was on a night down at the village club. The two Stans and me, recently affiliated – albeit temporarily (so temporarily that we were not invited again) – decided to ride our bikes the 1.5 miles or so from the camp to the club for an evening's entertainment. No thought was given to lights on the way there because it was a heady summer's evening and the smell of freshly cut straw still hung in the air. There was some kind of function on at the club that night, but I cannot remember exactly what: I wouldn't be able to remember anything by the end of the night and I was still under age! Anyway it included a number of Forces games such as 'Lancasters and Spoons' (explained later), which can get a little enthusiastic as the night wears on.

One game, 'Donkey Derby', involved winding a length of string attached to a wooden horse around a short piece of broom handle so as to mimic a race. I, with my expert 'wanking wrists', volunteered for this game and my pony duly romped home and won us a bottle of imitation champagne that we wasted no time in opening, spraying and 'glugging' immediately. The concept of not mixing one's drinks was totally alien to me and I began to feel unwell. I can't remember how many times I was sick, but enough to pebbledash a new decor into the cubicles of the 'Working Men's Club'. It was suggested to us, rather forcefully, that 'You might like to consider leaving – right now.'

I agreed with a single nod, as my vocal capacity to string a coherent sentence together had long since abandoned me. I fell out of the door after Stan and Jake and into the darkness of the night, followed by a trailing voice that said something about 'How dare you come down here and win the fucking bingo?' Stan and Jake were pissing themselves laughing while trying to unlock the bikes for our journey homeward. I had on my serious head and was trying to work out which way I was facing and how to get one leg in front of the other without eating grass. A good deal of pointing at each other and commenting on the state of each individual ensued as we tried to untangle our bikes.

Little Jake gave a huge tug, which just pulled me on top of the other two bikes, and I was back on the ground once more. Big Stan was 'shushing' us with a finger to his lips that looked more like a snake than a finger and was making more noise than all of us put together. The bikes finally separated and we swapped them about until we each had our own. I knew which was mine as it was the only one with lights on – but there were three of us. Little Jake had a moment of inspiration and slid the lamp off the front of my bike and onto his.

'I'll go at the front, you at the back, Bob, and big Stan in the middle – sorted.'

We couldn't argue with that: little Jake with the white light, big Stan with no lights and me following up the rear with the red. We set off like ducklings following their mother and all was well until some bright twat suggested we race, when all hell broke loose! Red at the front, white in the middle, then red in the middle, white at the back and 'no lights' blundered into the darkness as best he could; there was a good deal of unfair shoving and hanging onto the back of seats while we jostled for 'pole' position, giggling like schoolgirls. The road was empty at that time of night and it was just as well; to the right of us was a recently ploughed farmer's field some five feet below us, down a short embankment of dried grass.

Little Jake and I were now neck and neck in the 'pole' stakes. As we leant over the handlebars ever further, in a racing pose, we heard a massive rustle from behind us, as big Stan had a 'wobble' and went on safari into the farmer's field – down the embankment with some kind of 'Tarzan' war cry followed by a thud and muffled groan. Jake and I sped on regardless, expecting him to catch up before we made it back. Jake powered on, as my remaining energy had gone into laughing at big Stan's detour, and he claimed victory from a heap on the grass next to married quarters. I finally pushed my bike the remaining few yards past Jake as he lay on the grass, and I headed for home.

'See ya in the NAAFI tomorrow dinnertime,' I said, looking over my shoulder.
'Where's big Stan?'
'Fuck knows; he went on safari a bit back,' I chuckled. 'See ya.'

When we all finally met up in the lounge bar of the White Crane Club it transpired that big Stan had spent the whole night in the farmer's field, waking in the early hours of the morning after sleeping it off, and wondering how he had got there. We took the opportunity to spin him an elaborate yarn to increase his guilt and wonderment.

❖ ❖ ❖

Boeing 747 The 'Guzzomi bird'.

Departure Lounge BZN.

Sunrise at 35,000 feet.

Ascension Island.

Coastel 2 – The jump.

Walk the chain R/H end.

Author at minefield.

Penguins in a minefield.

Stanley Bay.

Stanley Jetty.

Stanley Town hill; dangerous to vehicles.

Whalebones near Stanley Church.

Doublebond Painted Penguins (left), My original 'Guin (right)

A real King Penguin

Initiation – 'On your head!'

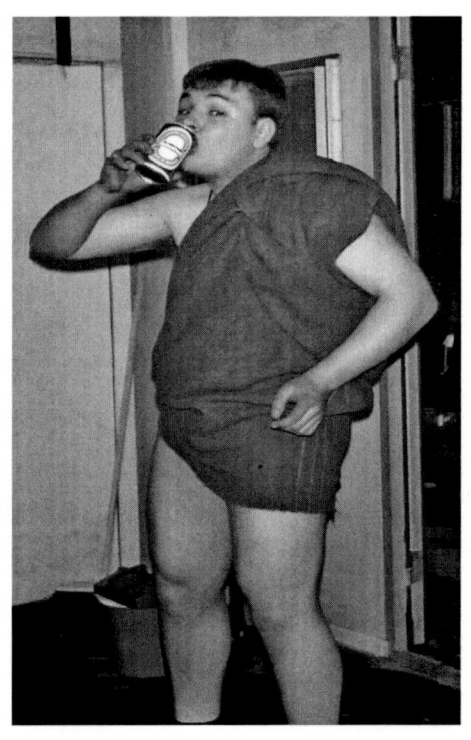

Toga Party – No sheets – left very itchy.

Can-am before Tate & Lyle injection.

Can-am after – Two sugars please!

Army BV206 – E.O.D. [Bomb Disposal].

E.O.D. blowing up a bomblet.

Mercedes Unimog on its nose.

Another 'mog' on test.

Above right – Tina the turd taxi.

A view of 'Two Sisters' mountains.

7.62 round found at San Carlos.

Argentinian Ammo boxes – Port San Carlos.

Bristow Helicopter or 'Eric'.

'Wokka-Wokka' – Chinook Helicopter.

Sea lion dashing for the sea.

Basking walrus on rock.

MTSS Unimog Wrecker.

Upsy Daisy – An Army recovery.

Coffee Jockey vs. seagulls.

Argentine Pucara full of bullet-holes.

Argentine Ak-Ak minus barrels.

A British frigate patrolling waters.

23 Squadron Phantom – Boom wheee!

23 Squadron flypast.

1312 Herc Det Air to air refuelling.

1312 Fat Albert on the ground.

11. Lubrication Bay

The lubrication bay or 'lube' bay was, as it name suggests, where all things oily and greasy took place. Being moved here was not a promotion but at least a step in the right direction, and it got me out of the bike bay and towards the main hangar. Like a kid in a sweetshop, getting covered in the slippery and sticky stuff was pretty much an everyday occurrence for me and I loved it; the dirtier I was, the more work I felt I'd done.

This feeling was not reciprocated amongst the rest of the chaps; I was constantly chastised in the tea bar for looking like 'the artful dodger', and was told to 'Go wash, ya little minger.'

The bay was massive in comparison to the tyre and bike bay; the ceiling must have been a good twenty feet up where the sealed sodium lights hung regimentally along with the heating pipes, which had blobs of a brown something-or-other scarring their surface. At twenty feet wide and thirty feet long, this expanse had me feeling like a pea in a tin, and I wandered around stroking the new equipment as if I knew what I was doing.

It contained a number of forty-five-gallon oil drums with pneumatic oil dispensers connected to a blue air line (100 psi); these made a fantastic 'chugging' sound as the oil was sucked up into the dispenser and forced along the retractable flexi-hose and into the engine or gearbox as required. A meter indicated the amount of oil that had passed through, but experience would eventually teach me that this was a rough estimate and there was no short cut to checking the exact level.

Many a time I would overfill an engine, having to remove the sump plug a second time and drain out some of the new oil. The work was monotonous and, daydreaming, I would often find oil pissing out of a gearbox or back axle because I had relied on the meter and the amount of 'chugs' that equalled a set amount of oil. On reflection, I think I spent far too much time daydreaming and not nearly enough time actually paying attention.

Pretending to be a garage owner, with the appropriate oil-stained rag hanging out of my pocket, I beckoned the imaginary vehicle into the bay, marshalling its owner to the left and right over the pit and saying, 'Hold it there; that'll do ya.' Taking the rag from my pocket I wrung my hands through the cloth, tut-tutting and shaking my head from side to side, saying, 'Gonna cost ya, mate.'

I had been in the bicycle bay for about a month and thought I knew it all. 'Lubrication: piece of piss. Oilcan everything that moves, top everything up that needs topping, change the oil and filter, and Bob's yer dad's brother!'

My stay here would be a lot longer than in the bike bay and I was under the scrutiny of a corporal – people who until recently I had revered as gods. To my surprise the corporals didn't like been referred to as such, and invited me to call them by their first names! I thought I'd really made the club – but my familiarity was soon sent packing. I couldn't work it out: first-name terms, but demanding the respect and authority that a corporal deserved? That turned out to be decidedly less than they thought they should have, given the relatively small pay rise in comparison to the responsibility that went with it.

I was confused but eager to please, and did what I thought was my best. Each vehicle had a laminated card that explained what required lubricating and what needed changing, e.g. lubricate all doors, hinges and moving parts, etc., change engine oil and filter, and check gearbox and axle levels.

On the days when I couldn't be arsed to check everything – mostly on a Monday morning or a Friday afternoon – I would skip things I thought I could get away with. For instance, taking your cloth and cleaning the oil filter and level plugs was as good as checking and changing them; after all, if the corporal wasn't gonna check my work, why should I bother? It was a bad attitude, I know, but I was still only seventeen.

I would love to be able to say that the RAF made me grow up quickly and that they gave me a sense of responsibility – but they didn't. They just provided a very expensive playground for an inquisitive mind that was having a ball, and I loved it. Among the pneumatic tools was a powered grease-gun that would be attached to the many grease nipples covered in dust and dirt – assuming that you could find them as per the laminated sheet. Let's face it: the ones you couldn't find you missed out, and you would lie convincingly that the amount of nipples greased matched the amount on the sheet; only the most tenacious of corporals would check that you weren't pulling a fast one, and I learned quickly who would check and – more importantly! – who wouldn't.

The grease-gun was capable of firing a jet of grease a considerable distance, up to the ceiling in fact – which is what the brown blobs were. In summer wasps and all manner of flying, biting critters plagued us and I took immense delight in depositing a dollop of XG279 (general-purpose grease) onto anything that even threatened to bite, sting or just get in the way of everyday servicing.

All seemed fine until an inspection was due and I had to clean the spots of grease from the window, which now resembled a leopard in full camouflage. One such day, when I was feeling particularly frisky (in the sense of getting the better of the corporal), I had a Ford 'Cortina' over the pit for a three-thousand-mile servicing. I got the card out of the slot and was proceeding with the monotonous indicated tasks: oil, filter, etc., etc., when my corporal entered the bay and asked how I was getting on.

'Yep, just about finished,' I said, waving the card in the air.
'You checked the gearbox and axle levels?' he questioned.
'Yep.'
I hadn't.
'Brake fluid level?'
'Definitely.' Even I wouldn't piss about with brakes.
'Oiled all doors and hinges?'
'Yep – the works, Pete, ready for your test drive,' which meant we got off the camp for a 'jolly' (a ride anywhere other than on camp).
'Clutch fluid level?'
'As per the sheet, mein Fuehrer; let's away!'

'Was it low?'
'Was what low?'
'The clutch fluid.'
'No, just normal.'
'Show me where you checked it,' he said.

I lifted the bonnet and pointed to where the master cylinder should have been – but it wasn't there!

'Er – er, let's have a look at that card again.'

I tried and I was rumbled; the car had a cable clutch and was not hydraulic, so the level couldn't be checked. Shit ...

Pete went over the car with a fine toothcomb and I forewent another tea break actually doing the things I said I had, wondering when the day would come that I would actually be able to get away with something. It would be a very long time in coming.

Officially, vehicles were to be driven only by qualified personnel and had to be 'marshalled' over the pit. This was not always practical or possible at the time I wanted to begin a servicing, so I would sneak into the driver's seat and wait until the coast was as clear as it was gonna get; I would have opened the large lube-bay doors, which slid on rollers in a quarter-moon shape inside the bay. When no one was looking I would 'fire up' whatever I was in and hurtle towards the centre of the bay, slowing before I approached the pit.

Sometimes the thick 'pit boards' would be in place covering the pit, preventing people and vehicles from straying into it accidentally; it was a good six-foot drop to the bottom. I know this only because I was five-foot five at the time and when in the pit was still six inches short of seeing over the top of it. If I couldn't be 'marshalled' over the pit, I had two alternatives that I used. If the pit boards were in place, I would open the driver's door and hang out, almost upside down, so I could see the wheel closest to the edge; given that all vehicles were wider than the pit, it was a scientific impossibility for the left-hand wheel to fall in while I drove the right one as close to the edge as I dare.

For the other method, when the pit was 'open', i.e. the boards were not in place, I would drive the vehicle towards the pit at what I guessed to be the centre, stopping short of actually going over it, and place something behind the front right wheel to stop it rolling back (a hammer shaft was reliable). I would leave the car out of gear with the handbrake off, go down the steps into the pit and manually drag said vehicle over the pit, being able to steer it by pushing the tyres in and out until it was far enough over to begin the servicing (I have no doubt that there is some Rodney somewhere shitting himself not knowing what goes on. Don't worry sir; long as the job gets done on time, no one's hurt and your arse isn't in the sling, that's all that matters – right?)

In the bottom of the pit was the 'Dalek', a cylindrical container about three feet high on castors, with an extendable funnel on its top that could be lifted close to the sump plug so the waste engine oil did not splash out all over. There was a definite knack to using this piece of equipment, and again it would be down to experience – and hatred of having to clean the white pit walls and remove the black engine oil, which ran freely over the gloss paint.

If you placed the funnel directly beneath the sump plug, the sheer weight of the oil in the sump would cause it to 'jet' out, missing the funnel completely and covering the walls and floor. If you tried to judge how far it would squirt out, inevitably it would come out more slowly than you thought and run down the side of the 'Dalek'.

The trick was to undo the sump plug slowly and, as the last thread came undone, tilt the plug at an angle, obscuring part of the hole and allowing the majority of the oil to escape into the funnel before removing the plug completely. Sounds simple now, but I had to learn everything the hard way. Spare a thought for the fact that most of these vehicles had recently been driven and the oil was often still scalding hot! One particular incident that sticks in my mind is when I missed out on yet another tea break. While changing the oil on a Mini, I dropped the sump plug as the 'Dalek' rolled away from me; I stuck my thumb over the hole and tried to scoop the plug towards me with my foot. I got it close enough, but couldn't quite reach it without letting go of the Mini; I was stretching as far as I could, with only inches between me and the plug – but alas, it was not going to be. The oil was still quite hot and I quickly swapped thumbs to allow the first one to cool down. I couldn't get to the 'Dalek', and I couldn't get to the plug! Oh shit ...

Ritchie, my new corporal, strolled through the door just at the right moment; I tried to look nonchalant as I mimicked leaning against the underside of the car, while my thumb began to glow. Ritchie came down the steps and into the pit to see what I was up to.

'Pass us that, Ritchie.'

I pointed to the plug, hoping he wouldn't cotton on.

'What this?' He twiddled the plug between his fingers, smiling broadly.

'Come on, Ritchie, I've been stuck here ages.'

It was like the Dutch boy and the dyke, and the game was well and truly up.

'And ya gonna be stuck there for a lot longer for being a tit.'

He placed the sump plug just out of reach, tantalisingly close, and watched as I attempted to stretch myself far enough to get it.

'Is that oil still warm?'

'Yes, it fucking is – look!'

I showed him my cooling thumb, which still had a threaded circle on its end.

'Yeah, 'tis a bit. Anyway, it's tea break – see ya in fifteen.'

As he climbed back up the steps of the pit and made for the door, I thought he was only kidding and would be back to assist me. The bastard didn't!

Slowly the realisation that I would be cleaning the pit walls again became a reality and there was nothing for it. I let go of the Mini and approximately a gallon of oil squirted all over the place. What else could I do? And I couldn't get a bollocking for it, because a) it was me who was going to clean it up, and b) Ritchie could have helped if he so desired, but had chosen not to. I sat on the steps of the pit, mumbling to myself and making a mental note that come the revolution, brothers, Ritchie would be first against the wall.

I grabbed a roll of blue paper towelling and began the mopping-up operation. Ritchie came back in with a mug of coffee, and for one miniscule moment I thought it could be for me. No such luck; the bastard had the audacity to rub salt into the wound as well, teasing me with the coffee. That was it; the gloves were off as far as I was concerned. I dragged my toolbox over to the front of the Mini, replaced the sump plug and refilled the sump with oil. I took an oilcan back down the pit with me to lubricate the handbrake cables, while Ritchie got a laminated sheet and began checking my work, I could see his work boots at eye level as he circled the vehicle up top, and kept stopping at random points.

A mischievous glee washed over me and vengeance was mine! Taking the oilcan I began to fill up the back of his boots, silently and softly, making sure each shoe got an equal amount of oil as he walked around the car. It took quite some time before it began to dawn on him that all was not well. I think it was the 'slurping' sound that finally clinched it, as his socks became awash with oil.

'What the fuck?' was the first exclamation, followed by 'Ya little bastard!'

He took his boots off and left little oily foot prints on the concrete floor as he disappeared through the door. I was still having hysterics down in the pit and my eyes were watering big style – the kind of laugh that comes back to haunt you about an hour later and sets you off again. At least we were even – or so I thought!

Ritchie came back in the bay with clean feet, no socks and ordinary shoes. Well, that just set me off again and I lost it; this was high jinks, one-upmanship, and in my book I was winning. I could barely control myself and wondered if he'd told anyone what I'd done. 'The little bastard filled me boots with oil' – surely he must be able to see the funny side of that? Ritchie casually walked over to where my toolbox was perched on the edge of the pit, and with a single shove toppled it over the edge. Its entire contents of over a hundred and fifty items spilled out onto the pit floor.

'Aw, for fuck's sake, Ritchie: there was no need for that.' And I stopped laughing.

Right, ya bastard, we're back where we started; and I would come up with something even more devious this time. I made sure I had the necessary tools and equipment as the day drew to a close: a drill, a tap-and-die set and a ten-millimetre grease nipple. Everyone locked their toolboxes at 'cease work', because things could go mysteriously missing during the night.

I drilled a small hole in the side of Ritchie's toolbox and tapped a thread into it that would accommodate the grease nipple. 'Kerchung-kerchung-kerchung' went the pneumatic grease gun as I filled Ritchie's toolbox to the gunnels with grease. I knew it was full when it began to squeeze out of the joints, and with a quick wipe with a rag I replaced his box so it looked as if it hadn't been touched, although it was a good deal heavier to carry than before. I could barely sleep that night and was dying to tell someone, but I couldn't. No proof equals no blame: could've been anyone!

The following morning we all changed into our overalls as usual, although the excitement and anticipation was killing me as I tried to look casual. I went to work in the lube bay and Ritchie wandered around with his clipboard, surveying the vehicles I was working on for any obvious parts they would require when next in for a servicing. He had no reason to go into his toolbox, and I was deflated to say the least.

A couple of days went by and Ritchie's box still lay untouched; I was beginning to wonder if I'd been rumbled.

Friday came and we had a tidy-up, which was par for the course and it was usually a slack day. If there wasn't much on we could get away an hour or two early, depending on what mood the 'chief' was in – but that's where 'poets' day came from (piss off early, tomorrow's Saturday), and we would propel ourselves at breakneck speed to the NAAFI if we got away soon enough. As I collected my bike from the rack, I noticed that Ritchie's toolbox had gone and so had he!

My plan could well backfire now, if he'd taken his box home to work on his car (which was allowed, with permission). Oh dear ...

Now settled in the lounge bar of the NAAFI, I can recall occasions when, as the bar was closing, several bottles of Newcastle Brown Ale were purchased (sometimes up to six), and we would sit there until the airmen's mess opened, go for tea and then return to the NAAFI to carry on drinking until the bar opened again in the evening, leaving one of the married guys to look after the ale. As the beer was quaffed my tongue loosened, and I had to tell someone what I had done to Ritchie's box and of the events preceding that with the boots and my toolbox. They didn't believe me at first, and I said 'Wait and see.' It would all be out in the open on Monday if not before.

'NOVAK! YOU'RE FUCKING DEAD!' was the greeting I got on Monday morning from the staff car park outside our workplace. Ritchie had been waiting for me there, and I have no doubt that had I not scuttled around him and made it into work I would have got a good hiding. He was seething, and I knew this week was not going to be a pleasant one. I got every shitty job going and then some; 'fisticuffs' was a chargeable offence and too much bother if caught, so Ritchie just made my life an absolute misery for the next week – justifiably so, I suppose, although by the following Friday I was ready to crack.

I thought in time he would see the funny side of it and eventually he did, telling everyone in the tea bar what a conniving little bastard I was, and to watch out! 'Lil' ol' me'? Surely not! The tea bar rippled with giggles and laughter and I was beginning to be accepted as one of the lads; I thanked Ritchie privately for being honest.

'Fuck honesty,' he said, 'I wanted to tell them before the rumour machine blew it all out of proportion – I'm not having you make me look a c***. Your card's marked and it's not for a dance, ya little bastard!'

I kept out of Ritchie's way for the foreseeable future and in time, although I'm not saying he forgave me, he did learn to tolerate me in small doses – very small doses!

At the first sign of winter all the snow-clearing vehicles, which had been standing idle for the rest of the year, were hauled into the hangar for a check-up. Ritchie was busy changing the brushes on a 'Sicard' (a runway-clearance machine) when I popped over to offer my help. He declined, saying 'Get back to your lube bay, ya poisonous little dwarf.'

He was having difficulty with the brushes and I offered a suggestion that I thought might help. Ritchie stopped what he was doing, stood up in front of me, all six-foot-plus of him, pointed to the lube bay, and said 'Get!'

'But I only ...'

'Get, ya twat!' Ritchie's voice was getting louder as his fuse was getting shorter.

'If ya put a jack under there ...' I began.

Ritchie came for me and I backed away quickly out of the hangar, with Ritchie in pursuit. I was still protesting my innocence and genuinely wanting to help as Ritchie and I were nose to nose (well, nose to belly button anyway).

'Say one more word and I'm gonna punch ya fuckin' lights out! Just one fucking word!'

I breathed in as if to begin a sentence: Ritchie pulled his fist back!

'OK, OK.'

I held my palms up like a dog with its tail between its legs; that was the closest I'd come to being punched before I actually was, but not by Ritchie.

I went back to my lube bay to reflect on things, thanking my lucky stars that I hadn't been 'twatted', and to finish the servicing on the diesel coach now covering the pit.

I grabbed the power grease-gun, extending the flexi-hose so it lay beneath the bus, and wandered down the steps to grease the prop shaft. Most of the grease nipples were 'in line' and if one was pointing to the ceiling, they pretty much all were, making it almost impossible to get the grease-gun on. If the bus was moved forward about a foot, they would all be pointing to the floor, making life a sight easier.

A little trick I'd observed one of the corporals doing was to flick the ignition key, while leaving the vehicle in gear; this would jerk the bus forward the right amount to get at the nipples – like 'monkey see, monkey will do'? And so this little monkey stood behind the driver's seat with the coach in first gear and the handbrake off, and flicked the key! This being a diesel, though, the engine 'caught' and began chugging the bus towards the back wall of the bay; the inertia had sat me on my arse and I scrambled for the keys as the wall loomed in front of me, snatching the keys to the off position, I was horrified to find it didn't make any difference; this was an old coach with a cable stop, which needed to be pulled fully out and held there until the diesel stopped completely. The wall was now inches away and the only thing I could think of doing was diving over the driver's seat and pushing on the brake pedal with both hands.

The position I now found myself in could not have been conceived in a thousand years of 'Twister': squashed between the seat, steering wheel and driver's compartment, upside down and in some considerable pain ... but the bus stopped! I was having a bad day. Collecting myself, my heart pounding like never before, I put the bus in neutral and wedged myself between the wall and the front bumper to push it back enough to be able to get down the steps and complete the job. I must have looked ashen, and someone commented that I wasn't looking well as I walked through the yard, a bit dazed. Job done, the bus was driven away for a quick test and the bay was empty.

As if all of the above was not bad enough, there was one more thing to happen that really made this a day to forget. The 'Dalek' had a measuring glass running up its side to indicate when it was nearly full and required emptying; I had seen the other lads do this by connecting the 'blue' air line to it near the top of the container. As the air went in, the waste oil was forced out. I trotted down into the pit and checked the level; it was almost full, holding some ten gallons or so.

Climbing back up the steps I uncoiled the air line and laid it alongside the pit, with the tap on the wall in the 'on' position. I went back down and connected it to the 'Dalek': there was a 'hiss' and a 'whoosh' as the entire contents of the 'Dalek' spewed into the air like a gushing geyser! I ducked instinctively, with oil raining down on me from a great height; I was absolutely covered from head to foot, and the 'Dalek' was still hissing as I stood there dripping. Ritchie stepped through the door as I stood there in a 'Wurzel Gummidge' pose.

'What the fuck 'ave you done?' he said, looking at me in disbelief.

'I dunno ... I just put the air line on and –whoosh.'

'Didn't ya think to connect the waste pipe first?' he said, pointing at the two-inch-diameter pipe hanging on the pit wall.

'I wondered what that was for!'

Ritchie went over to the wall and turned off the air line; the 'Dalek' made a dying whistle as its final few drops popped up into the air. If I'd broken into song with 'Mammy, how I love ya, how I love ya ...' I wouldn't have looked out of place. Ritchie erupted with laughter, sticking his head out of the door and shouting for everyone to come and have a look. They did; and I felt as meek as meek can be and very, very silly.

'Ya better get this cleaned up before the chief sees it, or you'll swing for this.'

'Isn't anyone gonna help me?' I bleated.

'Get to fuck,' was the resounding reply from all concerned!

The oil had sprayed in a circular pattern, covering the pit floor, walls and concrete floor of the bay. The only clean area was where I had taken the 'hit' from the oil, acting as a kind of shield. I mopped up the oil as best I could and went through about six rolls of blue towelling and countless rags. It took an absolute age; I was still there long after everyone else had gone home, cursing and shouting at the top of my voice.

The job done, all I had to do then was clean myself up, which took another age, and the smell stayed with me for days and days. I had the piss ripped out of me for weeks after that, but it was a valuable lesson; it subsided only when someone else committed a mortal sin in the main hangar by jacking a Mini up through its floor, having missed the jacking point. Like a pack of baying hyenas, the lads would psychologically pounce on anyone who 'fucked up'. It could be demoralising at times, but the secret was never to let anyone see it was bothering you, or they just did it all the more.

Tea breaks and lunch breaks were the worst times, when you would be made to feel a complete berk in front of the rest of the lads and a 'let's see who's dropped the biggest bollock this week' competition was formed.

It was usually the inexperienced and younger members, but even corporals can have bad days, as the following describes. Ritchie had taken a Ford 'Cortina' on an extended test route (ten miles) which took him into the countryside of rural Lincolnshire, along winding roads and up a hill where the performance of the handbrake was to be tested. It was quite a steep hill, and Ritchie had stopped the car part way up when a pensioner drove straight into the back of it, giving the Cortina a good crunch! Ritchie leapt out of the car to see the damage that had been done; it was considerable, but no one had been hurt.

'Ya dozy bastard – didn't ya see me indicating? Look at the state of it,' Ritchie crowed.

'I've been driving fifty year and not had an accident,' the codger said.

'Well, ya should 'ave 'ad a rest, you old git,' Ritchie replied sarcastically.

Ritchie limped the rearranged Cortina back to camp and I offered a little 'thank you' up to the Lord for divine retribution. He was forced to complete a dreaded FMT3. (accident form) that explained the incident in minute detail, so the RAF could decide whom to nail to the wall. I'm not sure of the outcome, but I don't think Ritchie was at fault.

The yard would fill up with vehicles, making it almost impossible to get to the one you wanted without having to move one or two, and just as you'd cleared a path some 'knobhead' would park a Land Rover in front of it. It was just such an occasion when Ritchie was moving an aircraft-refuelling vehicle; with the yard being heavily covered in snow, we were always told to 'get someone to watch you back': but there wasn't always anyone around, and Ritchie took it upon himself to reverse the refueller on his own. I heard the large diesel engine rev up and saw clouds of fumes from the exhaust at the front of the vehicle as he built up the pressure in the air brakes; a loud hiss denoted the handbrake was off and reverse was selected shortly afterwards. The truck moved backwards a little and then encountered some resistance; thinking it was just piled-up snow behind the rear wheels, Ritchie took another go at it. There was still resistance; the engine revved higher and the rear wheels began to 'skip', but still without any rearward movement.

'Whoa, whoa, fucking whoa! What're ya doing?' the Chief screamed at Ritchie. Ritchie applied the handbrake with the same loud hiss and walked to the rear of the truck, where the airfield caravan (a kind of motor-home) was on two wheels, teetering at an angle of thirty degrees and held up by the truck. It was on the blind side of the truck, the mirror being obscured with snow. Ritchie put his head in his hands, which dropped to his chest. Another FMT3 – and it was all his own doing this time.

The worst part of it was that to get the caravan back onto its wheels was going to cause even more damage to both vehicles on the way down, but it had to be done and Ritchie inched the truck forward under the supervision of the Chief. I think they may have put a couple of jacks at the front and rear axles of the caravan to hold it up and stop it sliding against the truck, thus reducing any further damage. To cut a long story short, Ritchie got a massive bollocking, but I don't think he got 'done' for it.

The 'D'ya remember when?' crowd always livened things up, as story after story was told of when someone had caused a major 'boo-boo'. It was OK to admit that we were fallible; just how fallible, though, was a closely guarded secret.

~ Drop and Give Me Twenty! ~

The lads would play 'arrows' (darts) with games such as 'killer', 'cricket' and '501 straight in-double out', while the card school was usually in full swing at dinnertimes playing 'trumps', 'crash', 'chase the ace' or 'hunt the lady' (although it wasn't called that!). Some sat quietly and read newspapers or books; 'wank mags' were ever-present, and comments flew around as to whose 'missus' that looked like. Some quite personal details would push the boundaries, until a scowl or a look told the protagonist that he was close to the line! I've only ever seen a few scuffles and they were not usually malicious, more like play-fighting; but when it did get out of hand the scufflers would be paraded in front of the boss and asked to explain. It was usually down to who threw the first punch, and not necessarily the one who'd won.

I'd been at Cranwell about three months now and was making friends easily, although there was no sign of me getting a room in a block yet; I was still sharing the converted house with Danny the bird scarer. This had the effect of separating me from my workmates; they would often leave their doors open in the corridor of the 'H' blocks and would converse to all and sundry as they to'd and fro'd to the showers, washrooms or the utility room, which usually had a coin-operated washing machine and dryer. I still felt 'out of the loop' a little and wanted to be in amongst it, as most of the gossip happened after work but before 'Emmerdale' and 'Coronation Street' started. The lads loved the soaps and many a discussion was had about the previous night's show during tea breaks; and God help anyone who resembled a character in the show: the nicknames were merciless.

❖ ❖ ❖

12. Winter Games

The winter months were now approaching and snowballs were a constant threat; tea breaks turned into a massacre between the 'erks' and the NCOs. I got scrubbed in the face more times than I care to mention, got held down and had snow forced up my trouser legs and down my back; I was pissing freezing, but kept well away from the tyre bath and scarpered across the road and into the woods at the first mention of the word.

The air-raid shelter across from the yard and at the beginning of the woods was the perfect barrier as I was pursued round and round by the three little pigs; one stopped and went the other way, and I squawked loudly as I was caught.

'I'm fucking off home if you soak me in this weather – I mean it!'

I was unceremoniously dragged towards the bath, kicking and screaming, getting louder and louder, until the Chief poked his head out of the door of the main hangar and put a stop to it. I was immensely relieved and thanked him profusely.

'How come it's always you getting a dunking, Novak?'

'I dunno, Chief,' I said, thinking I'd made a friend.

'You wanna try keeping your ears open and your mouth shut for a change.'

I was deflated once more, and any idea that he might have been looking after my welfare dissolved. I knew I was cheeky, but thought he was going over the top a bit. I got the feeling he really didn't like me; no matter – he was just one of many, and the lads ripped the shit out of him behind his back, so it wasn't entirely my fault.

One day I was assisting another corporal, Billy, outside with a 'Sicard'. I mentioned this earlier; it was basically a massive rotary brush, powered by a V8 Chrysler engine and with hydraulics that enabled the brush to be swivelled at an angle via a remote control box kept in the cab of the vehicle towing it, so enabling the snow to be brushed off the airfield and onto the grass. At the rear of the 'Sicard' was a jet-blast nozzle, which could be swivelled by the remote and which blasted the snow away.

The remote was connected to the machine by about twenty feet of cable and was the size of a shoebox. Large buttons covered its front, with one that brought the revs up from idle to maximum; it made an unholy racket when at full pelt, with the exhaust gases coming straight out of a pipe, no silencer. It would often cough and splutter when going from idle to full revs, and occasionally it would backfire and huge flames would shoot out from the pipes.

Billy was trying to adjust the throttle linkage and had me pressing the button on and off while the engine was not running; the large solenoid clunked as it operated the throttle and it was time for a running test. The yard was covered in compacted snow, which made walking across it a little precarious. The 'Sicard' was fired up and allowed to idle until it reached working temperature; the whole thing would shake as the brush went round slowly, maximum throttle being prevented by a temperature sensor until it had warmed up. It also had a low-oil-pressure cutout switch fitted, which could be quite troublesome. Wearing ear defenders, I pressed the 'rev up' button and the monster roared into life. I was terrified of this thing; you couldn't hear yourself think when standing next to it, while the brush was galloping around at a phenomenal rate of knots and the jet blast blew snow into dust devils across the yard.

The Chief came out into the yard with his ever-present clipboard, making notes of jobs that needed doing or people that needed doing, and he began to cross from one side to the other. I was pissing about with the buttons on the remote, making the brush swivel from side to side; as he crossed behind the machine I pushed a button that I thought was the brush – but the blast nozzle swivelled round unexpectedly, blowing the Chief off his feet and his clipboard into the air! His legs were doing the 'cartoon shuffle' as he tried desperately to remain upright. He lay in the snow, his grey overcoat thrashing him to death as the blast whistled around him.

I hadn't seen any of this, but Billy was laughing and doing the 'cut throat' gesture that meant 'kill the engine'. He waved me forward, bent over double with laughter, barely able to catch his breath, and pointed to the rear of the machine. The Chief was still on his knees collecting up the remnants of his clipboard; I looked on in absolute horror while Billy pissed himself. He didn't like the Chief either.

'Nov-a-a-a-a-ak' the Chief growled, getting to his feet – and I gulped. Billy was now in fits of laughter, hanging onto the machine to stop himself sliding away, while I just stood and trembled. If he didn't like me before, I was certainly not 'flavour of the month' now.

'It was an accident, Chief.'

He could see the fear in my face and I wished I had planned it – but no, it was completely unintentional. Fortune smiled on me as he turned his attention to Billy, who was still 'rocking'.

'And you! You should know better! Set an example! That's what you should do – set an example.'

Billy couldn't give a toss, and had been a corporal since Pontius was a pilot and had an autographed copy of the bible.

He was my hero and I looked to him for guidance as a son does to a father. He was getting on in years and could tell a convincing tale of just about anything. I'm not sure if he was passed over for promotion or just didn't want it; he was happy being 'one of the lads' and was a fantastic and knowledgeable fitter. As the 'Arthur Daley' of Cranwell, if there was a 'scam' going Billy was never far from its source. He was amazingly resourceful and could put his hands on just about anything; if you needed something, Billy could charm the birds from the trees to get it for you – for the right price, or for a favour in lieu.

He seemed to know everyone and moreover everyone seemed to know him, especially people in Stores. The most prized possession was a pair of soft leather flying gloves: very difficult, almost impossible to get hold of – 'like rocky horse shit', to quote one person. Billy was even able to get me a second-hand engine for my Mini – only £15 from a local scrapyard – when I eventually acquired a car.

~ Winter Games ~

Above all he was very funny and very fair. One particular incident, which still makes me laugh today, is when Billy moved into the 'singlies' block after some domestic crisis; he was as placid as they come and I never saw him lose his temper in all the time I knew him. The room he moved into had a noisy neighbour who would play his stereo very loudly. Billy had asked the perpetrator to turn it down, which he did initially, but it soon returned to full volume once more. Billy had asked him at least three times more before marching into his room with a pair of pliers and cutting the plug off the stereo.

Some minutes later the lad had put on another plug, sticking two fingers up at Billy and saying,

'What ya gonna do about that, old man?'

Billy pushed past him, and with the same pair of pliers cut the flex off flush with the back of the stereo, replying; 'Put a plug on that, ya clever twat!'

That was Billy all over: confident, clever and as dry as sticks.

I think it was at about the six-month point that my name finally came up on the waiting list for a single room, and I was duly allocated one. This was heaven for me, even though the room was much smaller than the shared house. It would have been about ten feet by eight feet, with fitted wardrobes and a bench on one side, a sink with cupboards above and below and a single bed on the other, leaving a three- or four-foot space in the middle of the room.

It was compact but homely, with a small reading light above the bed with a shaving socket built in. The window opened 'up over' and looked out into the road facing another block. Directly outside the window was a large tree that would rustle and coax me off to sleep; sleeping with the window wide open in the summer, you could hear the chatter of airmen returning from the NAAFI as you dozed in the transition between sleep and wakefulness.

Occasionally you would hear a woman's voice, which got the curiosity hackles up, and I would hang out of the window to see who was doing what to whom and for how long! No members of the opposite sex were allowed in each other's blocks, although nobody stuck to this rule except me, 'cos I didn't have a girlfriend. All the gorgeous ones were snapped up immediately and only the 'mooses' were left; although I was incredibly naïve and shy, I still had my standards – and my virginity!

We were rapidly approaching Christmas and the snow was thick and picturesque on Cranwell's' landscape. Once again tea breaks were a treacherous time to be out and about and any passing bandsmen were fair game, as we launched a surprise attack on anyone unwary enough to be passing.

Officers were a favourite! To knock an officer's hat off commanded royal respect, but I was never brave enough to do it. What I did do though, on a number of occasions when a pretty female officer was passing, was to tell the lads, 'Wow, she is beautiful!' They would flock to the fence like hungry starlings, and as I hid out of sight I would yell at the top of my voice, 'Get your tits out for the lads!' Several highly flushed faces disintegrated into nowhere, like the shrapnel from a grenade.

A massive snow-fight began between the main hangar staff and the outside bays; raiding parties would shoot forth, grab unsuspecting airmen by the dozen and 'scrub' them.

I did my best to keep out of it as I was always targeted, but to no avail; decked and scrubbed for the umpteenth time, I finally took the law into my own hands. Climbing aboard the bucket tractor, used for filling the snowploughs with grit, I scooped up the biggest bucket of snow you could imagine, so big that it made the rear tyres of the tractor go 'light'. The hangar staff fled for safety indoors, slamming the door behind them, but as usual there was always a rat in the camp, and they tried to push someone outside to be covered.

I parked the tractor outside the main door with the bucket raised above it and vowed that the next twat out of that door was gonna get the lot! I had my hand on the lever ready to tip it out, and when the door opened, I let fly. An avalanche poured from the bucket and I saw a couple of hands going up instinctively to protect their owner's head – but one hand had something in it?

I was jeering and bouncing up and down in the tractor's seat in utter ecstasy until I saw the clipboard. No! It couldn't be! Not in a month of Holy Jesus Sundays – could it?

It fucking was, though! I just stared in shock.

The Chief brushed the snow off himself, glaring at me maliciously. I held my wrists up together as if about to be handcuffed.

'Fucking office – now!'

I climbed off the tractor and headed for the office, head bowed, sullen, but propelled by a hand in the middle of my back that made me skip a few steps.

I looked around and there was still snow melting off him in little drizzles. I didn't know whether to laugh or cry, but decided the former would not help my cause at that exact moment in time and I would keep it for later. I was paraded in front of the Flight Sergeant, and the Chief definitely wanted me charged to the full extent of the law.

But with what?

The Flight Sergeant talked him round, explaining to the Chief that he would be made to look foolish when the charge was read out by the CO. My arsehole relaxed a bit when I realised I wasn't gonna get done, although I would be on 'teas and keys' duty for the next month; still, it was better than a fine and having my service record blemished – although that would happen soon enough.

I'd settled into a routine and was reasonably happy, although still not working in the main hangar. I'd been getting driving lessons from the lads and took every opportunity to drive whatever I could as often as I could – trucks, buses, forklifts: you name it, I drove it. I had my provisional licence and passed my test first time when a visiting tester came up form RAF St Athan where I had done my trade training. I had bought a Hillman Imp for £150 from a guy who was getting posted (I was paying him £50 a month), and I sneaked about the camp in it after work for a while, but it was a complete 'shed'. I didn't know just how dangerous it was until I wanted to go home to Durham in it.

Every time I put the brakes on I could hear a scraping sound coming from the front of the car. I got one of the lads to have a look at it one dinnertime and it was made clear it was a death trap; I was advised not to pay the seller any more of the money I still owed. The front 'wishbone', an integral part of the suspension, had rotted away from the main chassis and was coming away from the car each time I applied the brakes – and I'd already filled the fuel tank to the brim, ready for my first long journey. The grapevine had brought the problem to the attention of the senior NCOs and, to my surprise, help was offered in the form of one of the sergeants, who would weld up the chassis after work. I was ecstatic.

I drove the little Imp over the pit and the 'sarge' dragged the welding gear from the main hangar into the lube bay and began welding up the job. The fuel tank on the Imp was at the front of the car and just above the wishbone! As Sarge carried on welding, the heat caused the fuel to expand; it began leaking out of the filler cap and running down the side of the car! I was beside myself as the neat fuel dripped onto the floor; I was really worried and told Sarge what was happening. I grabbed an extinguisher, just in case, but he never even batted an eyelid and said it was the fumes that burn, not the liquid. He carried on as if nothing was happening; sparks were flying everywhere as the nozzle dipped into the molten metal and I was convinced we were going to be blown to kingdom come at any second.

I was mopping fuel up with rags as fast as it ran out, but Sarge finished the job and the car was made safe for my first journey home in my first car. The little Imp was only good for 50 mph, and I remember being stuck behind a coach on the A15 as an Austin 'Princess' zoomed past me, overtaking the coach as well. Not wanting to be outdone, I floored the Imp and nothing happened; slamming it into third I began to creep alongside the bus, but not before a car coming in the opposite direction was approaching at a rapid rate of knots! Time was running out and a decision was needed quickly. I leapt on the brakes, swerving back in behind the coach as the approaching vehicle's windscreen came past half on the road, half on the grass verge, with two fingers firmly pressed up against it, the horn sounding and the main beam blinding me for what seemed like ages. I had been nearly wiped out on my first journey in my first car, and I kept checking the mirror in case said driver decided to come back and "ave a go' at me.

He didn't and I pushed on home. It took four and a half hours to do a hundred and fifty-five miles, while the temperature gauge of the little aluminium engine danced in and out of the red as it consumed water like a thirsty dragon.

You would think that the heater would be extra-hot in this condition, but no: the engine being at the rear of the car and the heater matrix at the front did nothing to enhance its already poor performance, so the windscreen misted up and I froze. The journey was decidedly unpleasant, but nothing could have removed the beam that stretched across my cherubic face, putting the Cheshire Cat well and truly to shame, as I drove through the council estate I had left only a year earlier. But it was late and it was dark, and there was no one to recognise me in my 'new' car. I bumped it up the kerb and drove onto the grass alongside Dad's Ford 'Escort' Mk 1, wondering how long it would be before I had a better car than he did. It turned out not to be long; and to top that, for £150 I sold him a piece-of-shit Morris 'Marina' that used more oil than a sweaty chip shop. That was for forcing me to get rid of my motorbike, after almost running into a police Transit van on the way to the 'pit heaps' (scramble track).

'Bring the police to my door, would ya?'

He clouted me all the way from the front of the house to the back yard, where he took the bike off me and locked it in his shed. I remember thinking, 'If you think that's gonna keep me off it, "you've got another think coming"' – which was one of his favourite sayings, along with 'I didn't get where I am today by …'

Whatever was happening at the time? When I found out he would be working overtime the whole weekend, it would mean he wouldn't have time to go into his shed and engrave the pint glasses that he sold in the pub for … you guessed it: 'beer money'.

I unscrewed the mesh from his shed window that had once been a child's fireguard, scooping out the putty and removing the 'tacking' nails that held the pane of glass in place. I opened the bigger window and climbed though, removing the nuts from the captive bolts that held on the outer clasp and pushed open the door, rescuing my beloved Yamaha 80cc field bike. I made space quickly in my 'coal house' shed and stashed the booty before anyone could see. The low fence between our house and the family next door was not high enough to obscure their view from their living-room window, so I was in constant danger of being discovered by one of the four girls they had, who would delight in dropping me in the shit at the first available opportunity, even though I had been out with two of them (not at the same time though). Maybe that was the problem.

I put the glass back into Dad's shed and put a couple of screws in the mesh to make it look good, knowing I would have to put the bike back before Monday. I was up early Saturday morning, shortly after Dad had gone to work, got the bike out and took it straight to the petrol station and filled it to the brim with the money from my milk and paper rounds.

Even Mam hadn't seen me, and I was assured of a great day's scrambling. I'd met a couple of the lads up 'the heaps' and gave a few of them 'backers' around the course and lifts here, there and everywhere, even as far up as East and West Rainton, where there was an access road to once-busy pit works. I was absolutely soaked and covered in the darkest mud, being coal waste, and returned home about ten o' clock in the morning, leaving the bike at a mate's to change my jeans for a more comfortable pair. I walked into the kitchen; Mam was busy with clothes all over the kitchen floor, since Saturday was washday. Gawping at me is sheer disbelief, she barked:

'What the hell have you been doing to get in that state?'

'Garry's got his bike up the heaps and we're sharing goes,' I said.

'Get them off, right now! You're not trailing them through the house!'

There were clumps of mud still 'clagged' onto the legs and arse of the jeans, where we'd been splashing each other with wheel-spins and 'power slides' through the deep puddles.

'But Mam, me underpants are soaking as well.'

'Off!' she repeated.

'The door's open, man!' I protested, as there was always a gap where the hose of the dryer was poked into the yard to avoid condensation.

'You've got nothing I haven't seen before.'

'Aye – but not this big!' I joked, trying to take the awkwardness out of the situation.

If anything it was smaller than usual and still as bald as a coot. I turned away, sliding the jeans and pants off together in one movement and kicking them backwards towards the washer, then scampered off up to my room with just my socks and T-shirt on. It must have been a comical sight and I could hear Mam laughing as my lily-white arse and cupped 'nadgers' disappeared into the living room and then thundered up the stairs to my room. Returning a little later in fresh socks, pants and a light blue pair of jeans, I threw the wet socks I had taken off at Mam. They bounced off her chest, falling into the washer; I gave a football cheer, punching the air and saying 'Come on!'

She dived into the scalding water of the washer, shouting:

'I've got whites in there, ya stupid boy!'

She threw them back, but I ducked and they made a lovely 'plopping' sound as they hit that back wall and slid down behind the dryer. She made after me, but I was already out in the yard hopping into my Wellingtons and leaping over the fence to freedom.

She could never catch me, and on the few occasions I was close enough to be hit she would half-heartedly swing at me. There was no malice there – not like Dad, who would put his left hand out, saying 'Ya see this?' and clatter me with the right one while I wasn't expecting it.

I'll never forget the day he chased me through the small garden fence and up the top of the garden, where I leapt over the corrugated iron back fence and goaded him from the other side. The little gate had a typical garden catch that needed to be tilted backwards to open it, and it had a hole in it where a small lock could be put through it. I put a bolt through it, and as Dad chased after me he tried to open and come through the gate in a single movement! The gate stayed shut and he cantilevered head first over the gate, landing in a heap on my side of the fence. I let out a massive guffaw and was finding it difficult to get over the back fence, howling like a hyena; I managed to get one leg over the fence, but was dragged back unceremoniously into our garden. I couldn't see for the tears of laughter and was frog-marched by the scruff of the neck, laughing all the way towards the house and being clouted at every step and every syllable.

'You - de - vi - ous - lit - tle - sod' (seven clouts). I was pleased he wasn't more literate! Propelled into the kitchen and grounded for a week, my ears were ringing and the back of my neck was decidedly warm. Oh, happy days?

I'd had a great weekend on the bike and decided to replace it while Dad was in the pub Sunday night. I gave it a bit of a splash to get the majority of the mud off, and after it had finished dripping I put it back into his shed and reversed the process of getting it out. Replacing the nuts on the clasp, I climbed back out of the window and went to replace the pane of glass, but as I tapped in the pins it cracked from left to right, falling in half to the ground and disintegrating. Aw, shite! I was in for it now.

I put the mesh back up and just prayed he wouldn't need to go in there before he went to work tomorrow. I would use the remainder of my wages to buy a new pane and replace it before he got in from work, thus being none the wiser. Monday, after school, I bought the correct size pane from Greenhow's hardware shop in Houghton-le-Spring, along with a tub of putty. I raced home and began repairing the shed. Ever so carefully this time I put the glass in and kneaded the putty into place, using some muck from the garden to discolour and age it. It was a futile attempt; I even dirtied the fresh pane trying to make it look like the others. The more I thought about it, the more I should have said I smashed it with the ball and replaced it. Anyway, I put the mesh back and hoped for the best.

When Dad returned home I made him a coffee, which must have alerted him, and he began questioning me suspiciously, but to no avail; after all my effort, I had to see it through. Whenever he couldn't find anything I was culprit number one and accused without thought, and on fifty per cent of occasions it would be justifiable.

'You got my soldering iron?' he said, after rummaging through the cupboard under the stairs and all the other cubbyholes where he would hide his things from me.

'Might be in the shed,' he added, and moved towards the hook where his keys would hang when he was in.

'I'll check for ya – I think the petrol tap's still switched on – on the bike – ya wouldn't want it burning down.' I had to keep him out of there at all costs.

'Go on, then,' he said, thinking I just wanted to have a look at the bike – he was still in the dark! I searched and searched, and knew that if I didn't find it he would come and look for himself and smell the fresh putty that was ever-present: linseed oil is a very distinctive and pungent smell.

At last a plug dangled out of one of the many boxes and I wrestled it free like a poisonous snake, looking over my shoulder to make sure he wasn't coming. I'd got away with it this time, and wondered how long the smell of the fresh putty would linger. In a flash of inspiration, I pulled the rubber hose from the bottom of the fuel tank and allowed a few drops of petrol to stain the floorboards; at least that would disguise the smell and might even worry him enough to take the bike out altogether – but no such luck. I put the word out that the little 'Yammy' was for sale and I got £60 for it: more than enough to get blind drunk in my mate's shed, but that's another tale altogether.

Alan was a piss-taker's gift! And he was my best mate (accidentally or unknowingly?); we were inseparable before I joined up. He tells me that when I first came home on leave from Swinderby he had been keen to see me in my uniform, but that I dismissed him, saying that I didn't need him any more. I can't say I remember this, but for it to stick in Alan's mind – and let's face it, not much else did – I guess it must be true. I felt ashamed that I was capable of such maliciousness.

I called for him Saturday morning and he was defiantly 'stand-offish'.

'Oh, you won't want a drive in my new car then?' I said, turning on the step and heading back down his garden to climb the fence once more.

His eyes widened and I could see his resolve diminishing.

'What sort is it, then?' he questioned nonchalantly.

'A racing "Imp",' I said, mimicking a handbrake turn.

'A what?'

'A Hillman "Imp"; it's got an aluminium racing engine in.'

It was true; they did use the Imp engines for racing because of their lightness and overhead-cam configuration – but the only racing thing mine had was the time it had left before its next (and final) MOT. Alan was still stood in the doorway with his 'hacky' terry-towelling socks hanging over the step at right angles to his feet, giving him a comical look.

'S'pose I'll 'ave a look, then,' he said, disappearing into the kitchen to put yesterday's clothes on. Alan's hygiene left a lot to be desired on a few occasions, but it was more to do with his upbringing and financial circumstances than a desire to be scruffy.

His parents had a liking for the bottle, as many North East families had; what were all these industrious miners to do after the closure of all the pits? – not that his dad was a miner, but life was tough for the family at the bottom of our garden. Fights were a regular occurrence and Alan would often appear with a good deal of bruises; I really felt for him. I thought I had it bad when my old man would clout me round the back of the neck or 'upside' the head, but this was in a different league altogether.

I showed him around the little Imp and fired it up, revving the tits off it, which was not the brightest thing to do with a cold aluminium engine. I had now started carrying bottles of water around with me to top it up, as the temperature gauge kept creeping up into the red. We drove around everyone we could think of to show off that we had a car, and the girls that had ignored us before were now firmly planted on my back seat; they couldn't escape, as it was only a two-door.

I raced around and around until they complained of feeling sick and I deposited them where we picked them up, saying we would be back later that night in case anyone wanted 'a ride' (nod, nod, wink, wink). It's amazing what wheels will do for ya! Still, a snog, a fumble and a bit of 'tit' was better than nothing and it was a scene straight out of 'Rita, Sue and Bob too'; steamed-up windows and 'lover's balls' was at least something to tell the lads on my return.

Sunday came and I packed my stuff up ready for the journey back to Cranwell, although taunting Alan by getting him to top the water up at the front of the car had him declaring:

'The engine's gone, Bob!'

'It's under the mat,' I said.

Alan's head disappeared into the boot, lifting the mat. I blasted the horn and Alan slammed his head on the bonnet, while I sat in the driver's seat pissing myself laughing.

'Ya twat!' he said approaching the driver's window and still rubbing the top of his head.

I wound it up quickly, thinking I was about to get covered in water, locking both the driver and passenger doors. He went to the back of the car and opened the small rear window that opened like a tailgate and showered me with the bottle; the catch was bust and every time I closed a door, the air pressure inside the car would push open the window momentarily.

'Touché, wanker,' I said as he danced around the car in delight; it wasn't often that Alan got me back, but he had his moments and when he did it was time for exaggerated celebration. He splashed the rest of the water over the car and I put the windscreen wipers on in defiance. I got the bottle off him and went to the kitchen to refill it; when I came back out he was down the bottom of the street, ready to make a rapid exit into the cricket field, giving him a good hundred yards' head start.

'Come on, ya tosser, I'm not gonna soak ya.'

Lifting the boot lid (engine compartment), I began checking the oil and water.

'I don't trust ya!' he shouted – and with good reason: I was extremely imaginative when it came to getting my own back.

'Come on, I'll show ya where ya check everything,' I replied, emptying out the remainder of the water so he could see.

'I know you – you'll have another bottle down the side of the car.'

He was right. Damn, he's catching on quick: most out of character – I was usually able to get him at least twice before he 'rumbled'.

Mam had made a delicious Sunday dinner (as she did most weekends) and Dad's was in the oven waiting for him to come home from the pub; that was how it had been for many a year and Mam was fed up with it. I recall the time he was late back and his dinner had dried up; when he complained to Mam she took the plate off him and back into the kitchen, where he thought he was going to get some gravy on it, but she put the dinner, the plate and knife and fork in the bin and went out. I was amazed; he was crestfallen and went to bed. Oh well, at least I had somewhere to go now; I wasn't trapped in an atmosphere of disgust. I have always been of the belief that if someone is going to spend a couple of hours making you something, the least you could do was to turn up on time for it! I left Mam a note thanking her for the dinner and saying I would be back in a week or two.

It would be dark in a couple of hours and I didn't want to be out on the road at night, so began my journey at about 1.30 pm. It was reasonably uneventful, apart from taking a different route back as I missed the turning for Doncaster and Gainsborough. Eventually I turned onto the camp roads and felt a sigh of relief and comfort knowing I would be back in my block, which was always warm and cosy (sometimes too warm). and could pack away my clean washing that Mam had done, make myself a coffee and sink into the bed.

If there was time, a couple of beers in the NAAFI were always welcome, and exaggerated stories were bandied around as to what people had got up to over the weekend. It was always an adventure, listening and then commenting on what had gone on. One question was always asked:

'You get laid this weekend, Bob?'

I hated this question; I wasn't experienced enough to bluff my way through it and they knew it.

'Ner, just a bit of tit, but I'm working on it.'

'Cherry, cherry, cherry boy – who's a little cherry boy?' They would grab my cheeks, wobbling them back and forth like an auntie would. I hated that as well.

I sat and listened to the conquests that the older lads had apparently experienced and how they had 'shagged' half of Lincoln City's agricultural students: Felicity Kendal look-alikes, one said.

'Piss off; more like Mrs Slocombe look-alikes,' was the reality check.

Feeling exhausted after the long drive in the cold once more, I made my excuses and headed back to my room, but not before being accused of being a 'lightweight'. I couldn't keep up with the lads, no matter how much I tried; I'd like to see some of them drink me under the table now, though.

❖ ❖ ❖

13. A Christmas 'Do'

As Christmas approached, I was becoming more and more excited at going to my first 'do' (party). Still under age, I would be allowed to let my hair down, but someone was tasked to keep an eye on me and prevent me from getting 'arse-holed'. They failed miserably and I made a complete exhibition of myself. The party was to be held at the 'Hare and Hounds' pub in Fulbeck village, Lincolnshire.

It was about five miles from the camp and where a couple of MT staff had bought houses; I seem to remember it was, as most villages are in Lincolnshire, a picturesque and sleepy place. On the day of a party we would pack up work early, after the obligatory sweep of the whole building, and then have a few beers in the tea bar to start things off.

Back to the block for a shower and a change of clothes and meet at the RV (rendezvous) for the coach to the pub. Ricky, an absolute monster of a man and a rugby player, was given the task of looking after me. He was a bit like 'Taff' at Swinderby, and kept putting me in neck holds and tweaking various parts of my anatomy until I squealed. Even sat on the bus next to him, wedged between him and the window, I had to look up to meet his eye line. He would squash me up against the coach every time we rounded a right-hand bend, collapsing my lungs; I tried to push him off his seat on the left-hand ones, but it was futile. Writing this now, it amazes me just how many memories come flooding back in the clearest detail: Ricky had incredibly bad, pockmarked skin and hideous boils on his neck. To complement these he always had an aroma of 'sweaty arse' about him; I have no idea why that was so, but I did something about it later on that evening!

The coach pulled into the car park and we wobbled off into the pub; most of the SNCOs or 'Snecos' (senior non-commissioned officers – sergeant and above) had arrived by their own means with accompanying wives, some of whom were very pretty and glamorous with their flowing evening gowns and sparkling gems. I was introduced to some of them, but was far too shy to even speak. The Chief brought his wife over and introduced me as 'the little waster that had caused him all the grief'.

I thought, 'Fuck you, mate: this is the one night you can't tell me what to do!' There was never a thought given to the ramifications of my actions; I was having too good a time. After 'slying' some extra drinks, a pot of money was deposited behind the bar and we just ploughed our way through it until it was all gone – then we would have to pay for our own. I was well on the way to being pissed and it was only seven o'clock! Thankfully, sitting down to our Christmas meal some of the room in my stomach was taken up by food, which was a welcome break from all the drinking – although wine flowed around the table like water and I partook of it all. There were crackers and party hats along with the shit jokes and piss-taking, especially of the 'Snecos', as this was the only night we were gonna get away with it – or so I thought.

But the hierarchy would hold grudges, and that would be another costly lesson I would learn. Food fights were a constant danger, and I do declare a lone sprout shot past my eyes and into the lap of the woman on the end; I stopped chewing and thought all hell was about to break loose, but it didn't – she just picked it up and sent it back in the direction it came from. Wow! I thought: this was fantastic; we really couldn't get wrong tonight? But as I launched a pea across to the other table, giggling like a schoolboy, a hand gripped the back of my neck!

'Best behaviour, Novak! Or else ...' It was Ricky reining me in.

'But she ...' I began.

'You just worry about yourself,' he said, straightening my collar from behind, patting me on the back as if I was choking, and tilting my party hat back over my head with the force.

'Aye, no worries, Ricky; chill out, man.'

'You better not drop me in the shit tonight, Bob,' he replied, with the wagging finger making an appearance.

'As if,' I said, raising my thumb in a hitchhiking gesture and smiling innocently.

The meal was beautiful and the chatter exciting. I was as full as a fart, although the thought of the disco did nothing for my confidence and I just sat in one of the comfy chairs getting more and more drunk. I glanced around the room, noting the oak beams on the ceiling and various stuffed animals on the wall mounted on plaques. One particular plaque caught my eye; it was a huge moose's head. He doesn't look very happy, I thought, and I began talking to him.

'Hey, moose – what's it like up there? Having a good time? It's a great party, isn't it?'

Ricky came back to check on me;

'What ya doin', Bob?'

'I'm talking to the moose!' Ricky looked around, thinking I was referring to a woman.

'Where?'

'Up there,' pointing to the wall.

'For fuck's sake: go and sit back down.'

I wobbled my way across the dance floor, bumping into the many dancers and apologising as I went: 'Sorry, sorry – 'scuse – whoops there, comin' through – room for a little 'un.'

My glass had almost emptied itself by now and I peered into it despairingly. Before I could make my way to the bar, a couple of the lads came and asked me to do 'one of those things ya did in the hangar'.

'What things?'

'Ya know – one of those gymnasty things.'

'Oh, you mean a "flick flack"?'

Having been a gymnast at school, I had performed one of these manoeuvres at work, on the concrete floor, for the unbelievers.

'Yeah – one of them.'
'What here? Ner – not enough room.'
'See – I told ya he couldn't do it,' the second guy said.

And that was it; never dare a drunken airman to do anything, for verily, he will perform.

I took a long run upon the soft carpet, doing my 'Arab spring' before launching myself into the air and completing the 'flick flack' onto the middle of the dance floor; my landing left a little to be desired, but on the whole I thought the manoeuvre to be a successful one. I was wringing my hands in triumph as if dusting them.

'I think you'll find that was OK?' I chided.

They both nodded. And then they nodded again, and again, but they were indicating to look behind me. As I turned, Ricky and another monster put an arm each under mine, lifting me off the floor and marching me towards a quiet corner of the room, with one saying, 'You're either very brave or very, very stupid.'

I was thrust down onto the floor in front of a slightly built woman holding the side of her face and sitting in a chair, a trickle of blood barely visible.

'Apologise!'
'What for?'
I was bemused.

'APOLOGISE!' Ricky repeated. The woman was gently sobbing; I thought she was just drunk. In the confusion I still had time to realise how pretty she was when she raised her head.

'APOLOGISE FOR WHAT???'

Ricky articulated the sentiment that unless I wanted a moose's head enema, I should apologise, immediately and profusely.

'Sorry,' I said to Ricky.
'Not me ya twat – her!' pointing to the damsel in distress.
'When you did that somersault thing – you kicked her in the mouth!'

My world collapsed around me; tears streamed from my eyes, some from drink but most from having hurt a pretty girl. I was devastated. I ran out into the car park, finding an unlit place and sobbed like a child – like the child I still was. Ricky came to look for me and only discovered me from the crying, much as I'd tried to hold it in.

'Come on, Bob – it's not the end of the world,' he said, seeing how traumatised I was.

I began babbling incoherently, but he managed to calm me down and get me back inside. My face was red raw and it was obvious I'd been crying. There were lots of comments that I was still young, and couldn't hold my drink; they were all true.

But I was sincere in my second apology to the girl and she forgave me, putting a slight smile back on my face by noting that my eyes looked like – and I quote – 'sheep's fannies'. She stroked my cheek and I could feel the lump in my throat, like a conker still in its prickly shell.

We sat and talked for a while; I found out she was one of the drivers and that she had a boyfriend who was away on exercise. If she hadn't had a boyfriend, it would've been one hell of a way to meet – but then again, I wondered if he would kick the shit out of me when he got back, being RAF Regiment.

I was forced to have black coffee and was feeling a little perkier by the end of the evening – so much so that I decided to try a final pint. I bought it and put it to my lips, but nothing happened; my stomach was refusing to allow any more alcohol into my system, and I wandered around with it as it slowly warmed up. The coach arrived to take us home and we took the seats we had on the way there; I sat near the window again, clutching the pint I'd sneaked onto the bus, I'd fucking paid for it, and come rain or shine I was gonna drink the bastard! To this day I cannot believe what on Earth possessed me to do what followed, and I'll never fathom the logic that went into doing what I did.

Ricky made his way up the coach to sit next to me, turning and preparing to sit. As his arse approached the seat, I tipped the full pint of lager onto the red vinyl and Ricky plopped into the frothy puddle!

'What the fuck?!'

He stood, pinching the wet pants from his arse cheeks.

The back of the bus exploded with laughter as Ricky grabbed me by my hair, dragging me off the bus and banging my ears on every seat as we went. I was half laughing and half in pain, but it was fucking funny. The door to the coach was dragged open and I was propelled out and into the snow, doing a kind of 'para' roll as I landed. A couple of the 'Snecos' were making their way back to their cars, looking towards me and shaking their heads. One comment I heard was 'I doubt that lad will ever learn!' to much mumbling and nodding of heads.

I was eventually allowed back on the bus after a good scrubbing with snow and we set off for home. The piss-taking was in full flight now, and a fight broke out as we approached the camp.

The driver was told to stop and the culprit was ejected into the snow as I had been earlier, only this time the bus pulled away and left him to walk the mile or so back to the block. The guy in question was what we in the North call a 'Worky Ticket' – someone who is basically trying to get himself thrown out and was constantly being charged for fighting or for sleeping in. It finally came to a head when the 'snowdrops' (RAF Police, so called because of their white hats) were called to the NAAFI after Tim had started another fight.

The coppers dragged him outside; this was high entertainment, as he began writhing around on the ground and taking lumps out of the coppers. Biting one of them on the finger as he was pointed at, he hung on like a pit bull, with the 'snowdrop' squealing like the proverbial pig! We all thought this was fantastic, as all the RAF Police seemed to do was ride around in a Land Rover and put a damper on anything you were doing, particularly if you were enjoying yourself.

Tim broke free and escaped, kicking over Danny the bird scarer's Kawasaki on the way past into the large parade square car park. The squealers gave chase and 'decked' him not long after; they threw him into the back of a 'Sherpa' van and off he went, banging and rocking it from side to side. You would have thought they had just caught a Tasmanian Devil!

We went back into the NAAFI, applauding as we went. Tim was obnoxious, but we liked the 'snowdrops' even less, with them being 'acting corporals' and failed 'civvy' coppers in our eyes – just glorified traffic wardens and general party poopers.

As we finished our drinks in the NAAFI and began walking out, the 'copper' van rolled up with a police dog-handler and Alsatian in tow, looking for witnesses of when the other one got bitten. No takers there, then; 'Little Jake' started giving them some cheek and was asked to produce his ID card, which he duly did but showed it to the dog, saying:

'What've ya brought him for?'

'In case there was any more trouble,' the copper replied.

'I was talking to the dog,' Jake said.

We fell about laughing, but the copper had a sense-of-humour failure and asked Jake if he wanted to joint his mate in the cells.

'Can do – it'll keep me away from the missus for a night!'

'Right, in the van,' the copper said.

We flocked around Jake and told him to 'Shut the fuck up and don't spoil a good night.' And amazingly, we talked the copper out of locking him up – probably too much paperwork?

Jake and I hit it off immediately. We were kindred spirits; he was similar in build and height to me and had a wicked, impish sense of humour much like my mischievous self. He was married, with a couple of kids, but that never stopped him from doing anything. The rumour that even the goldfish stopped swimming, as he would shag anything that moved, gave me a laugh, and he openly admitted that he would 'fuck the crack of dawn' if only he could be bothered to get up early enough! (I found this statement a bit crude.)

We used to go back to his house and get 'hammered', and he would allow me to stay over till Saturday morning, when his missus would make us a hearty breakfast if I wasn't going home at the weekend. I would baby-sit for him on the rare occasions he took the wife out; she was the butt of many of his jokes and on occasions I did feel sorry for her. They would leave me plenty of cans in the fridge and free rein of the kitchen, and a couple of porn videos.

Jake would ask if I'd 'galloped the maggot' when he came back and he was always funny. I felt embarrassed, but it never bothered his missus. One such evening Jake returned rather the worse for wear and asked if I wanted to see a trick; I was extremely dubious, as once committed I would inevitably have to see it through.

'Go on then,' I said cautiously.

He disappeared into the kitchen and I leapt up from the couch and partially hid behind the living-room door, thinking a soaking was coming. Jake returned from the kitchen with a pack of Cheddar cheese biscuits and shouted for the dog, laughing at me being on edge.

The dog bounded in from somewhere and Jake threw it a biscuit.

'Yeah – so what? All dogs will catch a biscuit,' I said.

'No – just wait and see.'

The dog took the biscuit behind the couch and there was a crunching sound; nothing new in that, I thought, until Jake pulled the couch away from the wall, where the dog was grinding the biscuit into the carpet with its arse. There were small piles of biscuit everywhere! I was in hysterics saying,

'How the fucking hell 'ave ya taught him to do that?'

'Didn't have to; he was like that when we got him.'

What a party trick. Jake's devious mind was in overdrive and he took the biscuits back into the kitchen and spread mustard on one – English mustard, mind – for that extra 'zing'. He threw it to the dog, same as before, only this time the dog shot out from behind the couch and flew out into the garden, dragging its arse across the grass with its hind legs swept forward, overtaking its ears. It was quite possibly the funniest thing I've ever seen, along with the airman jumping out of the locker, and those images still make me laugh.

Jake was very defiantly a bad influence and I was spending too much time around him, according to the boss.

Many late nights at his place – or early mornings would be more accurate – were making getting up in the morning ever more difficult. I began to sleep in and was late for work a couple of times: not by much, but it had come to the attention of the Chief! Combined with all the wanking I was doing, my boss suggested that I should go to bed with boxing gloves on.

'Why? Is it better like that, Flight?'

My gag fell on stony ground, and I was told in no uncertain terms that if I was late again I would be charged. Sure enough, after another late night I slept in. If you were one of the good guys and were still missing by 8.30 am (we started at 8 am), one of the lads would try and wangle a road test so he could give you a knock before the 'Snecos' realised you were missing. That worked on a couple of occasions for me, but I was getting worse and my attitude was slipping. If you were a 'tosser' like Tim, you were left to stew in your 'pit' and eventually someone would be told to go and get you. The time I was told to get him he threw shoes at me until I went away; I returned with a corporal and he got charged again.

I opened my eyes and the clock said 8.45 am! Oh, bollocks! I began thinking of the excuses I could try this time leaping into my uniform, washing and brushing my teeth at the same time, I fled for work. As I came out of the woods (a short cut) like a bullet from a gun, the Chief, clipboard at the ready, smiled one of those 'I've fucking got ya now' smiles as he crossed the yard.

'Chief – Chief – you'll never guess what's happened!'

'Not interested,' he said, writing something on the clipboard.

'I fell through a time warp and missed the tram!'

His pen stopped writing, and I could see his shoulders shaking trying to keep a giggle in, not making a sound. Without looking up from his board he said,

'Get yer overalls on and get to work – this is your very last warning, Novak!'

Phew, I was relieved and in those overalls 'toot sweet', as industrious as a beaver in a monsoon. One of the sergeants took me to one side and told me that the Chief really had it in for me: no more chances. OK, I thought, enough's enough; I'll buck up.

I opened my eyes the next morning! Eight thirty am!

'Knock-knock-knock' went the door.

~ A Christmas 'Do' ~

'Yeah, I know,' I mumbled.
'You've fucked it this time, Bob; you're getting done!'
'Yeah, right; I'll be up to work soon.'

If I was getting 'done', there was no way I was rushing around like an idiot; remembering the 'might as well be hung for a sheep as a lamb' saying, a few more minutes wouldn't make any difference. I strolled up to work and was marched in front of the boss, who took my ID card off me and recorded all its details, saying I would be getting charged with contravening Queen's Regulations for failing to attend a duty.

It didn't sound all that bad, but I would be up in front of the MTO (mechanical transport officer).

'Prisoner and escort, by the left – quick march,' said the corporal, as we made our way from our section to the MT yard. Prisoner, I thought? – blimey, I only slept in, not murdered someone! When you're on a 'fizzer' (charge) you are marched without your beret on, so that all and sundry can see you are about to be punished; it definitely felt a bit weird. Obviously without a beret on I could not salute, but had to give an 'eyes right' as the escort saluted the officer on the opposite side of the road.

'Eyes front.'

Check, turn, I counted in my head. Into the MT yard and up the stairs to the boss's office. I was shaking; this was the first time I had been in 'proper' trouble and I didn't know what to expect. The lads made the most of this and frightened the life out of me by telling me what would happen. It was a tissue of lies, with talk of court martials etc. – and all this 'aggro' for a few extra minutes in bed! Like most military things, it was OTT (over the top).

The officer read out the charge and asked if I understood it; yes, I did. Did I have anything to say in my defence? I'd been advised to reply in the negative to this, and to keep my gob well and truly shut.

'Will you accept my punishment?' the officer said.

And the advice this time was to reply in the affirmative, although I really didn't want to; but to refuse would mean going to a higher authority and the punishment would be much more severe. Reluctantly I agreed, not knowing whether I was to be jailed or fined, or both; and the mere mention of the dreaded Colchester word (military prison), sent shivers down my spine! I was fined £20 and given seven days' 'jankers' (extra duties and daily parades).

'Prisoner and escort – about turn!'

And that was that; piece of piss, I thought – and it would all happen again all too soon. And for the same thing; what a 'knobber'.

I wasn't bothered about the fine, as it would be deducted directly from my wages and I never had any money left at the end of the month anyway; far from it – I would be skint a couple of weeks after pay day and borrowed where I could. Usually overdrawn, I was on a downward spiral until the boss eventually took my chequebook off me and helped me to get my finances back in order.

There was talk of an individual who had a similar attitude to money to mine, but he apparently thought that while he still had cheques in his book, he still had money in the bank. A pinch of salt required with that one, but as they say, 'Life is stranger than fiction.'

The constant parading at the guardroom twice a day in 'number one' uniform was a real pisser, and I hated it. It meant being inspected by some snotty officer who revelled in ripping the shit out of you, making notes that the creases weren't sharp enough or that the shoes were not polished enough, and on a number of occasions I had to return to the block and have another go before returning to the guardroom again half an hour later to go through it all again.

I suppose it should have acted as deterrent enough: but you don't plan to sleep in, do you? Maybe less beer or less wanking, and definitely less contact with 'Jake' – or a combination of all three – was advisable. But I was 'young, dumb and full of cum', according to one corporal; I thought that was a bit personal, and shrugged it off.

I was more or less ordered to stay away from Jake, as the bosses thought he was trying to 'work his ticket'. But I was damned if the RAF was gonna tell me who I could, and more importantly who I couldn't, socialise with – a rule too far in my book; I rebelled and almost took a tumble for my loyalty to Jake.

While working one Saturday morning, Jake came up to the section for his toolbox to do some private work. I was told not to let him in. The gates were locked and he stood the other side of the fence, asking me to let him in.

'I can't,' I told him.

'Come on, Bob – I only want me toolbox.'

'I can't Jake; I'll get done if I let you in. Wait there and I'll go and get your box.'

'OK,' he replied and off I went. I got his box and opened the gate to push it through to him, but he wandered past me and headed for the changing rooms for some overalls and came back a few minutes later.

Monday morning I was summoned to the flight sergeant's office.

'Did you let Jake Smith in at the weekend?'

'No, Flight,' I tried confidently.

'Are you sure?'

'Yeah, boss; he just came for his toolbox and I got it for him.'

'You wouldn't lie to me, Novak, now would you?'

He was glaring at me now.

'Straight up, boss; you said don't let him in and I didn't.'

'I'm going to ask you one more time, Novak, then you'll be over the road in front of the MTO again.'

I'd reached my zenith and knew the game was up.

'Oh, that's right; he just went in for some overalls.'

'So you disobeyed a direct order?'

Now I knew I was in the shit; disobeying an order meant jail time. Strangely, he said:

'I recognise your loyalty towards a workmate, but this lad's gonna drag you down; people are giving you advice and you're choosing not to act on it! I don't think you're a bad kid, but you've got a lot to learn and a long time to do it; you're coming up to your yearly assessment, and if you want to get on you're gonna have to knuckle down and stop fucking about.'

~ A Christmas 'Do' ~

'I'm sorry, boss; I just didn't know what to do for the best.'
'Who's doing your assessment, me or Smith?'
I hung my head in shame and it didn't require an answer; I could feel myself filling up and it reminded me of the talking-to I got when I was caught stealing 50p from Mam's purse when I was a kid. I didn't get shouted at, but the shame of what I'd done felt the same. I remember leaving the office in deep thought and blanked Jake as I passed him on the stairs up to the boss's office; he looked at me, holding his hands out in a 'what've I done?' gesture.
'I nearly got fucking done for you!' I protested.
'What for?'
'Saturday morning; I told ya I couldn't let ya in!'
'Bollocks, yer having me on.'
'Go and see; you're next in line for the bollocking!'
Jake shrugged his shoulders and sauntered into the office, and I heard raised voices for a good while. When Jake finally came out his face was as red as thunder. He hated being bollocked, but knew he couldn't retaliate without getting further in the shit. We cooled our friendship for a bit after that, but we eventually drifted back together as time passed, although I was a little wiser towards him. He was waiting for me to get him back and was decidedly untrusting and stand-offish.

He'd bought an old Jaguar car for £150 and it needed a lot of work, which we would do at dinnertimes in the car park and in the Motor Club, a kind of enthusiasts' garage, quite well equipped actually. On the wall were many adverts offering cars and motorbikes for sale and spare parts available. Jake was doing something to the Jag and I was looking at the adverts, where a piece of white card told of Jaguar spare parts by the hundred and to contact a Mr Cox. I told Jake about this, he dismissed it immediately.

'Here Jake, I'm serious: cheap Jag spares.'
'Yeah, fuck off; I'm not falling for that shit!'
'Here, look, contact Mr Cox on this number.'
'If you think I'm phoning that number and asking for Cox, you've got another thing coming!'
'It's genuine, ya melon.'
'Well, you phone the fucker then, and ask to speak to "sucks" when he answers.'
I was absolutely floored; this was Jake all over. If he got any sharper, he'd cut himself. I laughed for ages and ages. He still didn't believe me, but the 'ad' was genuine.

I did get him back at another 'do' at the rugby club. Things could get royally out of hand here and I was soaked with beer while playing 'Lancasters'. In case you've never played it, I'll explain. A number of chairs are placed in the shape of a large, multi-engined aircraft and volunteers are recruited to be the pilot, co-pilot, navigator, gunner and tail gunner, along with the four engines of the Lancaster. People sit in their respective places with a pint of something. The script goes something like this.

'Pilot to co-pilot: ready for start-up.'

'Starting engine number one, skipper.'

The person at that position makes coughing and farting noises as if starting the engine and then settles into a regular hum. The same follows for the other three engines, until there is quite a loud roar as the aircraft taxis to the end of the runway ready for take-off. I am number four engine and enthusiastically take part in the scenario; the constant banter among pilot and co-pilot, gunners and air traffic control is highly amusing. As we come under attack the pilot pushes the throttles to full and all engines are now making an unholy row; while the gunners are firing at imaginary bandits at three o'clock and Kit Kats at four o'clock, the aircraft is hit and number four engine catches fire!

Dozens of pints are thrown over it to put it out. I was fucking drowned in beer, lager, coke and Christ knows what else. Jake was in on the gag and I was determined to have my vengeance. When the laughter had died down and I'd gone to the toilets to mop up some of the beer, I sneaked outside and swapped the cables of Jake's bike so that front brake was back and back was front. At the end of the evening, I challenged him to a race from the top of camp, where the rugby club was, down to his house, a good mile away. Jake leapt onto his bike while I unlocked mine; he set off at a phenomenal speed with me giving chase, goading him.

We were for ever doing skids on these bikes and Jake approached the T-junction like an express train; sticking his foot out to do a sideways skid, he went to lock up the back brake, grabbing the lever with full force. The front wheel stopped immediately, catapulting Jake over the handlebars and into the middle of the road; the bike bounced over him, catching him in the 'knackers' as it somersaulted out of control. He lay in the road, clutching his 'jewels' and groaning.

Oh, this was a high coup! I had to get off my bike; I couldn't see where I was going for having fits of laughter. I gave myself the stitch, I was laughing so much. Jake was not amused. Eventually getting off the floor and mumbling something or other, I'm not sure if he was 'hamming' it up a bit, but that 'nipped arse-cheek, John Wayne walk' was about as funny as it gets.

'Quits?' I said, hopefully.

'No fucking way, Novak – this is war!'

I must have laughed all the way home and he was getting fed up by the time we separated: the 'onion giggle' that keeps repeating on you. I couldn't wait to tell the lads tomorrow. We were always 'up front' about admitting that we'd been 'had', and the inventiveness never ceased to amaze me.

One Friday afternoon we got an early knock-off, and I'd packed my bag the previous night and put it in the car so I could go straight home from work to beat the traffic. I had a 1.3-litre Mk 2 Ford Escort by then and I was really proud of it; it was a tidy motor with a little sports steering wheel on. I climbed in and fired up the engine, selected first gear and lifted the clutch. The revs went up but nothing happened. I put it in neutral and tried again: revs up, no movement. I tried all the other gears – still nothing. Thinking it was something drastic, which would definitely scupper my plans for going home, I tried again and again. As well as the revs going up, the 'speedo' was registering different speeds as the revs increased. I could hear the lads roaring with laughter and pointing to the back of the car. Jake stood with his arms folded in a triumphant pose. The crafty bastard had sneaked a jack down at dinnertime and put the back axle on bricks, so the tyres were just off the ground.

'Aw, you fucker! You knew I was going home!'

'I know: that's what makes it even funnier.'

A round of applause rippled from the lads for Jake's inventiveness, and I set to work getting the bricks out.

'You'll pay for this, ya big dog's cock!' I said, but never knew whether it was an insult or a compliment. I was always doing that, saying things I didn't know the meaning of.

One of Jake's favourite tricks was to put the steel toecap of his boot under the tyre of a vehicle being driven into the hangar, causing it to bump in the air; the driver would think he'd hit something, and get out and wander round the car for ages. Jake would be lurking somewhere nearby, giggling away.

He did this to me just before tea break one day. but I'd spotted him lurking around and knew he'd be up to no good. As I drove the Cortina into the hangar he put his boot under the tyre of my blind side, but I was ready for him. I yanked on the handbrake and removed the keys, leaving him stuck under the wheel. We all went for tea and Jake hobbled in a few minutes later, minus one shoe, to rapturous applause.

Jake was definitely an outdoor chap, with a passion for motorbikes and shooting. He had an air rifle and we would stop by his house and pick it up before going on the ten-mile extended test route. Many a pheasant had the wind put up it as we drove in the countryside – but with a rifle in the car we were sailing very close to the wind, and it would be jail time if we were caught.

So I returned one weekend with an SP50 Diana .177 air pistol that was much easier to conceal. I used to keep it at Jake's and he would wrap it in a duffle coat when we picked it up. It was a 'gat' gun and required the barrel to be compressed by pushing it into something solid to cock it. A threaded 'stop' screw at the rear would be opened, a slug (pellet) put in the barrel and the screw replaced. The sights were shite, the gun was shite, and we rarely hit anything we were aiming at. I shot a pheasant one day while out on test and it just leapt in the air and fucked off, like the 'Road Runner'.

'Ya missed, ya bell end!'

'Here! You try then, ya clever twat, if ya can do any better.'

We swapped places and Jake hung out of the window like Bodie and Doyle of the 'Professionals'. He shot at everything, announcing that the gun was shite and wouldn't stop a 'spuggy' (sparrow).

'It smashes bottles,' I said.

'Ner, not powerful enough. You could even shoot me and it wouldn't hurt.'

'Wanna bet? Yer on!'

We went down the tip and Jake put on the heavy old duffle coat.

'No shooting me in the arse, ya wanker!'

'You're not serious?'

'Yeah, I am; twenty yards away and in the middle of me back.'

'I'm not fucking shooting ya, Jake.'

'Come on, ya big pouf – are ya chicken?'
'No comebacks, mind?'
'No; come on, then!'
I loaded the pistol and dropped onto one knee to ensure that I was steady.
'I'm not sure about this, Jake ...'
'Just get on ...'
THWACK!'
The slug hit him in the centre of his back and he fell to his knees with a groan. Reaching around with a hand, he began rubbing where he'd been hit.
'Are you all right, Jake?'
'Aw! That would definitely kill a fucking pheasant if you'd have hit it,' he whined.
I was dying to laugh, but thought better of it. Walking back up the track to where I was he said, 'My turn!'
'Get fucked, ya knobber; look at the state of you!'
There was no way I was handing it over. The next few days I saw the bruise in the middle of his back go from golf-ball size to a good six inches across, with every colour of the rainbow radiating outwards from its centre. Good show, Jake.

❖ ❖ ❖

14. Main Hangar

My little old presence was requested in the boss's office once more – 'on the mat', as it was known. I thought of asking to have my own personal one made with my name on it, but wasn't sure quite how that would go down. I stood in his office with my hands behind my back, wondering what I could have possibly done this time to warrant another visit.

For a second I thought that Jake might have 'grassed' me up about the pistol thing: but then dismissed it. Jake would never grass! – would he? Surely not; I mean, as an accomplice he'd be in as much shit as me! And the air pistol was kept at his house – so no, I convinced myself not.

'Sit down, Novak.'

A gentle finger movement accompanied the instruction, as if tapping the ash from an imaginary cigarette.

'You've been with us approximately nine months now, give or take a week, and it's been ...' (pause for effect – look up and over the glasses sarcastically) '... an interesting time. Not quite what I'd hoped for, but nevertheless, we have to see if all that money spent training you at St Athan can be put to good use. In three months' time you will be having your first assessment, and I can joyfully say that I am eagerly looking forward to it. Career assassination ...' (pause: wave of the hands and lean back in the chair contented) '... or indeed enhancement is an acquired art, in which I take a great deal of pride.'

I hadn't the faintest idea what the old fart was ranting on about, and started to daydream out of the window. But I'd been invited to sit; surely I was in the clear, otherwise I would have still been standing.

'Your career lies in these hands, young Novak. What I write about you on your assessment will follow you around for the rest of your time with us, however short.'

I must have pulled a questioning face, because it prompted another explanation.

'These hands have sent young men, good young men, on to be SACs, J/Ts, corporals and sergeants, and if you want the same, unless you stay 'off the mat' for the next three months, I will not be giving you a glowing report! Far from it. To that end I will need to keep an extremely close eye on you – closer than ever before, and to do that I will need to look out of my window every day and see that cheeky face of yours hard at work. You start in the main hangar on Monday.'

My face must have lit up like the jackpot of a fruit machine, eyes agog.

'D'ya mean ... I ... me ... in the ... down there, with the lads?'

'Yes, as of Monday you will be my newest mechanic.'

No one had ever called me 'mechanic' before and it was only then that I realised I was one – and a qualified one at that, with City and Guilds (Part 1). No more oil changes, grease-guns and monotony: I was joining the big boys' club.

I leapt to my feet and shook his hand; this took him a bit by surprise, but he reciprocated nonetheless. I don't think he'd ever seen anyone so excited to be told he was going to be working in the main hangar. It pleased him and I assured him I would not be giving him cause for concern between now and assessment time; I meant it, but it wouldn't happen. I turned to leave.

'Did I say you could go?'

I went to sit back down.

'That's all; you can go now.'

Eat your heart out, Frank Spencer; my performance was tenfold. I thought I would explode with excitement, and ran out of the office to tell everyone. By ten 'o clock tea break the grapevine had proved as reliable as ever, and the news was common knowledge.

'Weld your boxes up, lads; the poisonous dwarf's made it to the hangar!' was one comment, followed by a collection of rather imaginative put-downs. No matter: I was on a high now and shot off at dinnertime to phone home and tell them the good news. I explained how big the hangar was, and its layout.

It was like that massive barn on 'Those Magnificent Men in their Flying Machines', only made from steel and with double doors at both ends, which pushed apart so planes could fly right through. Workbenches everywhere, with a twenty-tonne press and a hydraulic car ramp; pits in the bays next to the offices, and jacks and axle stands by the dozen; book after book of APs (air publications) – most were parts catalogues or repair manuals: like a Haynes explains, only a hundred times more in depth. The place was capable of accommodating between ten and fifteen vehicles at a time comfortably.

'I wonder which poor twat's gonna be looking after him for a year?' I heard someone say, as I returned to the tea bar.

'What d'ya mean?' I asked innocently.

'You don't think they're gonna let a tosser like you loose on all this equipment on yer own, do ya?'

I was crestfallen.

'You'll work with someone more experienced, a J/T or a corporal, until you've got the hang of things.'

'Who?' I barked.

'That's for the bosses to decide.'

I looked around the sea of faces and imagined it would be like at school when no one would pick the useless kid – after all, I'd insulted most of them at some point before now. You see, what I hadn't realised is that unless you are a wizard mechanic, or have some other discernible skill, you've just got to take it; until you had 'got some in' (that's time/service) you were not to give it out. (Well, you know what you can do with your silly rule – what's good to give is good to take, in my book.)

But oh God, if it was Big Ritchie, I could see myself getting 'twatted' before the first week was out.

The Chief put his head around the door of the tea bar and all faces looked up, as they always did to see if it was another piss-worthy lamb for the slaughter or a 'jammy' job, like getting off camp during working hours: a 'skive', or going on a 'jolly' for spare parts to another camp, or a breakdown – basically anything that broke the monotony of the day.

'Young Novak here needs some apron-strings to hang on to – any volunteers?'

He was fucking loving it; not a single hand was raised. I looked around the room again, forlorn, pleading with my eyes; the heads dropped like ninepins. Little Jake put his hand up as a last resort (he was one rank above me), only to be shot down in flames by the Chief.

'You're lucky you're still here, boy; put you and him together? You should be at other ends of the planet, never mind the section. At any rate I need experience and responsibility, neither of which you have.' He was wrong; Jake had experience by the bucket load but responsibility mmm... I wonder?

I always imagined Jake knocking him out one day and I wish someone had done; he was like one of those blokes who was unhappy at home and took it out on everyone he met, except ranks equal and above – that's right, a creep.

'Right: eeny meeny miny mo.'

I could actually see people duck as the word fell on them; fuck off, I wasn't that bad, was I? Or was I? I began to take stock of my nine months; mmm, ner – they're only kidding, aren't they?

The job eventually fell to a short, stocky corporal called Larry who didn't seem bothered either way, as I would find out to my cost a little later. A cheer went up for the reprieved and then a lot of laughter, but it really did unnerve me; that's the fine line between being cheeky and being insulting, and I hadn't learned it yet. And so our student–teacher relationship began by me doing all the fetching and carrying of all things heavy, jacks and axle-stands: I got to steam-clean everything outside, even in the rain, and wash everything greasy in the paraffin bath. This was definitely not how I thought it would be.

But I listened intently as I passed him a variety of tools, as he lay underneath a range of different vehicles. I perched on his locked toolbox like a gnome fishing. I wondered why he didn't use his own, but he said,

'They would get mixed up and we wouldn't be able to tell whose was whose.'

The truth of the matter was that if we lost any of mine, it would be me getting in the shit for it and not him – something I wouldn't find out until our first toolbox check just before assessment time – and there was also the fact that he did so much 'govvy', or 'private' work, after hours on other people's cars that he didn't need to bring his box in at all: we just used mine.

I think he was getting as sick of my incessant questioning as I was of doing all the donkeywork.

He asked me one day if I wanted to help him change a water pump on a Renault after work for a few quid (now you're talking!); I readily accepted and carried my box down to the band car park after work. The car park was large and was always full of cars in different states of repair, although they always had to remain mobile, i.e. with the wheels on, in case of a security threat. If any vehicle were left unattended for some length of time, and the SWO (Station Warrant Officer – 'God'!) had clocked this on his many travels, the owner's records would be checked and then if he or she did not move said vehicle fourteen days after the registration number had appeared in SROs, then 'the scrap man cometh and maketh disappear'.

Larry appeared with a few instructions.

'Unbolt this; watch out for that; don't lose or drop that, and I'll check on ya in a bit.'

I did as instructed, got the old pump off without any trouble and cleaned the engine block where the new one was to go on. Larry came back after about an hour; as I was sat on the wall twiddling my thumbs and feeling quite proud, he threw a tube of 'Hylomar' (water-sealing compound) at me. He said to use it liberally and to put the new pump on in the reverse order I'd taken the old one off, and he would check on me in a bit. I refitted the new pump carefully; I was keen to impress, but eager not to fuck up on the first job, as this could be the first of many, I thought. I walked back up to the section and borrowed a watering-can, topped up the little sky-blue Renault and was waiting for Larry to return, remembering my hallowed warning, 'Do not try to start the engine till I get back!'

I waited and waited: no Larry. Time was getting on now and I had had visions of having been paid and being settled in the NAAFI by this time. It was getting on for eight pm. I'd been down the car park on my own that long that the 'teas and keys' man had thought I'd finished and had locked up the section. I still had my overalls on and was filthy. My room keys were in my uniform in the changing room, as were my wallet and ID card, so I couldn't even go to the guardroom and get them back out; anyway, I don't think I was even on the key list yet as an 'authorised drawer'. Where the fuck was Larry? I hadn't a clue where he lived, even whether he lived on camp or not. I only knew where Jake lived, and that was a good twenty-minute walk away; in overalls, without ID, I would be asking for trouble.

It was getting dark now; what was I gonna do? No 'pay as you go' mobiles in those days – in fact no mobiles at all, unless you were a rep or an executive, or just a 'flash' bastard. An RAF Police Land Rover circled the car park and I dived for cover between the car-park wall and the car; I waited, motionless, until the familiar sound of its exhaust and engine note disappeared into the distance towards the OMQs (officers' married quarters), which meant they would be back this way before very long. I tried to think it through logically; I'd already put my toolbox in the Renault, so I could 'kip' in there – but that would be ridiculous. I could run back to the block and hope I'd left my window open, but the sight of a person running out of hours on a military camp always aroused suspicion, and in overalls and without ID I'd have an awful lot of explaining to do. I was furious. Just then I heard the sound of another car approaching; thinking it was the 'snowdrops' on the flip journey I hit the deck once more, listening intently, but this was no Land Rover – it was a civvy car. Could it be Larry? No such fucking luck.

It was one of the lads from the block coming to get something out of one of the cars he was fixing up.

'Fucking hell, Bob: that's what I call overtime!'

As I approached his car, I saw it was one of the junior technicians. I explained what had happened, and he laughed knowingly as soon as I mentioned Larry.

'Come on, I'll give yer a lift back to the block, and if ya window's not open I'll get the master key off the block corporal.'

The window wasn't open and there was a bit of explanation required, a lot of secrecy pleaded for on my behalf, and many favours owed. The block corporal let me into my room and I got washed and changed, although my beautiful white sink would never have quite the same shine ever again after the ingrained muck was rinsed around its basin. I thought about going over to the NAAFI, but of course I had no key to lock my room; yes, I could lock it from the inside without a key, but not the outside. I slid the large sash window up and clambered onto the windowsill, commando-style, checking the coast was clear while humming the 'Mission Impossible' tune.

I rolled out of the window and onto the grass below, sliding the window down gently so as not to lock it, and galloped over to the NAAFI as though prohibition was on its way back in. Ta-da!

Getting back in, though, was a sight to behold. It had gone midnight when I finally left the NAAFI with the regular stragglers; we separated like satellites and made our way to our respective blocks, mine being the furthest away but one. There were still lots of lights on and lots of TVs chattering away, but I would have to be quiet if I wasn't to attract unwanted attention.

I slid the window up again, put my top half through, grabbed hold of the 'comfy' chair each room was issued with, and tried to pull myself in. The sash swished down onto the middle of my back, trapping me in a most provocative position. Needing my arms to keep my front up left me with little means of trying to raise the window; I wiggled my bum from side to side while pulling myself forward, hoping to Christ no one was looking. It was working, but I was scraping the front of my shins on the windowsill, while the bottom of the windows did my calves in – but hey, I was in! Setting the alarm clock with the one eye that was barely still focusing was the next challenge – and my watch alarm, and the little travel clock on top of the reading light; I could not afford to sleep in.

The alarms all went off at the same time the following morning, give or take a minute or two, and I looked around for my uniform with my wallet and keys in. There was just a pair of scruffy overalls lying on the floor, stinking the room out. Oh yeah, I remember now; so I had a choice of climbing out of my window so the door could remain locked, or walking out through the door and coming back to lock it when I got to work. But what if I couldn't get away?

Like any large organisation, I'm ashamed to say it had its share of light-fingered petty crooks. I'd managed to purchase a rather magnificent twin-deck stereo tape player with VU meters and lots of buttons; I definitely didn't want that to be nicked. So in my spare number two uniform I opted for the window, making sure I wasn't caught. I had a spot of brekkies and wandered up to work with the rest of the rabble. Larry was as nonchalant as expected, and just asked if I got the car finished.

'Yeah, I did, and I waited for you coming back till nine pm – what happened?'

'Oh, after my tea I fell asleep on the couch, and it was too late when I woke up.'

'Well, thanks a lot.' I told him what had happened.

He pushed a fiver into my hand, which shut me up, but it wouldn't have done when Billy told me he charged the geezer £15 for doing the job. I knew I was under scrutiny and decided that remaining calm was the better part of valour, but that I needed to be a bit more wary. I kept my head down, as I was working in the bay right next to the offices and old beady-eyed sod's nose was never far from the windowsill – it was like working in a fish-tank.

Everyone was waiting for you to drop a bollock, so they could pounce on you. Every mechanic and fitter passing my bay to Stores had some form of advice – some good, some not so good and some downright dastardly. It was only a matter of time before I fucked up.

'You want to make sure the flluffle valve is set before you jack it up,' one said.

'Yeah, and make sure the splonge selector is in neutral or you'll never get it back together,' said another.

This was the baby mechanic's nightmare: having so much to learn, but then showing how little you actually knew by asking someone on the quiet – in confidence, you thought – how to set the flluffle valve, only to have the whole tea bar rip the shit out of you for a solid fifteen minutes at the next break.

This is the way it was, and believe me, I've been to Stores for them all: tartan paint; a bubble for the spirit level; skyhooks; a long stand; a left-handed screwdriver; a cordless extension; a set of worry gauges – you name it, I went for it. The gentleman in Stores was a retired flight-sergeant fitter and a very knowledgeable chap, and I should have shown him more respect than I did. Larry said there are two things you never do in stores – one: never take a tool back dirty, and two: never, ever fart in Stores.

Why? After all, trouser trumping was something I was particularly good at, and still am – ask any of my ex-partners. It was a Monday morning and after the usual weekend of beer and curry, I'd gone into Stores for a large, adjustable spanner, saying:

'Eh up, Dick, this one's for you!'

P-a-a-a-a-r-r-r-r-p! As I raised an arse cheek up to the level of the bench, Dick picked up the biggest adjustable spanner from the tool board and threw it full force directly at me. I ducked instinctively and the spanner just missed me, sailing over my head and thundering into the door, the open jaws biting into the woodwork.

'Ya filthy little bastard – get out!'

And I was back on the mat. Now I don't care how serious things get: if you are gonna try and bollock me about farting and expect me to keep a straight face, you've had it, mate.

The boss did his best to describe the complaint put forward by Dick and every time he approached the word in question, a massive smile would spread across my face. I was thinking, if he utters the word 'fart' I will collapse in a heap of giggles right here on this mat.

~ Main Hangar ~

'I cannot have you upsetting my civilians! Broke wind,' he said, 'of a particularly odious nature!'

Well, that was about as posh as it got for me and I giggled uncontrollably. No amount of threats was going to take the edge off it and the boss reluctantly admitted defeat, sending me on my way by saying he would let Dick loose on me himself if I ever did it again. Of course I would: I was a daredevil, cheeky minx! And it's not all good news, as anyone who's ever sneezed and farted at the same time will tell you how painful it can be. God forbid going the whole hog and actually following through; I'm sure that most of us have done that at least once, although girls won't ever admit to having 'skiddy' pants – oh, come off it!

Whenever Larry sloped off somewhere to do one of his dodgy deals, I would wander around the hangar asking every one else what they were doing: why, where and when. I was like the kid with the 'Fisher Price Activity Centre': 'What's that do?' 'What's this for?' 'What happens if I push this?'

'I push ya face in, that's what happens if ya push this; now fuck off!'

I was just inquisitive and couldn't take it in fast enough. I would even volunteer to get things for them, or search through the endless list of part numbers to see if they were in stock, if it meant I could watch for a while. This is when I was reminded that you watch with your eyes and not your tongue. 'OK, I'll be quiet.'

But I just couldn't resist; so another lesson had to be learned. It came in the form of helping one of the sergeants with a Mk 8 fire truck out in the yard (a 'Green Goddess').

'Get on that crawler board, get under the truck and take this special spanner with you Can ya see the rapid-drain valve?'

'What's it look like?'

'It's the big shiny nut that the spanner fits, in the middle of the truck – got it?'

'Yeah, I see it.'

'It's got a left-hand thread on, so to tighten it you turn it in the opposite direction; if you turn in the normal direction you'll get soaked.'

The last bit of information convinced me that he was telling the truth, otherwise he would have said nothing – and he was a sergeant.

'It's a bit stiff,' I said.

'Just give it a right old tug, ya little wazza – she'll come!'

Tug – whoosh! – oh, she came all right! I floated out from beneath the fire truck on my wooden crawler board, pursued by a thousand gallons of water and with the 'sarge' in stitches.

'But you said ...'

I had to walk back to the changing room like John Wayne to change my overalls. Bastard! He stuck his head around the door:

'It's very simple, Bob: when people tell you to shut up, you shut up – OK?' I nodded.

You got to see some fantastic sights in the hangar; it was a hive of activity. There was always someone needing a hand or a lift, and I picked up an awful lot really quickly: how to bleed a braking system; how to change a Land Rover gearbox (there was a definite knack to that); how to strip and rebuild a wheel-hub assembly – but not before completely fucking one up so badly that the vehicle was off the road for a month before a new one could be ordered and refitted. I was not flavour of that month.

It was time for my TATs (trade ability tests); this was to see whether what you had learned at St Athan had remained with you, or whether you had a colander for a brain. It was mainly a practical test, with close attention being paid to safety, and my job was to change the engine on a Hillman 'Hunter'. It was my first one, although I had helped out with several Land Rover engine changes, which were pretty easy as you had a good deal of space to work in; once the bonnet was off my only problem was reaching the damn thing, and I often used the spare tyre that lived on the bonnet as a step. No trouble this time; I checked that the handbrake was on and the car was in neutral. The first thing was to disconnect the battery; remembering the old adage of 'earth off first and on last' would keep you from 'shorting out' your spanner on the chassis. Being observed this closely by a corporal with a clipboard was decidedly unnerving, but he had to check. I tried to work systematically; the sign of a good fitter is one who has all the nuts and bolts at his fingertips when he needs them. One way of doing this is to replace them once you have removed whatever it is you are removing: for instance, once the alternator is off the engine, you put its retaining bolts back in the block so you know where they are, because as sure as God made little green apples, if you put them on the floor someone – usually yourself – will kick and scatter them all over the place, and that looks bad. Crawling around the floor looking for an important component will not instil confidence in anyone.

I got someone to help me off with the bonnet so that everything was reachable and accessible; there's nothing worse than working endlessly under a bonnet that blocks out the light and hinders your progress: if it's easier without, get rid of it.

During lunch break I took the opportunity to pilfer a roll of white masking tape from the painters. I would write a number on the tape and affix it to any wires I would have to disconnect and with the help of my notebook would know where to reconnect them. It might sound a bit amateurish, but if you have to leave a job and come back to it later, you would be amazed at how quickly you forget things. There is nothing the lamb slaughterers like better than to hear an engine turning and turning without any signs of firing up; it attracts experienced mechanics like lions to the whimper of a wounded animal. Many a saboteur has looked on in glee (myself included) having deviously 'nobbled' your engine, just to see whether you can discover the fault – see how good a fitter you really are.

I got some drip trays and put them under the car, my mind racing all the time in case I had forgotten something. I drained the cooling system and disposed of the fluid so as not to leave a tripping hazard; I got a big tick for that one. I took off the air filter and any cowling that needed to be removed and carefully put them in the boot: that was another tick for neat working. I took the front grille panels off and stowed them ready for the main unbolting. I checked and checked that I'd disconnected everything; it's so easy to leave a single wire attached. The one to the oil-pressure switch was a particular favourite, because it was a single wire usually on the side of the engine and easily missed – but woe betide anyone who started to remove the engine while something was still attached.

I removed almost all of the bell-housing bolts (holding the engine and gearbox together) and placed them in a small cardboard box. Another tick. I could safely remove the engine-mount nuts, as gravity would keep the engine in position. I was nearly ready for the lift; over to Stores to get two 'lifting eyes' that would be attached to the engine using its existing 'head' bolts, so I would get a balanced lift and not have the engine swinging around wildly, which is what you see amateurs doing with a bit of rope. I fastened the lifting chains to the portable lifting hoist and had a final look around, supporting the gearbox from underneath as I took the weight of the engine with the hoist. I removed the final two bell-housing bolts and the engine slid gently forwards, freeing herself of her mounts. I was ecstatic; I hadn't forgotten anything! A 'baby' mechanic usually leaves a hidden bolt somewhere and frantically tugs at the engine, shaking it to death, thinking it should be free; after all, this might be the first time it's been separated since manufacture. But no – it had gone well.

That was the easy part, though; anyone can take something to bits. The skill comes in putting it all back together without forgetting anything, then having it start when you turn the key. Because splitting an engine from a gearbox is such a big job, it is always advisable to check the condition of the clutch and release bearing while the engine is out; this may save you having to take the gearbox out a few months later. I did this only because Billy whispered it in my ear as he was passing; big tick. Thanks, Billy.

The replacement engine sat in a large wooden crate, which I opened, then gazed at the motor's highly painted finish. Sometimes you get only a 'short' motor, which means the cylinder head from the old engine has to be swapped over onto the new; but no, this was a 'full motor' and all I had to change were the inlet and exhaust manifolds, the fuel pump, the alternator and the dreaded distributor.

New engines came from the REME (Royal Electrical and Mechanical Engineers) and were often covered in grease or greaseproof paper or some kind of grease-impregnated paper, which was an absolute bastard to clean off. It was obviously for preservation, as once crated up they could be in storage for years. I swapped the components and prepared to refit the new engine. It was on the hoist and lined up ready, when:

'You gonna put that in like that?' Ritchie questioned.

'Yeah, why? Have I forgotten something?'

'Not my place to say,' he said tapping his pen against his clipboard.

I looked around the engine: alternator, yes; manifold, yes; looks good. I went to push it towards the car.

'Wouldn't do that if I were you!'

He tapped his pen even louder. I just couldn't see it.

'It must be something small; I've checked all the other things.'

'You got a tick for telling me about the clutch, didn't you?'

'Yeah.'

'So where is it?'

'Where's what?

'The clutch!'

I swung the engine around on the hoist and pointed at the flywheel.

'There ... Oh!'

It was still on the old engine, fuck it! I quickly swapped it over and got the clutch-aligning tool from Stores to show that I knew how to use it properly, but it cost me a cross – bugger, it had all been going so well. Billy whispered to put the car in gear, so the primary shaft on the gearbox wouldn't spin as I tried to engage it with the engine. Nice one, Billy. I tried gently to rock the new engine onto the gearbox, up down, up down, push pull: nope, it was having none of it.

I couldn't see anything obvious and tried adjusting the hoist height slightly; plop, it went on a little way, but was not fully engaged. Rattle, rattle, jiggle, jiggle, grrrrrr ... get on, ya fucker!

Ritchie handed me a 19mm ring spanner from my box, with a knowing look. I held it up, puzzled; what was I meant to do with this? 19mm (3/4 AF) was way too big for any of the bolts I'd taken off. The only thing it would fit was the front pulley bolt ... oh, right: I need to rotate the engine slightly to line the splines up – I'm with ya! I put the spanner on the pulley and with a turn and a push, the full satisfying 'plop' as engine and gearbox were once again married.

Quick a bolt, a bolt! It has been known for them to separate all too easily and you have to go through the whole process all over again. I was feeling quite chuffed, but another whisper from the 'Billmeister' told me to make sure the clutch was working before reconnecting everything; if it's not, there's less to do if the engine's got to come back out. He was an absolute fount of knowledge and was getting some scowls from big Ritchie.

'Cut him some slack, Ritchie, ya lanky streak of giraffe piss; he's only a kid!' Billy said.

Whoosh! That came right out of the blue and I shrugged my shoulders, showing my palms to Ritchie.

Everything reconnected and refitted, I topped up the coolant, which left just the battery. A tip I had been told was not to try and reconnect the earth lead to the battery: just touch it to it first, then if you have trapped a cable or caused a short you'll get a big flash, rather than risking the vehicle catching fire. I stroked the cable over the lead terminal and got a flash, but was this a big flash or a small flash? – how was I gonna be able to tell?

I thought some sneaky twat might have come and turned something on during tea break; it had been known for all the electrics to be turned on while the battery was disconnected, to give you the fright of your life when you come to reconnect. I checked all the switches, ignition, lights, wipers, etc. – no, nothing on, but still it flashed.

'You'll have to help me out here, Ritchie; I'm not very good with electrics.'

This seemed to please him, and he walked over and pushed the driver's door shut. It had been the interior light trying to come on, so this would constitute a small flash; I would find out what a big one was soon enough. OK, then, ready for fire up.

'Wouldn't do that if I was you!'

~ Main Hangar ~

'Why not?' I said sarcastically, getting fucking sick of him.

'That's a brand-new engine. What haven't you checked? Something very basic!'

I thought of the basic checks: oil, water, tyres, screen wash. I topped the water up, and the new engines must come with oil in them, mustn't they?

'NO!'(big cross on my sheet). Tap, tap, tap went the dipstick on the front grille: dry as a bone.

Well, if no one tells you, how're you gonna know? So I topped it up and was ready for fire-up; a last check round and I thought I'd done it all. I was dying to hear it running.

'Ready,' I said.

'Sure you don't want to get your torch and have a last look around?'

He had that look on his face, so I did – checked all the leads and pipes, cables, bolts; there was none left over, which is always a good sign. It's something you rarely got when you did a Land Rover; quite scary the amount of bolts and screws you could have left after one of them.

'OK, then – if you're satisfied.'

He was still goading me, but I'd checked and rechecked. I sat in the driver's seat and Ritchie covered his head with his arms. I looked over the steering wheel in disbelief; what the fuck was he playing at? Was he just winding me up?

'WHAT?' I shouted.

'Carry on if you're sure.'

I'd had enough by now and decided to give it a go. I turned the keys to the ignition point: so far, so good – dash lights on and OK. I turned the key to the 'start' position and the loudest fucking clatter I have ever heard came from beneath the bonnet. It sounded as if the engine had fallen out onto the floor. My heart pounded in my chest, thinking I'd completely fucked it.

I leapt out of the car and ran to the front; Ritchie had his arms crossed and was laughing his tits off. He grasped the back of my head with a large open hand, gripping it quickly and pointing my face between the radiator and the front pulley to where the 19mm ring spanner that I had used to rotate the engine was now wedged between the bottom of the radiator and the subframe. I managed to get it out and it hadn't done any damage – but it could have gone through the radiator and I would have failed my TATs and cost the RAF a new radiator. I was shaking, partly with fright and partly with rage. We'd better be quits now, I thought, or the fucking gloves are well and truly off!

I went to the toilet for a sit down, to calm down; I wanted the car running today. If I left it overnight, there's no telling what the bastards would do to it before I got back in the morning. The lads went for three o'clock tea while I sat with the car; they were a bunch of devious sods at the best of times, but this was prime time to drop me in the shit. I used the fifteen minutes to inspect every inch of the car, over and over, until I was satisfied it was OK.

Ritchie came back after tea break and I wasted no time. I applied a quarter choke and turned the keys; it turned over a couple of times while the fuel pump filled up the carburettor and then 'brrrrum': the little Hillman jumped into life. I stared at the oil light on the dash; it would have to go out within a few seconds or else the new engine would be damaged irreparably. It took longer than normal and I was just about to switch off when it went out, and the engine ran almost silently, perfectly, with no leaks or misfires, I had done it!

We let it tick over until it reached normal working temperature; if you're gonna get a leak, that's when you're gonna get it. There wasn't any – and to add the icing on the cake, I got to take it on an extended ten-mile test route to make sure everything had settled into place. It had; it worked fine and I drove it back into the yard with the usual crap of, 'We were just coming to look for ya,' and 'How many times did it break down?' etc., etc.

Thanks lads – not! I'd passed the TATs and wish I could say the same about the BFT (battle fitness test), which was due after my assessments.

❖ ❖ ❖

15. Assessments

Looking back now, I must have always known I was going to write this at some point because I kept notes of all the funny things that happened and as each memory is expanded, it triggers lots more. I think I mentioned about getting a printout of the information held on computer about me and have recently contacted PMC (Personnel Management Centre) Insworth and got my remaining details printed and sent to me. It makes entertaining reading, I can tell you – and I will. My assessment figures give a condensed view of how my trade ability, versus my attitude, peaked and then descended to the depths from whence it had all begun. Here is my take on what the numbers meant followed by my actual record;

Trade:

5 = Newbie or 'knobhead' (green as the proverbial herb).
6 = Proficient and getting better.
7 = A damn good fitter, well on his way to promotion.
8 = A fantastic fitter, excelling in all aspects of his trade.
9 = He who walks on water (rarely seen).
10 = Never been known?

Personal:

5 = Naïve or couldn't give a fuck, and untidy.
6 = Smart, keeps his nose clean and works hard, but could do better.
7 = Works very hard, very presentable and does as he's told.
8 = A tongue-checking, bottom-licking crawler, smart as a new pin.
9 = Difficult to see where boss ends and airman starts.
10 = Never been known, or nepotism.

Conduct	Trade	Year	Personal	Promotion
Exemplary	5	1982	5	Not Applicable
Very Good	5	1983	6	Likely to be fit
Exemplary	6	1984	5	Likely to be fit
Exemplary	6	1985	6	Recommended
Exemplary	6	1986	6	Recommended
Exemplary	7	1987	7	Highly Recommended
Exemplary	6	1988	7	Recommended
Exemplary	7	1989	6	Not Applicable
Exemplary	8	1990	5	Not Applicable
Demob	–	1991	–	

As you can see, I started off well and was steadily improving in my trade, but became disillusioned later on, probably because my boss lied to me about the numbers he was giving me on my yearly assessment. He said he was giving me at least sixes and recommending me for promotion when he clearly wasn't, and I have to admit this did come as somewhat of a shock when I received the printout. So I guess he had the last laugh, and it seemed to take for ever to get my 'fitters' course' (promotion to Junior Technician).

I was well overdue for the course and got a written letter to confirm I would have backdated seniority for advancement to corporal (in my dreams!) This meant I would have less time to wait to qualify for the corporals' exam. Judging by the fact that I scraped through my fitters' course by the veritable skin of my knackers, getting to corporal was pie in the sky for me.

The trade knowledge was no problem; one or two of the lads even came to me for explanations on some of the more technical issues, especially electrics (initially weak in that subject I studied relentlessly) and fault diagnosis, which became fortes of mine. It was just as well, because when it came to the academic side of the course, I was struggling big-time, failed the maths dismally and was threatened with RTU (return to unit) without promotion. This was a shameful thing to happen to anyone, and it did happen to one of our troop – but more on that later.

I was called into the office and it seemed to be a fairly formal occasion. The boss commented on my first year's service and ability, together with my conduct and attitude. As you can see, my conduct for the ten years was exemplary except for the one year that I kept sleeping in, when it dropped to 'very good'; this automatically meant that my personal conduct number dropped a digit regardless. That is not to say that my conduct was exemplary; it was just that I was cute enough not to get caught, or was convincing enough to bullshit my way out of trouble. One thing that sticks in my mind was the constant and incessant reminders of my uniform and presentation, which culminated on one of the AOC's (Air Officer Commanding) inspections on the parade square, when I was demoted from the front rank to the rear because:

'Novak, you look like a fucking Toby jug with your arms sticking out. You are the wrong shape to be tidy: get to the fucking back! You are a royal disgrace! I've seen tramps with better creases than those!'

I was waiting for the usual and obligatory 'Get off my fucking parade ground!' but it never came; they must have been short of numbers. Bastard! I hated parades, and all the bullshit that went with them, as much as they hated seeing me on them.

It was on such a parade that I nearly came a royal cropper, when the AOC's official driver (a rather unattractive WRAF, and even that was being kind) reported to her superior that she was feeling unwell.

'Too late to be unwell now,' she was told, and so was forced to carry on with her duties.

She drove the AOC onto the parade square in an immaculate, gloss-black Ford 'Granada', ready for his inspection of the guard. Stopping the car at the rehearsed point, she got out of the vehicle and went round to open the rear door of the car. As the door opened and the AOC began to get out, she 'barfed' a multicoloured rainbow of puke all over the main man! The shock was incredible; she burst into tears and the rest of us pissed ourselves laughing as quietly as it is humanly possible to do. Unfortunately I have a rather loud voice, which has been commented on on a number of occasions and which has got me into more trouble than I care to mention. I let out an audible guffaw, which was heard by the SWO (Station Warrant Officer). He shot me a Mr McKay sneer straight from the TV series 'Porridge', and I knew I would be in for it later on.

The AOC got back into the car and was whisked away, to return some thirty minutes later as fresh as a daisy, while airmen fainted on the parade ground with ever-increasing frequency. To combat this the SWO decided a spot of marching would shake the cobwebs from our inactive minds; it seemed to work and I tried my best to get back in his good books.

It didn't work, and I was summoned to the guardroom later that day. I had planned my explanation over and over; after all, how on earth was he going to prove it was me? But then again, proof is never at the forefront of HM Forces' agenda when it comes to burying someone up to their neck in shit: more a case of reasonable doubt, and this instance was no different.

'I'd know that laugh anywhere, Novak! You are always the first with your mouth open and seldom have anything constructive to say – least of all anything remotely intelligible!'

There was no doubt he was an officer with a superior command of the English language, but it was wasted on me. I was, as I am still, a 'speak as you find' chap.

'Come on, sir: you must be able to see the funny side of it!'

'Yes, I can, but you is an erk and is not permitted to laugh. I is a Hofficer with thirty years' experience and can laugh at the Queen if I so chooses.'

This did nothing to calm my already active sense of humour, and I could feel myself beginning to 'lose it'.

'Something funny?'

He stared at me fixedly. I was screwing my beret up as tight as I could get it without being too obvious. He must have seen it.

'Get out of my sight, you 'orrible little airman. I'm watching you like a shitehawk! If your unsightly face comes before me in the next six months, yer for the high jump – clear?'

Churchill dog: 'Oh, yes!'

This was always going to prove difficult to do, as my liaison with Jake was still going strong and he suggested we should throw eggs and tomatoes from the sidecar of his 750cc shaft-drive Yamaha at the CND protesters who were picketing various camps throughout the UK. Well – it seemed like a good idea at the time. The protesters were camped on the grass verge of the A17, opposite the entrance to Cranwell camp.

They were very peaceful with their 'Ban the Bomb' banners and colourful clothing. The sidecar was on the left-hand side of the bike, which was perfect for us to do neat circuits of the camp, restocking at Jake's married quarter and then hurtling up the A17 at 70mph, where I would hurl the load at the protesters.

The first few shots were well wide of the mark, but by the third run I was on target and clobbered a couple of them with said merchandise, so that they were even more colourful. The tale was exaggerated to unbelievable proportions by the time the NAAFI had called 'last orders'.

This entire high jinks took place on a Saturday afternoon, and Jake was hauled into the boss's office first thing Monday morning. It never ceased to amaze me how the fuck they knew who it was; but then on reflection, how many 750cc Yamahas with sidecars were present on a relatively small Lincolnshire camp, hmmm? Anyway, give Jake his due; he fervently denied that I had anything to do with it and I 'blagged' my way through, saying I'd gone home that weekend. It worked, but I was sailing much closer to the wind than was good for my career or for me.

Jake just got a bollocking and we all had a good laugh about it; he couldn't give a legendary fuck and I admired him for that if nothing else: something else to tell the grandchildren. 'In the olden days before hover cycles ...'

I hasten to add that these high jinks took place after my assessments, and there was a good deal of juggling one's attitude and conduct three months prior to being judged. The boss read out what he'd written about me and I suppose it was close enough, if a tad unflattering; he told me the numbers he was giving me and got me to sign the form. I paid no attention to it and signed blindly, believing what I was being told; it was all over in a matter of minutes. Someone asked me how it went.

'Oh, ya know? School reports-ville – "could do better, easily distracted and immature".'

At least the last bit was accurate. Still, I thought, I was getting sixes and things could only get better as I would become more knowledgeable and headed for promotion. If I'd known how long that was going to take, I think I'd have chucked it in long before I finally did.

❖ ❖ ❖

16. A Day in the Life at Cranwell

As with any garage, there would be a number of vehicles being brought in with different faults throughout the day, with varying degrees of urgency. Often you would have to leave the job you were immersed in and go to a breakdown if labour was scarce or there were more vehicles in the hangar and yard than usual, in winter for example.

Mornings were always more entertaining than any other time, given the amount of alcohol consumed the previous evening. 'Leaving do's' and any other excuse for a party were usually held on a Thursday; this was to give the 'singlies' enough time to sober up if they were going home that weekend. Also it was the 'back end' of the week, when if things had gone to plan most, if not all, of the important work had been taken care of and it just left the routine servicing to be done. If it was an official do, say a 'Sneco's' leaving do, or a promotion, we would get an unofficial lie-in; loosely translated this meant that as long as you turned in at about first tea break (10 am) or thereabouts you would be OK. Of course there were always those who took the piss, and someone would have to go and get them, but basically you were immune from being 'done'.

Given the state of some of the airmen, if I had been the boss I wouldn't have let them within a hundred yards of any machinery, let alone high-pressure airlines and toxic chemicals. There was always a hard core of boss-impressing bottom-lickers who would be in on time, bright-eyed and bushy-tailed, as if nothing had happened. This always made me suspicious, as the quantity of ale they professed to have quaffed was not in evidence. Others sat in the tea bar with their head in their hands, drinking copious amounts of coffee and fizzy drinks to chase off the hangover; by lunchtime most would have returned to work, if still a bit unsteady and not in possession of their full faculties.

I witnessed one particular incident that I would love to say I had invented, but you just can't make up things like this. One of the J/Ts had brought a Land Rover into one of the bays with a suspected gearbox problem, which was par for the course for a Land Rover. The vehicle had just returned from an off-camp exercise with the RAF Regiment, who 'beasted' all vehicles, and it was still red hot. The J/T got a crawler board from the corner of the hangar, lay on it and slid underneath the vehicle, looking for any obvious signs of broken mounts, loose bolts or prop shafts, etc.

Someone shouted his name from the other side of the hangar and he lifted his head to see who or what they wanted; his noggin came into direct contact with the hot exhaust, burning a lovely bar shape onto his forehead. Instinctively he pulled away from the exhaust and his head slammed back down onto the crawler board, which propelled it back onto the exhaust again; two lovely marks now, and once more for good luck. It sounded like bacon sizzling, and a good deal of 'effing' and blinding came from beneath the long-wheelbase Rover.

I'll never forget the image of the solemn airman, with his hand clamped to his forehead, walking very deliberately to the toilets to dampen his burns and check his looks in the mirror. He now resembled a mountain zebra, native to Africa and remarkably similar to the wild ass in habitat and form. There was just no way to explain away a mark like that without some form of dubious justification that no one would believe anyway. Better to just hold your hands up, let the piss-takers have their fun and then it would be forgotten – hopefully.

Whilst I'm on the subject of making oneself look a complete and utter tit, the RAF Regiment, revered by some as professional soldiers but mostly ridiculed as 'not the sharpest tool in the box' – their nickname being 'Rock Apes', which I think comes from the Barbary apes on the rock of Gibraltar – I watched in disbelief as two lads carried the 24-volt batteries from a Land Rover into the hangar for testing. The clever one tilted the battery away from himself so that the acid ran down the front of his trousers, while the not-so-clever one tilted the heavy battery towards himself so that the acid ran towards the waistband of his OGs (olive greens, i.e. trousers). That would reduce them to a moth-eaten ball of fluff in the coming weeks, accompanied by an increasingly red and itchy rash – but the Regiment being the Regiment, it was better to suffer in silence than risk going sick and being called a pouf.

Morale was always high after a piss-up, and one had to be on high alert so as not to be caught out by the overzealous and enthusiastic piss-takers – namely myself and Jake. We were both SACs now and had a healthy dislike for J/Ts – mainly because they got paid at least a hundred pounds a month more than we did, but to all intents and purposes still did the same job.

DE (direct-entry) J/Ts were particularly despised, as they came into the RAF at that rank having qualified in 'civvy street'. In our eyes they were taking our fitters' courses away from us, and while it was true for the most part that they were intelligent, unfortunately the information stopped at the elbows for many of them! In short, they could talk a good job, but when it came to hands on and 'spanners in mitt' they hadn't a clue. Still, if someone had said to me you can join up as an SAC and get a hundred pounds less, or join as a Junior Technician, filling a gap the air force said existed because there weren't enough SACs clever enough to be promoted, I know what I would have said! 'Show me the money, honey.'

Mark, a particularly cocksure and devastatingly attractive DE (according to him, that is) complete with medallion and chest rug, came into work the morning after his stag do, where the lads had 'Immac'd' a love-heart in his chest hair after he'd fallen asleep in the NAAFI – a very foolish thing to do, fall asleep! Mark, still much the worse for wear flashed the bald heart shape to all and sundry with an accompanying 'wankers', got a crawler board and slid underneath a Leyland 'Sherpa' van and fell back to sleep, snoring loudly.

Jake and I looked at each other with glee and mischievousness hitherto unsurpassed. We got a load of traffic cones used for the brake-testing area and placed them around the vehicle under which Mark was carelessly knocking out the 'zzzzzs'. Once they were in place we released the handbrake silently and pushed the van off him, parking it in an opposite slot and leaving him asleep on the crawler board in the centre of the bay all to himself, surrounded by traffic cones.

He remained there for quite some time, as various ranks to'd and fro'd from the hangar collecting and dropping off various vehicles. It was only fair that we made a sign that read 'Last day of singledom', and placed it at his feet to appease the curiosity of passers-by. The boss eventually put a stop to things by the time we had rigged up a flashing amber light above his head and started taking pictures; it was just too good an opportunity to miss. That was the main driving force behind most of the mischief: opportunity and creative inventiveness.

Someone kept an eye on Mark and rounded us all up as he began to wake; we were standing in a semicircle away from the bay and the image of a puzzled airman, as he realised the magnitude of his fuck-up, looking around at the cones, sign and flashing light, will stay with me forever. We gave him a massive round of applause as he sat up on the crawler board taking it all in. The intensity of his blush was enough for Jake and I and we basked in our glory; it was the talk of the NAAFI for weeks. Whenever Mark came for a pint people would make little whirling motions above their heads, like the flashing amber light; but to give him his due, he took it all in his stride and the hair did grow back on his chest. As I've mentioned before, the barracking only ever lasted as long as the next fuck-up, which was never far away – and this time it would be me!

The trucks of the time were mainly Leyland or Bedford and usually of the six-cylinder, in-line petrol-engine configuration, with points (no electronic ignition) inside the distributor. They made a whining sound as they were revved up prior to changing gear, and you could hear them coming from miles away. Having worked only on four-cylinder engines before, removing the distributor cap and plug leads was a precarious procedure for an inexperienced mechanic; there is nothing more embarrassing than having a vehicle backfire as you attempt to start it after changing the spark plugs and points. It happened to me more times than I care to mention, and so I made it a deliberate quest to learn the firing order of every vehicle I would have to work on, purchasing a pocket tune-up book that contained all the vital and technical information for almost all the popular engines of the day. Points gap (or dwell angle, if you wanted to be more accurate) spark-plug gap, static and strobe timing, valve clearances (hot and cold), exhaust emissions (CO content) ... you name it, the little book had it all. It was an invaluable tool for me and Jake, given the amount of private work we did.

If Jake had put as much effort into being a conscientious mechanic as he did fucking about, he would have been a genius. One of the tricks he showed me concerned the six-cylinder petrol pantechnican truck. As we passed a petrol station, returning from a test drive, Jake would switch off the engine (no steering lock on this heap of shit), and then as it decelerated, still in gear, he would pump the accelerator pedal furiously. That would squirt large quantities of petrol into the hot engine but, as it was switched off, the fuel and gas would pass through the engine and collect in the exhaust system, unburned.

When level with the garage, Jake would turn on the ignition, which would result in a massive 'bang' as the stored fuel was ignited in the exhaust. People at the pumps would leap out of their skins as we hung out of the windows in hysterics, banging the side of the truck doors in contentment and delight at our success. On this particular day I had coerced Jake into letting me drive the truck. This took a bit of doing, as I did not have an HGV licence at the time, but what the fuck! I built the speed up as we approached the garage, switched off the engine and river-danced all over the accelerator, switching it back on as we came level with the garage. There was an almighty explosion that blew the silencer clean off the truck and under the rear wheels, which crushed it as the truck hopped over it; people got back up off the ground in the petrol station and I slammed on the brakes as Jake and I stared at each other, ashen!

'Aw, Bob – what the fuck 'ave ya done?'

'Well, it was all right when you did it,' I gulped.

The truck came to a stop and Jake looked backwards out of the window at the flattened silencer, lying in the middle of the road. He got out, walked back up the road, picked it up and flung it in the back of the truck. Amazed faces looked on from the petrol station, unsure of what had happened. We swapped seats and Jake drove the truck back to the hangar, sounding like a dragster without a silencer. The short journey back was otherwise a silent one, as we thought of what we were going to say on our return.

'It just come off in me hand, Chief!' Jake said, as the sound attracted the attention of all and sundry. I couldn't believe it and had visions of both of us getting 'done': but Jake was driving, wasn't he? I was in the clear. To my amazement, his story was accepted without much fuss and the gaggle that had surrounded the rear of the truck pissed themselves laughing as Jake retrieved the squashed exhaust from the back.

'It's due for scrapping soon anyway,' the Chief said, shrugging his shoulders and probably glad to be rid of an ancient vehicle that took up far too much time and budget keeping it on the road. 'BER' (beyond economical repair) was the chant, and it was decided that the old truck would have its engine seized up (by running it without oil till it stopped) and then be scrapped.

But Jake couldn't resist dropping me in the shit to the lads on the quiet, when unfortunately the story eventually filtered back to the bosses via the bottom-lickers and I was duly hauled onto the mat once more for another bollocking. However, I knew they couldn't prove a thing, and Jake was hardly likely to own up to letting me drive the truck, so it was just a case of biting the bullet, tightening my sphincter and riding out the storm – which I was getting better and better at doing.

I'd been going home to Durham most weekends, if not every other one, and the nymph-like, nubile body of my best mate's sister, who was just beginning to flower, had the testosterone coursing through my veins. At sixteen, her tight white jeans drove me wild and it wasn't long before I was paying more attention to her than I was to my best mate himself – who was getting increasingly pissed off as we were doing less and less scrambling on my bike, which is what we did most weekends, along with getting pissed on my money. In the end I let him take the bike out, while I took his sister out! She was still under age and looked it. I had to secrete her away in the corner of pubs and clubs, while I bought a pint

~ A Day in the Life at Cranwell ~

and a lemonade – swiftly followed by a second trip to the bar for a Bacardi and coke. I got some strange looks, as people questioned how she could lose her balance and wobble around on just lemonade.

I had every intention of taking advantage of her, but we were both virgins and I had less of a clue than she did. It wasn't to be; but we did some heavy petting – very heavy – so much so that on more than one occasion I shot in my pants and had to get changed. It got so that Alan and I would go out on the piss in the evening and I would sleep on his couch.

After everyone had gone to bed Jamie would sneak down and we would begin exploring each other. We went further and further each time, but still hadn't gone 'all the way'. We would still be awake at five or six in the morning, cuddling on the couch after another change of underwear, and Alan couldn't understand why I was so knackered all the time.

Months went by and we began writing to each other – well, I wrote to her, anyway. I was in a daze a lot of the time; even my mischief with Jake took a back seat for a while because of his incessant question of when I was gonna 'biff' her. I thought more of her than that now, and was prepared to wait until the time was right. I didn't know it then, but I was falling in love for the first time! The heavy petting continued, with further experimentation until we had done just about everything you could do without actual penetration, including oral sex – which I must admit is as fantastic as the deed itself, both to give and receive, providing it's done with tenderness and care and a good deal of knowledge of the female form, which I researched tirelessly in those early tender months with the help of the bearded chap and his missus in the book 'The Joy of Sex'.

Many a frustrated night was 'spent' (if you'll forgive the pun) wanking over that book, imagining it was Jamie and I. I took the book back to Durham with me and we leafed through the pages while on the couch in the early hours of the morning, and it was time to try. And try we did – and try, and try, and try! It was all to no avail. What could I be doing wrong? We had the condoms, the KY jelly and the baby oil for our pre-romp massage.

I thought my knackers would explode, but it was just too uncomfortable for her, and the last thing I wanted to do was hurt her. As I've said previously, I wanted the first time to be special and memorable; well, it was certainly that. Operation code 'no joy' on my return to camp, and I got all the advice that I could stomach, from married guys and experienced 'singlies' alike; but even when told in confidence it didn't stop the 'cherry boy' jibes from being hurled around like confetti.

It seemed like the biggest thing in the world at the time; you weren't a man until you'd done the deed. There was much bravado made in the tea bar of what I had managed to achieve up until then, but it was always thrown back in my face – 'cherry boy'; and in hindsight I learned that a gentleman shouldn't tell anyway.

I also learned over the course of time that the people who generally make the most noise about their sexual conquests actually make the worst lovers. If all you're going to do is roll off and fart, leaving your woman frustrated, it won't be long before the whole of the female community your partner socialises with knows that you're a crap shag – FACT!

Fortunately, not only have I never had any complaints about my lovemaking, but I received a letter from an ex-partner complimenting me on the time taken to pleasure her and the tenderness involved. Lord knows, I'm not usually the one to blow my own trumpet (if I could I would never go out), but I was pleased that she felt confident enough to tell me. If I was full of bravado I would've kept the letter, but I didn't – I sent it to the 'Echo'! (only kidding).

After a few attempts, we arrived at the conclusion that it must be something physical and not that we were doing something wrong. Jamie made an appointment to see the doctor and was told that she had an unusually thick hymen (if you don't know what it is, lads, look the fucker up! – again, no pun intended). A place was booked at the local hospital and I took some leave to be there for her.

I'll never forget a comment that she made when I went to see her before her operation. She'd been talking to a woman who was having stitches after being cut for a particularly big baby, and she remarked how funny life was. She was having hers opened, while the woman was having hers sewn up! And the usual gag of:

'Can you put a couple of extra stitches in, doctor? The husband's not a big lad!'

'Well, he was obviously big enough to fill a pram,' was the male retort, which I found absolutely disgusting!

After her operation she was understandably a bit sore and we were told to wait a week or so before trying – but we just couldn't. I was as gentle as I could be, but my God! Angels flew out of my bum that day! 'Up to the buffers' was how one lad described it, and I must admit I did have a bit of a chuckle at that statement. I was a man! – a 'blokey' bloke, a testosterone-snorting, fully fledged member of the 'charver' society now though!

It didn't feel any different really, although I was glad the 'cherry boy' jibes had subsided. That didn't really make any difference either, though; they just found something else to take the piss out of – it's just Forces life. But my God, did I have a reason to go home now; and I did, every weekend for months. We spent most of the time in bed or in the pub; it was a heady time. Not so for my best mate, though, who was becoming increasingly jealous of our new-found lust and the fact that the scrambling was taking second place – so much so that I'd been leaving the bike at his house, instead of carting it back and forwards to camp every weekend. When I came home one weekend, I found he'd sold the fucker and pissed up the proceeds. I was furious!

Eventually Jamie's mother could see that I was serious about her, and I was allowed to sleep in her bed (not the mother's, although she did try it on once – I was horrified). After a carefree night's lovemaking with Jamie, her mother strolled into our bedroom where a used condom was still hanging over the headboard; she put the two coffees on the bedside table, tut-tutted and walked out. I'd forgotten it was there and we didn't know who'd put the coffees there when we woke.

'Aw, fuck!' I said.

~ A Day in the Life at Cranwell ~

'Yeah, we did, didn't we?' she giggled.

She had a really sexy giggle and I'd heard her being described as 'elf-like' in the pubs; I was flattered that it was me she was going out with. She was beautiful, petite, funny and very, very sexy. We were a very tactile couple and I've never been shy of showing my affections in public – long walks along Roker beach hand in hand; sensual, passionate kisses that warm your very soul; trips to the Lake District – if this was love, it was great. We made each other laugh, were great in bed and life was just about having fun; like all males, with the streak of selfishness that runs through us all, I wanted it to last. I wanted to keep her all to myself – and even though we would marry, it would all end in disaster. I returned to Cranwell an engaged man, and bought rings to make it official. I couldn't stop twiddling with mine and looking at it, I was so proud. Looking back, I wonder just how much of what we did was expected of us, and how much we really wanted for ourselves.

I guess some girls are just not meant to be caged and the fact that we were both virgins when we met made the grass decidedly and temptingly greener for Jamie; she was discovering that she was a very, very desirable woman with all the right attributes in the right places. I had unwittingly introduced her to the playground I had enjoyed for a couple of years; not having been outside the North East before, she was like a puppy being let off the leash.

If I'd stayed around, things might have been different, but my getting posted to the Falklands a month after getting married would have tested the virtues of even the most faithful of couples.

Some of the placating advice I got on my return was, 'Well, it's better that it happened now and not ten years down the line when you've got a couple of kids and a mortgage!' Yeah! Thanks for the sympathy, you condescending twat!

I just wanted to be with her, wanted the things I thought everyone has eventually – a loving family, beautiful children, a nice home and a reliable but not necessarily 'flash' car. How naïve I was to think I would be lucky enough for that to happen to me.

'Too nice,' a girl at school had said. 'You're too nice to go out with!'

What the fuck does that mean? Just because I wasn't trying to rip their knickers off on the first date, I was too nice!

Christ on a bike! If I'd known they wanted shagging on the first date, there'd have been no stopping me; to quote one lass when I got my hand slapped away from her fanny, 'Hoy – manners – tits first!' I was never able to get it right. The ones I thought were nice turned out to be 'slappers', and the ones I thought would be easy wanted to court for weeks before even getting a bit of tit. Posh birds were the muckiest of the lot; thank the Lord for the grammar school!

I learned more about a girl's anatomy in a few short weeks than I ever would in any of my long-term relationships. A body is a body; all girls have the same equipment – different sizes, shapes and smells, but if you touch them in the right places with the right pressure and speed (and everyone is different), then 'the thrill of the chase' and 'the voyage of discovery' are what it's all about. It's a real test of friendship once you have learned all you can about your partner – but I digress: I told you I would.

I sneaked Jamie into my room clad in a one-piece motorcycle suit, still wearing the helmet and we 'christened' the room forthwith, minus the helmet for the sake of you kinky sods. The block being an all-male block, it wasn't long before we started experiencing problems of a toileting nature – although watching her piss in my sink was one of the kinkiest things I've seen to date. I had to sneak her to the toilet for 'ladies' time' and number twos; understandably it was never gonna remain a secret for long. There was a kind of 'Up yours, RAF – look what I'm getting away with'; but it wasn't long before I was back on the mat!

'It has come to my attention that you have a girl living in your room,' the boss said.

How the fucking fuck could he have known this? What wanker grassed me up? Obviously some jealous bastard – Jamie was 'way out of my league', someone commented.

'Oh, and I suppose you could do better,' was my retort. Unfortunately they got the opportunity to try it out when I was in the Falklands. But for now we couldn't live together in the block, and we couldn't have a married quarter, so I found a cottage that was up for rent, although it was not complete and was in the middle of being renovated. It was bare and cold, so much so that we had to warm the bed with a hair-dryer that eventually caught fire because of all the fluff that it had sucked in; still, we were in each other's arms every night and that's all that mattered.

The saddest thing about the situation was that I said, 'Why don't we just get married and get a married quarter?'

I guess no woman wants that kind of proposal, and in hindsight it was a thoughtless thing to say – but she accepted and the ball started rolling.

April the 6th came and we were married at Newbottle church, back in the North East. I was ecstatic. We had a married quarter to return to, and although we couldn't afford a honeymoon, I booked two weeks' leave to set up our new home. It was very basic, if a tad uncomfortable with the 'toy town' furniture; still, we did our immature best to play at house and we 'christened' every room, including the bathroom.

It was during my two weeks' leave that I got a knock on the door and a uniformed person told me I was going to the Falklands in two weeks' time. I had volunteered earlier that year and had been on the waiting list for some time. I went up to SHQ (station headquarters) to plead my case that I had just been married and was still on my honeymoon. It made no difference whatsoever; I had volunteered and that was that.

The military comes first, second and last. I returned and gave Jamie the bad news, and suggested that she go back home to Durham while I was away, or bring her brother down to Cranwell to stay with her during my four-month tour. It was during this conversation that we had our first marital row. She packed a suitcase and threatened to leave there and then; I flung it across the room, gouging out a large piece of plaster from the magnolia wall of the bedroom. She retrieved it, carried on packing and demanded a divorce! I was crestfallen, to say the least. It turned physical when I tried to get the case from her; she went to scratch my face and I punched her on the arm, sending her onto the bed in floods of tears. I can categorically state that writing this is making me feel sick, and the shame that went with what happened haunts me every day. A man hitting a woman is unforgivable and cowardly. To this day I have never again raised a hand to a woman unless in self-defence, and that has happened only a couple of times (as I will explain later). They say the best part of having an argument is making up; and we made love with a tenderness recently forgotten.

I was still gonna have to go to the Falklands, but wished things could have been different. The cruelty of it was that this would be my first tour overseas but, excited as I was about that, I didn't want to leave Jamie. She couldn't come with me either; it was an unaccompanied tour with no wives allowed. It was a shame; it was 1985, the conflict was well and truly over and she would have loved to travel – she told me so on many different occasions while we daydreamed our future into a marital utopia.

The reality was that I left my bride two weeks after being married and some of her family came to stay with her for a while. Once she left the younger one unattended while he tried to make chips, and almost burnt the house to the ground.

Fortunately no one was hurt, but the kitchen was destroyed. And who was the bill going to fall to? Yes, indeed – fucking me! Eight thousand miles from home, on a freezing, pissy island with no trees in the middle of the South Atlantic Ocean, working twelve-hour shifts, seven days on then one day off.

The temptation was just too much for all concerned. I'd left Jamie with a credit card and she proceeded to entertain my workmates, going to nightclubs and pubs in the city of Lincoln, some twenty miles away. It didn't take long before the funds had run out and she was spending it faster than I could earn it. When I finally returned, I would be £2,000 overdrawn and minus a wife.

That was bad enough, you may think, but for the best man at my wedding to 'shag' her, along with at least two other so-called colleagues, had me pulling my hair out in clumps; to this day I still cannot understand how I retained my composure and refrained from physical violence on the perpetrators. The RAF knew what was coming though, and magically gave leave to the conspirators, so by the time I was back to camp there was no one to be seen. Just as fucking well!

And if you think things couldn't get any worse, the best man was on my fitters' course that I so desperately wanted. Imagine that – having to spend six months living in the same building as the man who had not only betrayed you as your closest friend, but was part cause of the end of a marriage. I thought the RAF was taking the piss and tried to get it changed. I was told in no uncertain terms that the only way I would get it changed was if I didn't go on the course that I'd waited years for! That may have been the day that the seeds of discontent were well and truly sown.

I did go on the course, and tried to rise above it, but there wasn't a day went by that I didn't want to cave his skull in. They say 'what goes around comes around' – and, true to form, he'd pissed off enough people that someone on the course poured brake fluid all over his car, which peeled the paint off very effectively.

I would have loved to say it was me, but we never found out who it was, even when the RAF Police got involved. Someone out there knows who did it; it may have been one of the many women he two-timed and mistreated, who knows? I was just glad to see that wanker finally get his come-uppance.

It was clear to all concerned that I couldn't remain at Cranwell, and I was offered a choice – yes, offered; that came as a holy fucking shock as the military never offers: it just orders! I got the choice of two postings; I could go up to RAF Finningley, South Yorkshire, or down to London for a new fighter squadron that was being set up.

Rightly or wrongly I chose to be nearer home, and I'll never forget the day I knocked on my mother's front door and said, 'If you say I told ya so, I'll never speak to you again.'

She didn't; she just invited me in and gave me a cuddle, while I cried my eyes out for hours. It was a crossroads in my life and I often wonder what would have become of me if I had chosen the other posting.

Before we leave Cranwell, there are a few more tales I'd like to tell you – some things that happened before I went to the Falklands. With my little Ford 'Escort' I was free to roam the Lincolnshire countryside at will. I travelled far and wide, learning the location of every scrapyard within a fifty-mile radius. Escorts were a mechanic's dream car; they could be easily customised with the 'bolt-ons' or 'add-ons' advertised in 'Car and Car Conversions', or 'Triple C' as it was known. I'd found an old 1600cc 'Sport Escort' and took the dash out because it had a rev counter in, as well as the boot spoiler and steering wheel – all for £30: I was in heaven.

Looking back, it would have been easier to buy a 1600 Sport or a 2-litre RS Cosworth, which was my dream machine, but they were as rare as 'rocky horse-shit' and I never came across an RS that was within my financial range.

My little 1300cc 'Escort' had been 'morphed' into a kind of boy-racer-mobile (non techies: 'scuse the boring bit). It had a 32/36 DGAV twin-choke Weber carburettor; A2 camshaft; a 'bunch of 'nanas' exhaust with a 'cherry bomb' to finish that made it sound like a V8; uprated suspension and brakes; and a low-ratio 'diff' that meant it would outperform a Porsche 911 for the first twenty yards, before the valves started bouncing.

The only thing it needed now was a set of 'Wolf race' or four-spoke RS wheels, which couldn't be found for love or money. On one beautiful sunny Sunday, I had gone for a meal in the airmen's mess and decided a journey out was the order of the day. I would go exploring. I found a company called 'John Brown's Wheels', which was situated on a ninety-degree bend in the road in the middle of nowhere; I came upon it quite by accident and it was shut. It looked like an old petrol station, with a large forecourt and suspended white chains hanging between the small concrete posts around well-kept lawns.

The sign 'Beware of the dog!' creaked in the gentle summer breeze as I parked my car opposite in the lay-by. I strolled across the road and looked around for the supposed dog, but there was no sign of it at all.

Being a bit nervous of dogs from having been bitten in the past, I took extra time to make sure it wasn't there, walking up and down the road to see if it was secreted away somewhere. Nope: there was no evidence of said hound! I stepped over the low chain and walked towards the shiny wheels advertised for sale in the window. I was engrossed by the different styles and prices; 'I've just got to have some of those on my little Escort,' I thought, looking at the wheels and then at the car, imagining them on it: that would finish it off nicely. Just then I heard a tinkling sound, which was getting louder by the second! I looked left and right, but there was nothing there; the sound was getting louder and louder and I felt I should flee!

But which way? And from what? The hackles were definitely up and I began to panic. The tinkling was getting faster, but there was still nothing in evidence. I turned and looked over my shoulder to see the Hound of the Baskervilles lolloping towards me at an alarming rate of knots, with a thick chain around its neck and its teeth bared. This fucker meant proper business!

I remember feeling my arse cave in for a second before the fight-or-flight reaction took over – and in this case it was definitely 'flight'! I hurtled towards the low chain with the mutt in hot pursuit only inches from my backside; I was running like a banana, trying to curve my bottom from the sharpened teeth of my pursuer. I leapt over the chain into the middle of the road and there was a loud screech of tyres as I was almost run over by a passing car – but given the choice I would have chosen the car rather than the dog any day.

The driver gave me the 'bird' and some condescending comments about the fact that my parents weren't married, but I was just glad not to be dog's dinner!

I was shaking uncontrollably and leant against my car in shock, the kind of shock that I've mentioned that turns your willy inside out. The dog had stopped just before the chain went 'twang', so it was obviously extremely familiar with where it could get to without garrotting itself. Revenge was the order of the day, but with the amount of noise the dog was making I half expected some doddering old lady to come out of the attached bungalow and give me a bollocking, but no – no one around. I got my Sunday papers from the car, including the magazine, and rolled them up as tight as I could get them. Crossing back over the road, I made sure it was clear this time, noted the position that said hound could get to and stopped a little short of that. It was going berserk and if it did get off that chain I would not be here today writing this; but it had frightened me and I, being an intelligent human, was going to beat this dog around the nose with my paper until it submitted.

The chain was making some kind of musical note because it was being pulled so tight; I was swearing at the dog, daring it to come and get me, while it was beside itself with frustration, running around in circles and doing some kind of ducking manoeuvre that was designed to get its collar off. This unnerved me and time for revenge was running out; when it came for the final lunge I smacked it as hard as I could right across the nose and it sat down with the chain swinging slightly, not quite in the 'twang' position.

I was even more unnerved by the fact that it never yelped at the newspaper, but just sat there glowering at me. I have no doubt that if I were to return to that garage, assuming it's still there, that dog would remember me; Lord knows, it's almost twenty years ago and I remember it vividly!

I'd had a good day out, barring the dog, and called into the Motor Club to see who was doing what and to whom. Jake was in there along with a 'rock ape' who was changing the brake pads on his Austin 'Allegro', or All-Aggro as they were known. Jake was welding a new sill onto the Jag and asked me to give him a hand keeping the carpet from catching fire as the heat permeated through the floor. I kept squirting water onto the carpet with a plastic bottle, a kind of weed-sprayer type. Jake was lying on his side welding the sill and I was daydreaming as usual; I only squirted the carpet when I could smell burning, which kind of defeated the object. Jake leapt up from the floor, shouting for me to squirt him in the ear.

'Fuck off, ya kinky twat,' I said.

'No – no, ya knobber; a blob of metal's gone in me ear!'

It was true and I could even hear it turning his ear into a pork scratching, I squirted him in the ear, which must have looked really comical, and the 'rock ape' changing his brake pads was ripping the piss out of Jake. But divine retribution is never far away from the carefree mechanic: the 'rock ape' drove his All-Aggro towards the Motor Club doors and pressed the brake pedal, but the pedal went to the floor as he had not pumped out the free space created when you change a set of pads, and the doors were ripped clean off their hinges.

Jake and I looked on in disbelief and pissed our-selves laughing; he just pushed the doors apart and left. We shrugged our shoulders and carried on as normal.

Jake was as dry as a stick and I tried tirelessly to find him, to see what kind of mayhem he was creating wherever he was. A couple of instances come to mind that made me laugh. The first was the time he shoved a short, fat WRAF through a window when she became stuck as we were having an exercise ('pretend war'). They were using the end window of the WRAF block as the entrance to a 'clean zone', and this particularly stocky woman had become lodged midway from outside to inside. Jake and I were part of the vehicle-removal team and had been tasked with getting any rogue vehicles off the parade square, which was fantastic for us as we could use any means to get shot of them, including 'hot wiring' or cutting the handbrake cable and dragging them off to wherever. As we rounded the corner of the WRAF block, the sight of a huge fat arse hanging precariously out of the window, caught Jake's eye.

He stopped our section mini-van and walked over to the block with his gas mask on. He put his shoulder to her fat arse and heaved her through the window, where she landed with a plop in a heap on the other side. I was beside myself with laughter; my gas mask was steaming up and I was having hysterics. He got back in the van as if it was an everyday occurrence, shooting me a look.

'Not even with yours,' he said and we continued to get the cars off the parade ground.

The second incident happened whilst an imaginary air raid was taking place and we were gathered in the air-raid shelter in the early hours of the morning. It was pitch black and we couldn't see a hand in front of our face. Whenever the siren indicates an air raid, you had to take cover wherever you were, and our shelter accommodated several wandering officers. The words 'red rag' and 'bull'

~ A Day in the Life at Cranwell ~

were applicable to Jake; he just couldn't resist an opportunity like this! In the total blackness, a little voice came from nowhere.

'An officer is like a lighthouse in the desert!'

I could hear the shuffle of people trying to look at each other, but torches were not allowed in case they attracted attention. Someone flicked a cigarette lighter, but it was far too late by then. You could almost hear the puzzled expressions on people's faces.

'Brilliant – but fuck all use!'

Jake finished his comment; the shelter erupted into the kind of laughter you experience only a few times in your life. Needless to say, the officers were not laughing, but everyone else was: even the bosses. It was a high coup for Jake; we all knew who it was, but it was so funny he didn't even get a 'waggy' finger' for it.

All these tales were told over a few flagons of foaming ale in the NAAFI later on, and we came across a young lad whose dad was a 'squabbling bleeder' (squadron leader), quite high up in the Hofficer structure. The lad was a 'FLEM' (flight line mechanic), and he rubbed everyone up the wrong way, although officers were his particular favourite. Cranwell was dripping with baby officers and he was sick of having to salute them all. One inexperienced officer asked him why he wasn't wearing his beret while he was on the 'pan' (aircraft manoeuvring area), where it is forbidden to wear any kind of headdress lest it be ingested into an aircraft engine.

'Where's you beret, airman?'

'In my pocket, sir.'

'Why isn't it on your head?'

'Because I can't get me head in me pocket.'

'You can't salute me if you haven't got your beret on.'

'I would be saluting the Queen's commission, which you have not got yet, and it would be a complete shame to give it to an arsehole like you.'

He didn't even get charged! I was flabbergasted – I get done for sleeping in, and he gets away with shit like that! He was a 'Worky Ticket', as I've mentioned before, and he would turn up for work with his hair all different colours from the weekend – this was the punk era. He was ordered to get back to his block and make sure his hair was all the same colour, so he disappeared for an hour or so and returned with it all the same colour. The fact that it was 'Orville' green was neither here nor there to him.

He was busted for that one and I never heard much from him at all after that. I don't know whether he left or was posted; it was a shame, as we could've done with more of his kind. Blindly following orders can become exceedingly monotonous and very tiresome after a while!

To that end, anything that would raise morale was encouraged by the mischievous. We had a young J/T who had a particularly bad stammer, and his name contained an 's' which was one of the letters he stammered on. It would give us extreme pleasure to phone him from Stores and have him stutter his name down the phone for what seemed like an age. We would pretend to be officers and tell him to shout for someone's name with an 's' in it.

~ Drop and Give Me Twenty! ~

This could go on all day long, until he eventually refused to answer the phone at all and just got people to take messages. One of the funniest times I remember was when a real officer phoned up and he answered, thinking it was one of us, saying, 'D'ya know who this is?'

The officer, a bit bemused, repeated, 'No – do you know who this is?'

Sid, replying with all the candour he could muster, said:

'Well, if you don't know, you can go and fuck yourself!'

❖ ❖ ❖

17. A Day Out at Her Majesty's Expense

Any time that you got to spend away from your parent unit was as exciting as a good holiday: new people, new surroundings, different NAAFI – and all paid ... Fantastic!

My first visit came after about three years at Cranwell, where I had become an extremely proficient mechanic, outstripping a lot of the older guys. I simply had that annoying kind of inquisitiveness that wouldn't go away; I just had to know how things worked, and then when they didn't I could visualise what had gone wrong, cutting fault-diagnosis time by half and often more. Basically the more information you had, the less work you would have to do and the less time the vehicle would be out of service.

I'd become competent enough to be entrusted to going onto the duty fitter roster. This meant you could be called out at any time to recover or repair a broken-down vehicle and were on constant standby; sobriety was the order of the day – but that didn't stop the high jinks of the officers from getting out of control. One time I was summoned by the duty driver to a Mini that wouldn't start. I got the keys for the section from the guardroom and then my toolbox; the duty driver said the Mini was at the officers' mess, and could I drive the Land Rover myself?

'Yeah, no problem,' I said and duly drove up to the officers' mess. I parked the Land Rover and looked for the Mini, but there was no sign of it. I wandered around the place for a bit with my toolbox, still looking for it. A head popped out of the door.

'You the duty fitter?'

'Yes, sir, but I can't find the vehicle.'

'Come in; we can't get it started.'

I was perplexed – what was he on about? I was always nervous around officers; they had a tendency to drop me in the shit without my cottoning on quickly enough. So with my toolbox and in my dirty overalls I entered the officers' mess, to find the Mini sitting in the middle of the floor. I knew it couldn't have been driven up the small flight of steps and scratched my head, surrounded by 'Rodney' onlookers.

They wet their royal pants at my bemusement; for a jolly jape they had carried it in manually, up the steps and into the main hall. Officers hung drunkenly from the balcony upside down, and I thought how unfair it was that we 'erks' would get done for behaviour like this, but in Hofficer terms it was just as classed as 'high spirits'.

I got it running in minutes. I wasn't sure whether the wire from the LT (low-tension) side of the coil had been pulled off or had fallen off during the lift; either way I should have dropped them all in the shit for wasting my time, but I didn't – I thought it was an original gag and saw the funny side of it. Boys will be boys, and given how cheeky I could be myself it was a fair cop – but I would keep a mental note of the ringleader in case I got the chance to bury the twat ... Unfortunately, I didn't. That's us 'quits', Rodders?

Now that I was competent enough to be left on my own to make intelligent decisions, I was offered the chance to take the section van up to Otterburn in Northumberland National Park as a breakdown and recovery fitter. It was my first time away from camp without supervision, and I was both flattered and nervous.

I knew I was a good fitter, but the shit-meister was never far from your shoulder if you fucked up, and I desperately didn't want to do that.

One time that I particularly shone was when I discovered a serious fault on a Bedford MK, and that would start the ball rolling for all of them to be inspected. A female driver had commented on the difficulty she was having selecting the gears on her truck. I gave it a quick test drive – still without my HGV licence – and agreed that there was a problem with the vehicle. The pedal could be pushed almost to the floor and still it wouldn't free the clutch, preventing her from selecting a gear.

Initially I adjusted the linkage, which took up the free play, and that worked, but by the end of the day the girl had brought it back, saying the fault had recurred. One thing that has stayed with me throughout my mechanical career is that if I do a job, it'd better not come back with the same fault, as that implies you haven't done your best the first time around. I was as mad as hell at myself, but on further inspection, as I got her to push the clutch pedal down, the whole of the gearbox assembly was trying to move rearwards. This was unprecedented. The bell-housing on most vehicles is integral with the engine casting, unlike these trucks in which it was bolted on. The bolts that held it all together were behind the flywheel and a devil to get to, and they were coming loose – so much so that I had Cranwell design and fabricate a special spanner and courier it up to me forthwith.

One of the officer candidates at Otterburn was an ex-flight-sergeant fitter, who helped and advised me as to the best way to repair all the trucks. He wasted no time in rolling up his sleeves up and getting stuck in; of course this was a major 'Smartie points' exercise for him, but I was grateful for his knowledge and candour. He could have lorded it over me, but he didn't; he was a thoroughly decent bloke and I wished him every success in his future.

The phrase 'Too many chiefs and not enough Indians' is often bandied around in the Forces, when too many people are trying to tell more experienced people what to do, how, why, where and when! I have experienced this on several occasions and clashed every time.

'I'm telling you to do it this way.'

'But sir, we've been doing it this way for years, and it takes less time and it's safer.'

'Never mind that; I'm the officer and I'm tellin' ya to do it this way!'

What I said was 'OK', but what I meant was 'Fuck you, you ignorant, arrogant prick' – and when he'd gone I did it the way I'd been taught to do it by the people who knew what the fuck they were talking about, because they had done it safely, securely and competently for years.

~ A Day Out at Her Majesty's Expense ~

There is no substitute for experience, as long as it belongs to a person who is not stuck in the annals of time and who can appreciate the advancement of technology. Blimey, I never realised twenty-year-old feelings could evoke so much passion. But I am passionate: passionate about what I believe in – that people should treat each other with dignity and respect, that manners really do 'maketh' man, that it's nice to be nice; and if we could remove the fucking **GREED** from the forefront of our minds then the world would be a damn' sight better place in which to live. How much is enough? Just how many zeros do you need after your bank balance to feel secure? How shallow are you that you need to keep up with the Jones's? I despair!!!

But then again, I digress, and I feel I could be cheating you, the reader, 'cos up until now I hope we've been having a bit of a giggle. I don't want my personal politics sneaking into a lively tale – so let's get back to the tellin' of how it was, and I hope you'll forgive me for having a bit of a rant.

I arrived at Otterburn with my Mini-van full to the gunnels with oil, spare parts and tools. Dressed in my DPMs (disruptive pattern material – basically anything that makes you look like a tree on legs) I settled into the Nissen hut, with its cylindrical pot-bellied fire in the centre of the room – too close to the door, so that every time it was opened I was bastard freezing. Ya just never learn some things, do ya? For the journey to Otterburn we had been given a packed lunch, which contained a couple of sandwiches lashed with butter – something my mother says I used to lick off the toast when I was a kid, and leave the bread; now, though, it makes me vomit if I even know it's in the ingredients, so I traded my 'sarnies' for some more fruit: a couple of apples that I placed on the windowsill of our Nissen hut to keep them fresh. I sunk into the old springy bed, and before ya knew it I was gone.

'Crunch, crunch, crunch' was the sound that woke me up. I sat up and laid down again a second later; a sheep's head was in my room and merrily devouring my stock of fruit on the windowsill. Big, black face: how dare you relieve me of my traded fruit you ... you ... walking ball of fur? I tried yelling 'Mint sauce' at it, but it just made the roommates laugh; the sheep was completely unfazed by my antics and continued to relieve me of my fruit.

It had finished my collection and hung around to see if there was anything else on the menu. I was livid! But how do you chastise a sheep? By now the sheep had attracted a small audience and I was keen not to be outdone. I asked them if anyone had anything left in their boxes that they didn't want. A few sandwiches were thrust in my direction by the girls, who were scared of the sheep, and a couple of bits of half-eaten fruit. Well, it had devoured my entire stock; what harm was a couple more bits gonna do?

I gave the sheep the sandwiches and the remnants of a pear and an apple filled with the entire contents of a tube of toothpaste; it wasted no time in scoffing the lot, but the expression on its face after the apple was well worth the wait. If you've ever seen someone smacking their lips wondering if that last taste was enjoyable or repulsive, seeing a sheep do it reduced me to hysterics! Bob: 1; Sheep: two apples, half a box of 'sarnies', some more fruit – but 'nil' in the stakes of one-upmanship. Sheep are just never gonna get the gag!

Still, a sheep with clean teeth and fresh-smelling Colgate burps was truly a wonder to behold!

We usually went away for two weeks at a time and the students would hide food on the trucks they knew were going up to Otterburn; it was a kind of cat-and-mouse game, fair play to the inventiveness of the baby officers – but the DIs had seen it all before. Whilst over the pit in the 'lube' bay I personally retrieved a box of Mars bars, several condoms full of rice and – strangely – a few juice cartons whose contents I had no idea of, but it certainly wasn't juice. I just shared them out in the tea bar, chucked the rice and poured the slop into the 'Dalek'.

I used to rally the little Mini-van around the Otterburn ranges, hurtling over the cattle grids, which were treacherous when wet, and I almost lost it when going round a tight, right-hand bend. The Mini's little wheels lost grip on the cattle grid and I began to slide towards the thick steel gateposts. By some miracle it found some grip from somewhere and the entire contents in the back flew up the back wall of the van. It was a wonder it didn't tip over, and had it not had such a low centre of gravity I think it would have done. That settled me down for a bit.

There were night exercises, when we acted as an attack force scaring the shit out of the baby 'zobs' (officers) getting 'cammed up' (with war paint) and handfuls of blank ammunition. I was in my element until I was caught and interrogated; I hadn't bargained on that, and it was the flash from the BFA (blank firing attachment) on the end of my rifle that gave away my position. I wasn't roughed up or anything, just put in the 'stress position' for a bit (fingertips and toes at forty-five degrees to the wall – it gets bloody uncomfortable after a while). Message learned: don't get caught – shoot and move, shoot and move.

The roads were extremely narrow, with passing places, but it didn't stop the drivers racing the four-tonners on the slippery roads, and it was only a matter of time before a calamity happened. One of the drivers rolled a Land Rover and had to be carted off to Hexham general hospital with a suspected broken arm and cuts and bruises. The Land Rover was 'totalled', with the roof squashed down to the top of the seats; he was very lucky he wasn't killed.

Another driver went 'on safari' with a Bedford MK, slipping off the road and down an embankment into the shallow river at the bottom. We had to get the Army in to recover that one. The driver had the largest bump on his head I have ever seen, and it was his head that had smashed the truck's windscreen: another very lucky individual. The bosses had an emergency meeting with all the drivers; they got a massive collective bollocking and were under threat of jail if anyone else trashed a wagon. It worked, and the rest of the two weeks passed without incident.

We packed up the gear and made sure the hut was left in the same condition we found it in. A 55-seater coach turned up for the 'zobs' and we set off in convoy for Cranwell. It was Friday, and we would be passing the turn-off I used to go home on the A1. I know it was naughty, but I let the others get ahead of me; the fitter is always at the back in case anything breaks down. I sneaked off the A1 at Chester-le-Street and dashed home to see if I could pick up Alan for a 'jolly' down to Cranwell, for some company and a sly shufti at Jamie in her very, very tight white jeans (before we got together but oh boy!) and to show him where I worked. He wasn't in and was well pissed off that he missed out. It was a long drive back to camp (195 miles) and I wasn't looking forward to getting in my car and doing the return journey back to Durham. I caught up with the convoy at Wetherby and hadn't been missed; but if you deviate from the official route you are said to be stealing fuel, as well as being uninsured, so if you have a bump while off the route, you are in the deepest shit possible.

Back at camp I decided to forgo the journey back to Durham as I was knackered, and instead I was invited to the disco over at the NAAFI by a couple of the lads. As usual I was skint, so I turned their offer down; they said they would get me a couple of pints each, so I agreed.

I was well pissed by about ten o'clock; my eyes began to head off in different directions and I thought it was time I left. I had drunk all the beer bought for me, but just couldn't resist having a last slurp from the table of drinks I was watching while the lads bopped away on the dance floor. I had picked up a glass and begun to drain it, when I got a sharp tap on the shoulder. As I spun around I was punched full in the face, sending me spinning into a corner of the bar.

'Ya little bastard – drinking my pint after we've bought your beer all night!'

My nose and top lip exploded; I was covered in blood. The pristine white T-shirt I had on turned into a blood-and-snot, vomit-coloured Hawaiian number under the ultraviolet light. I'd inadvertently picked up the drink of the lad who'd invited me out, but regardless of whose it was, it still wasn't mine and I deserved to be punched – but not that fucking hard. I remember there was snow on the ground and I left a trail of blood back to the block. He'd broken my nose and burst my lip; it took weeks for the swelling to go down and I was not very popular. Still very immature, I had a long way to go and kept fucking up at regular intervals. Remarkably, I made it up with the lad who decked me, and he loaned me his Morris 'Marina' to go into Sleaford town one dinnertime to buy some spares for my 'Escort'.

Some dozy bastard darted for a gap in a Mini with a trailer on it and I was forced to do an emergency stop! The clown behind me wasn't paying attention and rammed the back of Kev's car, ripping off the rear bumper. I couldn't fucking believe it, just how much bad luck can a chap have? And wondered if I'd be getting another clout when I took it back to him; I wasn't insured for it and had to fork out the cash to have it repaired.

That was a very expensive lesson, but Kev was really good about it as long as I paid for all the damage. I was incensed, it wasn't even my fault; if the 'tosser' behind hadn't rear-ended me I'd have been in the clear – but I was more worried about getting caught driving uninsured. My licence was clean and I definitely did not want any points on it.

Kev's car was a curious, battleship grey/blue colour; it had been painted by one of our lads, who cobbled together a few tins of left-over paint and mixed them all together, which gave it a unique colour. We'd been out to a nightclub at Ashby-de-la-Launde and one of the lads came to pick us up at about 2.30-ish in the morning.

We piled in, falling all over each other, and someone was having a piss out of the window as we drove up the twisty and winding lanes. A blue light came from nowhere, and of course it was me that was hanging out of the window at the time. Oh, shit! The coppers pulled us over and walked around the car.

'What colour's this, then?' the copper said, puzzled.

'Blue, ya knob,' I piped up, and was dragged unceremoniously back into the car.

'Shut the fuck up, Bob, or you'll get us all done, ya knob-head!' someone said, and I was gagged and sat upon, being squashed in between two of the biggest lads. I could hardly breathe, which is probably just as well.

The copper bent down at our window and we all beamed at him innocently; he checked the documents and on production of our ID cards he lets us go with a cautionary warning and a 'waggy' finger. I just couldn't hold my drink and Kev scowled at me; I covered my nose up with both hands, just in case, while Kev just laughed.

My other 'jolly' out was to take a replacement Land Rover up to the North Yorkshire Moors where the RAF Regiment were doing some sort of exercise with high-ranking officers (squadron leaders and flight lieutenants). Somehow they had destroyed the reverse gear, and I was to take them the new Land Rover and drive the other one back to camp without a reverse.

When I finally got there it was late, and the 'animals' of the Regiment were busy digging the Land Rover out of a snow drift with a 30mph sign they had ripped out of the ground and were using as a spade. I shook my head in dismay; they were a law unto themselves. The best bit about it was that the officers were staying in a pub with a real log fire in the hearth. The senior officer decided that it was too late to begin the journey back, and that I would stay with them in the pub. I was given a single room and told to wash up and come down for the evening meal; that was fantastic and all free.

Whenever you stay at an establishment off camp you automatically get the same rate (daily allowance) as the most senior officer there; in this case it was a squadron leader and was worth £50 a day. I was elated, but told them I had expected to go back tonight and didn't have any money with me. The officer gave me the £50 and said he would claim it back on his return. I thought all my Christmases had come at once! After the meal they used their rates to start at one end of the optics shelf and they worked their way along it for the remainder of the evening, saying:

'Whose round is it?'

'Queen's round!' was the resounding reply and they each ordered some weird-looking coloured drinks. I stuck to a couple of pints of 'Old Horizontal', which was like treacle.

'Why is it called "Old Horizontal"?' I asked the barman, who was grinning wildly.

'You'll find out soon enough – how many have you had?'

'Two,' I replied confidently.

'I wouldn't advise having any more than three,' he beamed.

'Why's that?' I questioned.

'What time you want to be up in the morning?' he continued.
'Oh, I'll be OK; I've got an alarm on my watch.'
'No, you'd better have a call,' he said, wiping a glass.

I decided that on this occasion I should do as was suggested, as he seemed to know what he was talking about – and true to his word I fell asleep next to the fire, halfway down my third pint. It's called that because that's what it does to you. It was an experimental guest beer of some God-forsaken, unknown strength; I can't even remember going to bed – and what a thick head I would have in the morning.

The officers had a good laugh about it and I was lucky I didn't get sabotaged. Morale was high by the end of the evening and they had been staying there for over a week. The landlord told me that they'd practically drunk the place dry. I had a hearty breakfast and readied myself for my journey. It was easy to forget about the Land Rover not having a reverse gear and I had to push it backwards on a couple of occasions on the way back. Damn' heavy, those long wheelbases. I took the whole day to get back and got a bollocking for taking so long.

But if I could get out of a day's fitting, I would; I loved driving and was constantly badgering then to send me back to St Athan for an HGV course, but they wouldn't. It didn't stop me driving them, though, and I would harass the lads to give me a go at anything while out on test. Billy was giving a 55-seater coach an extended test one day and I went with him and begged for a go; he got out of the driver's seat while the coach was trundling down the road at a considerable speed, and came and sat next to me at the front of the coach!

'There you are, then – have a drive.'
'Jesus Christ, Billy – ya fucking mental, or what?'

He just laughed and crossed his legs nonchalantly as I launched myself towards the driver's seat, grabbed the steering wheel and plonked myself in the seat. It was well tough to handle; the gearbox was like a huge mixing bowl and I missed the gears every time I tried to change them.

I had to stop and start again from scratch. I got a bit better at it, but there is a definite knack to driving a big diesel: you have to let the revs drop all the way down before going for your gear, Billy explained:

'You drive a diesel on the rev counter.'

On Saturday mornings when I was on as duty fitter, I would get the biggest trucks and buses and drive them around the section. I would have been strung up if I'd been caught, but I was careful and didn't damage any of them. Even when I got to the Falklands I would drive anything I could get my hands on; there was a fantastic selection of vehicles there that I would never normally see. Unimog (Mercedes all- wheel-drive trucks - Plates 22 & 23); 'Eager Beaver' rough-terrain forklifts; BV206 (tracked off-road/snow vehicles – Plate 21); and of course the Can-Am on-/off-road despatch motorcycle (Plates 19 & 20). I was like a kid in a sweet shop.

❖ ❖ ❖

18. Islas Malvinas: Willies, Poo and Piss!

May 1985: 4-month detachment

I'd been married to Jamie for just two weeks. We had both been feeling numb and disillusioned since I found out I was going to the Falklands – to Devil's Island, BFPO 666 (British Forces Post Office) – so soon after our marriage. It was to be a life-changing day, in more ways than one, although I didn't really know it at the time. I had tried to get out of going by pleading my case at SHQ (Station Headquarters), and under normal circumstances my detachment would have been deferred – but because I had volunteered to go (a year or so earlier), there was no going back once the roster came around to me. Too many people were waiting to come home after their four-month tour.

I made out to Jamie that I was enraged with the RAF, and I was! But there was also a tiny curiosity and inquisitiveness at going overseas for the first time, the first time I'd ever been away from Cranwell for any length of time, and I kept this well hidden from her.

The day arrived for my journey to BZN (Brize Norton) in Oxfordshire. My heart was absolutely pounding in my chest. I heaved my overstuffed 'sausage' bags to the front door as the car's horn announced it was there to pick me up. We were in the tightest embrace we'd ever been in and Jamie was in floods of tears, and I have to admit that I would be lying if I said I wasn't. It must have been a pathetic sight – two young lovers torn from each other's grasp so soon after making lifelong commitments. I forgot about the Falklands for a few moments and the 'what ifs' hurtled through my mind as the car drove off and I stared out of the back window, waving childishly, watching Jamie's figure get smaller as I felt my vision narrowing and tunnelling. Could I stop the car and get out? What would happen if I just refused to go?

'Hang on a minute,' I said to the driver, who pulled up sharply. I got out of the back door and ran to Jamie as fast as I could; her face was red raw from crying!

'Don't go – please don't leave me! Just don't go – it'll be OK.'

She was sobbing like the child she still was, the kind of sobs a child makes when it can't get an inward breath and takes three large gulps of air at a time. She was actually crushing me with her arms – her soft, eighteen-year-old arms that had held me so tenderly the night before.

'I've got to go, love! – it'll soon pass, and I'll write all the time.'

She repeated her pleas, which made the walk back to the car seem to take forever. I couldn't look back; if I did, I would never get back in the car and it would be jail for me. What a way to start a journey.

The first few miles were silent, then the driver tried to cheer me up a bit; it was really touching – he commented on never having seen a couple so distraught before. I explained.

'That's just shitty,' he said. He scolded the RAF, trying to make me feel better. It didn't work.

~ Drop and Give Me Twenty! ~

I must have daydreamed the first part of our journey and only came to as I realised we were hurtling down the M1 and some considerable time had passed. I wondered what Jamie would be doing now? She hadn't been on camp long enough to make any real friends, even though the wives of the other lads said they would look out for her; she was just a kid and the other wives were so much older than her. I worried myself sick, and with good reason as it turned out. I rotated my wedding ring lovingly the whole journey and it had become quite hot as we entered the gate of BZN.

I smiled to myself as I remembered the gentle warmth of last night as we had lain cradled in each other's arms, after we'd shagged like rabbits all night long. I felt exhausted – but what a memory to go away with.

I was in my 'cabbage gear' (DPM) and dragged the two heavy 'sausage' bags from the boot. They were stuffed with every cold- and wet-weather item of clothing you could think of, including a 'Falklands parka', which was an extremely valuable commodity; I chose to hang on to mine even after I got back, having waffled my way into keeping it. I shook hands with the driver; he bade me farewell and I apologised for not being better company. Under the circumstances he was polite about it, yet a part of me knew it would be all over the station within seconds of his return – the 'Little House on the Prairie' scene etc. Unless you've have actually experienced the effectiveness of a Forces grapevine, I would be pissing in the wind (which is ironic if you read on!) trying to convince you of its capability to span distances unknown and still retain a certain, if slightly embellished accuracy. And all this was well before the advent of 'Tinternet' (thanks, Peter Kay) I wandered over to the check-in and was greeted (if you could call it that) by a corporal with a clipboard, which immediately made me think of the Chief back at Cranwell. My name and clipboards have a nasty habit of coming together, usually to my detriment.

'Put these labels onto your bags and get changed into your civvies; there's no uniform on this flight for security reasons.'

He waved the clipboard like an extra finger, as a puzzled look washed over my face and I could feel the gusset of my underpants getting a good chewing.

'What civvies? I've only brought uniform – I was told no civvies on Tri-Stars.'

'No civvies – no flight! The Tri-Stars have all been recalled for a safety problem and you'll be flying on that chartered 747 parked out there.'

He gestured with a nod.

'No! I'm deadly serious – I haven't got a single item of civilian clothing with me!'

'Then you're not going.'

My heart lifted for a brief second.

'And if you're not going – that means some other poor bastard's gotta take your place at short notice.'

I thought about telling him of how much notice I'd had and that I was officially still on my fucking honeymoon, but I thought better of it.

'And if you're not going, you're still paying for the flight – £1500! I've had all sorts of skivers through this airport on their way to where you're going, lad, and believe me, I've done it.'

I wasn't quite sure what to make of this. Was it bravado? Or did he really have the power to do that, and did he mean it?

He meant it!

'You've got hours yet. If you don't wanna get done, I suggest that you get yourself into town and buy some civvies!'

Well, by the grace of God I had recently opened a Burton's account and had a few quid left on the card, and so that's how it went. I had that same pair of £20 jeans, £10 jumper and £25 pair of trainers on for the whole four months I was there! (and photos to prove it). Still, it was better than £1500.

I sat in the departure lounge (Plate 2), twiddling my ring again – so much so that it was noticed and commented on by the group at our table, and before I knew it they'd whittled out of me that not only had I not flown before, but also I'd never been overseas. The rumour machine struck up with the full force of a County Brass Band and I was shitting myself long before I ever got anywhere near the plane. Bastards! The bar was closed and there was not going to be any drinking for any of the Forces lads, even when we stopped at Ascension Island to refuel.

There was a right old mix of passengers; you name it, they were on it. Civilian contractors, Army, Navy, RAF, and some very, very smart Gurkhas in suits and ties; they all looked remarkably similar, but their fearsome reputation preceded them and they are not to be ridiculed or tangled with in any way, shape or form. Stories of them sneaking up behind you, and if you felt your bootlaces being touched, it was already too late! I lapped them all up like the fool I was; I'm not much better now – I love a good story.

Eventually my adventure began and we were shepherded onto the plane and found a seat. The civvies were dressed in Hawaiian shirts as if they were going on holiday; mind you, some of them were allegedly being paid a 'grand' a week and they were totally blasé about the whole thing: so would I be for a 'grand' a week! When we were all settled in the plane was still only half to three-quarters full, so we got the chance to move about and sit next to some of the new mates we'd made in the departure lounge, but I avoided the rumour men like the plague. No alcohol again, and the lads were decidedly disappointed that there was – and I quote – 'no nancy-boy with a trolley to rip the piss out of'. When any kind of steward or aircrew did come to check on us at least three lads would 'mince' up the galley after him in unison, like the Marx Brothers doing the 'I'm Free, Mr Humphries' flounce. So they all took it in turns to mimic this instead, and we pretended to call the 'poof' backwards and forwards for an extra olive in our imaginary G&Ts.

When they were bored with all that they started in on the civvies, saying 'Can ya turn that fucking shirt down, mate? – I can't hear a word yer saying!' which I thought was particularly amusing.

The Gurkhas sat reading all the way and never batted an eyelid; I was told they could have taken over the whole plane if they wanted, and there were only about eight of them. I was fascinated by them, though, and while everyone else made a complete twat of themselves, they conducted themselves with a lofty decorum equivalent to royalty.

~ Drop and Give Me Twenty! ~

The flight took a total of about eighteen hours, with a couple of hours spent refuelling at Ascension Island (Plate 4). I'll never forget the magnificent sunrise at 35,000 feet; it's one of my best photos. The smell of the scorched air as they opened the doors at Ascension Island and the heatwave that wafted over us like a reassuring hand; it was early evening and the lads were champing at the bit for a drink, but still no alcohol. The ground crew wandered around in khaki shorts and open shirts and oh, how I wanted to stay there for four months!

I doubt whether there has ever been a situation where two more diametrically opposed things existed than when the door was opened at Mount Pleasant airport. 'Jesus H. Christ on a bike!' The polar bears were fighting the penguins, while the Arctic foxes humped the living daylights out of the white rabbits before scoffing them, and some kind of two-foot-high vulture (Johnny Rook) from the 'Jungle Book' looked on from the sidelines in fun. We all took a massive intake of breath, and to quote one lad, 'Fuck this for a game of soldiers!' A couple of the civvies refused to get off the plane at all and said they wanted to go straight back, lucky bastards. They were forced to get off while it refuelled, but true to their word they left the same day.

Because there are no, or very few, trees on the island, or large buildings for that matter, the wind howls across any open spaces at hurricane proportions, dragging a freezing temperature down to the minus 40s and 50s; piss will freeze when it hits the ground – there were piss 'jubbly's' as far as the eye could see. No one will ever believe that you cut yourself while slipping on a 'piss jubbly', or lacerated your hand on a frozen bogey!

There weren't any dogs on the island either – just as well if there weren't any trees, really! – but there were thousands of feral cats. I believe there is a virus that kills dogs, but doesn't affect cats? I couldn't say for sure, but I saw no dogs. We did, however, have a particularly bad-tempered cat named 'Panther' that would have made Garfield look like a Kindergarten Kitty. It made short work of the two sergeants who tried to shove it off the desk with a broom handle, spitting, hissing and flicking out the ten retractable talons in a 'Come an 'ave a go if ya think yer 'ard enough!' gesture.

The cat stayed! Panther had one good eye and an ear that had been chewed by something a lot bigger than itself. It was a motley, dishevelled bag of shit, but it was fed and was warm and dry for the most part, until an inebriated airman was 'dared' to throw it out into the cold (more on that later). The Argies left behind thousands upon thousands of tins of pilchards in tomato sauce that even the cat wouldn't eat. We even used to throw them into the minefields (opened, of course – penguins can't get the wrappers off, you know!), where the penguins still refused to touch them – no takers. There must have been something really dodgy about these pilchards. But I'm getting ahead of myself, so back to the journey for now.

We boarded a 55-seater coach that was hardly designed for the dolomite roads, which were widely potholed. When it froze, as it did almost every night, the dolomite would become like an ice rink and hard as diamond; it was extremely sharp, too, and I cut myself to ribbons on it later.

The journey seemed to be without end, and I stared out of the back of the bus as the reassuring glow of Mount Pleasant faded into the unfriendly darkness.

It was pitch black; I pressed my face up against the window like an expectant, excited puppy in a pet-shop window, rubbing a hole in the condensation. The only thing I could make out was a faint and distant light. Even in a coach with thirty other people, I couldn't help feeling alone; if we broke down now we would really be in the shit: in the middle of nowhere, no street lights, no mobile phones or radios, no way of summoning help! Who would even know we were missing?

Eventually we arrived at our 'Coastel' – a floating hotel was how they described it (Plate 5). My fucking arse! Oh yeah, it was floating all right – but 'hotel'? Nah ...

It was a series of metal storage containers welded together: more like a floating prison. The gangplank would rise and fall steeply as the tide washed in and out of the bay. Liver fluke teemed in the salty water, which we were told would have frozen over but for its high salt content. Thick kelp, which had been responsible for many a diver's premature death, pawed at the side of the Coastel's pontoon like the tentacles of a giant octopus, with the pervasiveness of the red weed from 'War of the Worlds'; but surely there was no danger from the liver fluke? Who would be fucking stupid enough to go into the water at these temperatures?

You guessed it!

A four-tonner turned up with our bags and we squabbled like starlings as to whose was whose. Once you had your bags, it was up the jolly gangplank and onto reception. 'Reception'!!!??? F-u-u-u-u-uck o-o-o-o-o-o-off. Some inbred 'hick' with buck teeth and a board full of keys, and who could barely string a sentence together, handed you a key and gave you thorough instructions of how to get lost on five different floors. Tempers were flaring as 'sausage' bags and airmen tried their level best to find their rooms and squash past each other in the sweltering, narrow corridors.

At last, I fell into a room with three beds in it – one bunk bed and one single bed. The single bed was already taken by the most senior person, i.e. the one who had been there the longest and had the most segments of his 'chuff chart' coloured in. Wouldn't ya know it? – the bottom bunk was taken too, so I spent the first two months hauling my little old five-feet-six-inch carcass up and down the end frame of the bed; there was no ladder. I thought of 'Fletch' from the prison series 'Porridge'. The very first thing I did, once on the top bunk, was to stick my pictures of Jamie on the ceiling right above me. I stroked her face and imagined that she could feel it from 8000 miles away.

The room was no bigger than the beds themselves and storage space was at a premium; maybe that's why there weren't any ladders. If it could have been fitted in there, it would; many, many things were squashed out of shape to accommodate them so they could be close to hand. It was the closest I could come to imagining being on a submarine, without actually going on one. Let me just give those 'matelot' submariners a pat on the back. I visited a sub later on, and can honestly say that there is not a gold pig big enough to tempt me to sea for six months at a time, when you don't know if it's day or night, where you have to 'hot rack' in your colleagues toenail clippings and 'knob-jam'. I used to think I was the only one to have ever wanked into a sock – but God forbid leaping into your bunk to find a recently soiled one in there before you! I suppose it must have happened.

Gear stowed, it was time for another game of 'Labyrinth' to find the mess hall, where we would get our 'Welcome to Devil's Island' speech. But there were enough bodies heading in the same direction for us to eventually locate it – although forlorn airmen were still arriving throughout the course of the meeting, which really pissed off the corporal because he had to keep repeating himself. When they were still coming in towards the end, he gave up and said, 'Anything you want to know – ask your room-mates.'

One thing that was no laughing matter was the ever-present danger of undiscovered mines and Harrier bomblets, mostly ours. We had to wear a specially wadded dressing about our person at all times, and if you were caught without it you were definitely for the high jump. The 'Argie' mines were of plastic construction and could not be detected in the usual manner with metal detectors; therefore another constant danger was that whenever the tide washed in and out it would move the existing mines up and down the beach without warning – something I wished I'd remembered.

Our first meal on the Coastel was as expected, cooked with a 'How fucking long 'ave I got left to do?' attitude – and it didn't get any better. Sometimes the packed lunches were more appetising than the cooked ones. Not to worry: Coastel 2 was right outside the Portakabin NAAFI (which we wrecked after an impromptu rugby match over a full can of lager. We had to give up an entire Sunday that was spent repairing it).

The 'chuff chart' was basically any picture, usually of a naked woman in a very 'open' posture, divided into 120 segments (give or take a couple) to represent the days done, which would be coloured in every time you had completed a full day. Many of the lads had the same picture and the usual topic of conversation at breakfast was where they were now on the 'chuff'.

'I'm at left nipple,' someone would comment.

'That's fucking ages yet – I'm on the minge! Days to do are getting few!'

'You can both fuck off! I'm right on the flaps and the "clitty's" tomorra!'

This would prompt a collective resounding moan that would proliferate and percolate throughout the breakfast crowd, followed by a few verses of Peter, Paul and Mary's 'Leaving on a jet plane'. Many a jubilant airman has been threatened with the most imaginative torture if he sang another fucking note of that song. I'm glad the RAF wasn't around when the Marquis de Sade was in full flight. Even 'Bendy Wendy' at BFBS (British Forces Broadcasting Service) was so sick of having to play it that she threatened a levy on whoever requested it – then it just became, 'I'm levying on a jet plane'. She just couldn't win; the lads were so sharp they could shave in their observations, and then some.

So after a couple of baby tinnies and a look at the Falklands money, which wasn't too dissimilar to our own, we headed back for a kip. It was tough enough to find your room when you were sober, but after a few tinnies all you could hear was:

'You're on the wrong floor, ya tosser!'

'Get the fuck out of my room!'

'Does anyone know where room ??? is?'

And woe betide you if you were the last one to bed, 'cos then there was no one around to help ya! And I've seen men sleeping in corridors, not knowing where they were or should have been.

I kissed Jamie's photos, as I did every night, and the gentle hum of the air conditioning knocked me clean out as soon as my head touched the pillow. I'd forgotten to pack an alarm clock though, and the two armourers I was sharing the room with thought it was a great game to vacate the room silently every morning and leave me knockin' out the zzzzzs until I was late. Bastards!

You really had to be on your toes here. If there was a chance of a practical joke, rest assured it would be grabbed with both hands and made the fullest use of. Morale was everything to the lads down here; work, sleep and drink, with the odd day off thrown in to prevent madness. And even then it didn't always work.

We worked from 7am to 7pm, or at least that was the official time; in fact very few people did and it was not ruthlessly enforced. That was for six or seven days a week with one off, depending on the workload. It worked well for the most part; you never got the same day off twice, which meant you could go down into Port Stanley itself on different days, although nothing much seemed to change.

The locals weren't keen to have us in the 'Rose' or 'Globe' pubs, which were proper spit-and-sawdust affairs with real coal fires; we were far too rowdy and they complained about the swearing! Fuck off! Fights were a constant risk; often they would break out over what seemed like nothing, usually just a 'throw away' comment – but it doesn't take much to flare a bloke up when he's 8000 miles from his home and family, with the only pastime being to drink. Signs were placed all over Stanley camp that read 7775 Miles to Blighty, etc.; it was a constant and sickening reminder, and I never quite saw the point of them. Still, anything was welcome that reminded us of home and stopped us from remembering the desolation of the island we were on.

I awoke to realise I was late, and my thoughts flooded back to Cranwell. The lads were still having breakfast, though, and I was just in time to meet up with the 'crew'. We met in the mess hall, as it was the only practical place where anything could get done on this floating rat turd. A few more speeches, and it was off to the four-tonner and my first day at work.

The banter was lively in the truck as we were thrown around like ninepins for the mile or so as we negotiated the potholes, which filled with water and ice overnight and made the roads extremely treacherous. Not a day went by without someone requesting a Land Rover, or the section Unimog, to pull someone out of a ditch. If you were unfortunate enough to slip off the road a forfeit was normally payable, if not mandatory, as 'hush money' for being recovered without dropping the perpetrator in the shit.

If the vehicle was badly damaged, that was a different matter. A box of Mars bars from the cooks, 'boogie box' batteries from Stores, even inter-service recoveries, would have to be coughed up for. I've got some great photos of the Army doing its utmost to recover some vehicles, only to have them laid on their side or completely tipped over moments later. FART Det. (Falklands Advanced Recovery Team Detachment) had the equipment to get most things out, although the Army usually dealt with the bigger stuff. Everything was a 'Det'; it just got tagged onto most things, and everyone knew where it was. Things like 'Hair Det' would be the barbers, 'Pig Det' the police post, 'Tyre Det' my tyre bay and so on.

Everything and moreover everyone had a nickname of sorts, some flattering but mostly condescending and in some cases downright derogatory, but if you kicked up a fuss about it the frequency of its use would be cranked up to insane levels. I've seen grown men and lads in tears; one of them would be me. The term FNG ('fucking new guy') was being bandied around all day long. I didn't want to look a twat, and figured that if I waited long enough I'd find out what it meant without having to ask. Big mistake!

There's nothing more infuriating than being called something you don't know the meaning of. 'FNG, FNG, FNG' was the chant, while a pointed finger singled you out. The ever-present 'Hitchcock' crows would amplify the chatter to a quite unbelievable volume; people would move in and out of your face while chanting and it began to feel personal. What the fuck could I have done? I'd only been here a day! So I adopted the attitude of 'If you can't beat them, join them.'

'What the fuck are you on about, FNG? Get some in, ya twat!' (meaning time).

I was perplexed. I hadn't a clue what they were on about but kept joining in; this just seemed to wind them up even more and I could feel myself getting agitated. The attacks got more and more personal, with things like 'Just been married, eh? – Ya don't think she's gonna wait for a c*** like you, d'ya? She'll have her knickers round her ankles faster than you can say "Galtieri's revenge"' (diarrhoea).

Regrettably, during the course of the four months they weren't all that far from the truth! I was thrown off balance by the vindictiveness and level of cruelty, and couldn't think what I'd done to deserve it. The fact was that I hadn't done anything;, it was just 'let's all pick on the new kid' and I wasn't prepared for that. Later that evening, when we were having our first piss-up, the attacks were getting sinister and I was quite unnerved. People ranted on about some kind of an initiation ceremony, and let me tell you – some of the tales I've heard would put the fear of God into you!

But like most things, it's fear of the unknown. As the ale flowed I was thinking of Jamie and twisting my wedding ring; Lord, what I wouldn't have given to be back home then: and it was only my first day! The hyenas began their attacks again, not just on me but on any of the new guys – really vicious, malicious, over-the-top attacks; something was gonna have to give – and it did. Smack!

I heard it, but I didn't see it and it was all over in a second. I didn't see who threw it and who copped it, but it became clear after they were restrained. It's the quiet ones you have to watch. Now that one of the lads had been swinging on someone else's neck, the hyenas turned their attention to little old me. Same sort of things as before; basically they probed you to find your weakness and then they blew the fucker clean out of the water, without the slightest hint of remorse.

When the sergeants began to join in, I was at breaking point. The next second I was in tears and that single indiscretion sealed my fate for the next four months. I was 21, going on 16, and took it hard. I was banished to the tyre bay, away from the main hangar, and was told I'd spend my whole tour there, which meant I wouldn't get my sticky paws on the fantastic range of vehicles. Well, ya know what ya can do with that shit! Fortunately there was always a regular turnover of staff, so I kept my head down and just did the work for the most part and started to win over some of the lads.

A couple of the hyenas left and things started to improve. I was hopeful of getting into the hangar at some point during my four months. Unwittingly sending me to the tyre bay was joyous, really, as it was the warmest place on the island! You can't get rubber solution to cure ('go off') in the cold, and I had a complete aircraft space heater all to myself. I would often go outside when it was 'brass monkeys' weather and stand there in a T-shirt, while the rest had their 'Benny' hats clamped to their cheeks and tightly fastened under their chins to stop them blowing away.

The island could have all four seasons in one day: in a morning, in fact – from blue skies and glorious sunshine to snow 3 or 4 inches thick within an hour. For this reason going anywhere alone was inadvisable, especially if you were heading away from the camp and into the wilderness, as was my wont. I loved to explore; anytime I was posted to a new camp the first thing I would do was drive around all the local roads, plotting a map in my mind and getting further and further away.

As with any remote outpost, contraband soon becomes a commodity and every section had something of value, except the 'Piggy Post' (police) and no one gave a fuck about them anyway. In fact, as we went through the police barrier one of our – shall we say, more adventurous? – colleagues would hurl heavy objects into the adjacent minefield from the back of the four-tonne truck. I'm glad to say he never succeeded in setting anything off, but it worried the shit out of us every time we passed.

My 'perk' was that I had the space heater and, as at Cranwell in the winter, I was never alone for very long, as people popped in for a warm or a chat all day long. Even if they weren't warming to me, they certainly were to the space heater. I also inherited a mould made out of 'Silicaset' (rubber sealant) and when it was filled with 'Doublebond', an epoxy resin, it made the cutest penguin figures you could imagine. Once they were cured, painted and mounted on a plinth with genuine Falklands beach stones, I was in business. I still have two out of a set of three today (one mysteriously went 'walkabout'), some twenty years on (Plates 14 & 15). I would usually swap them for batteries for my 'Walkman' or small tinnies; money wasn't that much use, as you could only spend it once every six or seven days and then only in the NAAFI or the General Store in Stanley itself, and that took all of ten minutes to look around.

The locals had a kind of Australian or New Zealand accent that made their 'look' even more comical; they were christened 'Bennies' because of those pull-down hats I mentioned that 'Benny' used to wear on 'Crossroads'. Not very flattering, and when news eventually got back to the CO he demanded that this practice stop immediately.

I then heard someone say that he'd given a lift to a local 'still' into Stanley.

'What's a still?' I enquired.

'Well, they're 'still' Bennys, i'n't they?'

The locals used to call all Forces members 'When I's' – because it's one of the first things you hear out of a service person's mouth: 'When I was in Ireland', 'When I was in Germany,' etc., etc.

On one of our many runs back and forth from work we encountered a civilian Land Rover that had gone off the road in the early hours of the morning. It was still dark and there weren't any streetlights here! The occupants were a bit dazed and had cuts and bruises, as the Land Rover lay on its side in a ditch. One of the lads, whose surname was Daniels, stuck his head out of the back of the truck and crowed:

'What's happened here, then?'

'There's been a crash, you fucking bell end! – Have you not eyes to see?'

The truck erupted with laughter, and from that day forth he was known as Paul 'Not a lot' Daniels. I'm not even sure if his first name was Paul, but it wasn't used anyway; he was just referred to as 'Not a lot'. If we needed a 'lecky' or a 'sparky' (that was his trade) we'd ask:

'Have you seen "Not a lot" Daniels?'

'He's in that "one tonny" Land Rover, working his magic.'

There were lots of references, of course, to Debbie McGee, rabbits out of hats and the like, but it always went too far; the rules of decency had long gone out of the window and swift justice was just a way of venting some of your anger at being stuck on this wasteland for four months. Nothing would be thought of someone getting punched for going too far, whereas back home it would be a chargeable offence and possibly a court martial.

As long as morale was high and the work got done, a blind eye was turned to almost all things criminal. Everyone went through the initiation and it went something like this.

Initiations to BFPO 666 were many fold; the first was to stand in a tray, put on the goggles, place the penis helmet on your head (Plate 17), and drink a can of beer in one go to a count of ten. Anything left was to be poured over one's head – without the helmet.

As the evening progressed and more alcohol flowed, stage two of initiation was to ride a bicycle over a narrow piece of wood, which crossed a small ditch. When I say 'bicycle', 'narrow' and 'small ditch', perhaps I should elaborate. The bicycle was merely a frame with two wheels – no tyres, mind – a loose seat and no pedals, just the two metal prongs where the pedals used to live. The narrow piece of wood could not have been more than four inches wide, and the small ditch was a good three feet wide by two feet deep with a fine selection of sticky substances at its bottom.

The crowd gathered to observe the skilful crossing of the ditch. Given the state of the bike and me, it was hardly likely. I balanced as well as I could before starting off, but not a single rotation of the wheel had taken place before the observing crowd had picked up the plank behind me and elevated it to an angle of 30 degrees, whereupon I slid arse over bollocks into the shite at the bottom of the ditch, to a raucous cheer.

The third and final part was to climb over the metal frame of the 'rub' (canvas hangar) which was a good 25 to 30 feet in the air, although I have to say this was done a few days later when I'd sobered up. Nevertheless, I was coerced into doing it and must admit I was shit-scared; the poles were slippery and the wind battered the outside of the rub constantly and vigorously, slapping and banging against the frame. As I neared the apex at the top I paused to look down, which in hindsight was not the best idea I've ever had, as I don't do heights all that well anyway, but when I did I saw the rest of the lads armed with mud bombs and any other small objects which could be easily thrown, like apples and oranges from the packed lunches. I clung on like grim death as I was pelted relentlessly for what seemed like an age; and it occurred to me that if I didn't wise up very quickly, this was going to be the longest four months of my life.

The airmen's mess was the only semi-permanent building on the camp, as I gather cooking in a rubber tent or metal container would have created a good deal of problems with smoke or condensation. The wind tore at its corrugated sheets, clanging them backwards and forwards, the sound akin to being surrounded by a hundred Maori warriors chanting the 'Haka', while the rain lashed the sides of the building – not at 45 degrees, but parallel to the ground.

Our many piss-ups were held in a ramshackle and makeshift tea bar. Any excuse would do; someone would only have to start a rumour that a piss-up was on the cards and the grapevine would do the rest. By knocking-off time people were jostling for a spot to sit in; basically if you got out of your seat for any reason it became fair game and would usually be occupied by the strongest or biggest, who would bolt for the space. Many a crushed airman was witnessed trying to get a seat – a kind of 'musical chairs' with violence. Then there were those who could disappear at least an hour early, without being noticed, to sneak off for the booze, as it was on a 'first come, first served' basis – that was the plan, anyway.

By the end of the evening it was those who were still standing and hadn't been punched or arrested who got the cans. Needless to say, anytime copious amounts of alcohol were quaffed there would soon be a need to relieve oneself; I can't remember exactly where the toilets were, but it was obviously too far for anyone to be arsed, so they just opened the door, where the light from the tea bar illuminated the side of the rubber hangar adjacent to the tea bar.

The positioning of the cabins meant that an alleyway of about ten to fifteen feet had been created between the tea bar and the 'rub', and this channelled the icy-cold wind like a vortex, speeding it up as it passed between the cabins. There was usually a pallet outside each building, so as not to traipse mud and congealed dolomite back into the cabin.

I relinquished my seat quickly so as not to be killed in the rush, and made my way outside for a piss. Christ, it was cold, and my willy shrank to an unbelievably small size. Smaller than usual? – much smaller! I began to wee against the cabin and in mid-flow the door opened and another desperate soul stood on the pallet. I shuffled away from the door to make room for him; the wind was now screaming down the alley as we both pissed like racehorses. He finished before me, and as he did himself up and opened the door to re-enter the bar, the light scattered on the wall where we had been pissing. I looked at the darkened area where the bloke next to me had gone; he must have been closer to the wall than me, because there was no dark patch where I had gone.

I first put this down to my miniscule 'tadger', but the horror of what had actually happened was about to befall me. The wind had blown all of my piss up the other bloke's leg! Upon entering the bar I was pounced on by said bloke, who rubbed my face on his leg like a tomcat marking his territory. The rest of the lads were in hysterics by then, and I have to admit it was worth it; there's something special about laughing out loud while trying to keep your mouth shut for fear of ingesting your own piss from someone else's leg.

This is the kind of incident that rockets out of control at an alarming pace, and it wasn't long before the contents of the mop bucket were being flung around the cabin – not that anyone had been doing any mopping, but it had become the makeshift piss bucket. Whoever filled it last had to empty it; hence there was some skilful management of one's bladder, like MFT. Just as things couldn't get any worse, someone who'd been outside had stepped in some police-dog shit (we were informed by the Piggy Post that it was of a finer quality than normal dog shit!) – or at least it should have been from the police dog. The phantom pooper used to leave little messages at night in the most disconcerting of places; I have to say he was never discovered during my four-month tour.

The cabin door flew open from the outside, a large, black boot flicked into the doorway like a Bruce Lee kick, and a huge chunk of dog-shit sailed across the room in slow motion, as the patrons parted like the Sea of Galilee, diving for the floor. With a sickening thud the turd claimed its rightful place on the wall, missing all but one of the bar's occupants, who stood there with eyes the size of dinner plates; the disgust and disbelief – the horror, the sheer horror!

The lad it hit grabbed a stick, scraping the remains of the new artwork from the wall and made after the culprit, who by now was halfway up the alley running for his life in total darkness. At least his eyes had adjusted to the darkness, whereas the shitty-stick wielder had just come out of the bright lights of the tea bar; he paused for a moment as the culprit was getting away. In a desperate attempt to wreak revenge without running blind he thrashed the stick with the ferocity and accuracy of a Kendo warrior and once more the turd was airborne; there was a good deal of 'effing' and blinding and a torrent of threats being thrown around like confetti. The warrior returned minus stick, not knowing where the poo had landed but still full of hell.

More alcohol was quaffed, but the now dehydrating poo began to drive people away, including me. Piss is one thing, but the minute bottom juice, 'clagnuts' or 'dangle berries' enter the picture, I'm off!

The Army allegedly has a game called 'freckles', in which someone supplies a poo and places it in the middle of the table; the poo is then slapped with the palm of the hand or some other flat object and the person with the most spots of shit on him buys the round. I say 'allegedly', because although I have heard this tale many times I have never come across anyone who is willing to admit taking part in this so-called ritual, let alone admitting to buying the round.

So as the miniature tinnies dry up, it's on the back of the Bedford four-tonner and the long, rickety road back to the Coastel. Much singing and high antics were par for the course, including dangling the newest airman out of the back of the lorry until he screamed, and people doing upside-down gymnastics on the metal frame of the canvas and dropping on their heads with a resounding thud to the cheers of the whole truck.

I began singing Leo Sayer's 'One Man Band', while two people swung like chimps towards each other on separate parts of the frame, kicking lumps out of each other. Someone struck a match to see who was singing, then lit the rest of the box and threw it at me; the yellow glow illuminated the faces as it burned fiercely, while I tried to flap it away like a seal possessed.

Now that people had an idea where others were, a good deal of punching, slapping and berets being confiscated in the darkness took place; the constant shuffling of feet meant both perpetrator and victim danced around the back of the truck trying to avoid another attack. It was extremely wise to wait until you could see what, if anything, had been put in your beret before putting it back on your head; some of us had to learn this the hard way, as some kindly airman had filled mine with piss!

So back at the Coastel we scoffed, showered and changed, ready for a few tinnies at the NAAFI. The married guys would usually take a lot longer as they were writing 'blueys' (a vital piece of A4 blue letter paper that could be folded into an envelope and posted anywhere in the world free of charge – the importance of a fighting man's morale should never be underestimated) to their wives and children; and for all that I was married, it had been for such a short time that I still had the 'singlies' mentality – although I did write home every day to start with, as I'm sure most guys did.

It soon became apparent that once you had discovered all there was to discover at Port Stanley, which took all of a day, writing was something the rest of the lads took the piss out of, saying, 'Ah, bless him; isn't that sweet?' The guys that had been married the longest either didn't bother to write at all, using the four months to get away form the 'walnut-faced, skanky old money- grabbing bitch' (to quote one individual), or else the parting seemed to bring them closer together. Either way you got the piss taken out of you for 'whatever'. For the most part it was like a school playground, only with violence and maliciousness on a few occasions; but the difference was that there was no friendly trouser-leg to tug on here for reassurance! ('Sir, sir: Basher Brown's just tipped me upside down by me legs and shook out me dinner money.')

'Grassing' just was not an option; if things had become so bad that you had to tell someone, it would be all around the place before you could say 'lickety split' (whatever the fuck that means). Basically you suffered in silence or else gave as good as you got, which is what I tried to do; but the other lads were so much better at it than me and I'd be stuttering trying to get out a particularly vengeful retort and be pounced on for that as well.

'That's easy for you to say, ya f-f-f-fat bastard!'

I wouldn't care; I wasn't even that fat at age 21 – puppy fat, yes, but not obese. However, the puppy never left me and has now turned into a St Bernard, lolloping about the place uncontrollably – I wouldn't mind if I had a barrel of brandy around my neck, but I've got a barrel of lard around my waist instead! It's just not fair.

As we sauntered down the gangplank for the short dash to the NAAFI, which was only a couple of hundred yards up a short embankment, comments were made on who would be brave enough to 'walk the chain' on the way back (Plate 6). I'd heard about this many times, but had only ever witnessed a couple of people actually trying it before giving up a few links into the dare. The Coastel was moored to the bank by two massive chains that were big enough to stand on every other link, depending on whether the tide was in or out. If it was in, the Coastel rose in the water, as did the incline of the gangplank, and it twisted the chain so it lay on a 45-degree tilt.

Only the alleged 'Special Forces' (and there were plenty who claimed they were, although I doubted them) would tackle it in this condition – all unsuccessfully, I'm pleased to say – for the following reason. Even if the tide were out, even if you weren't that pissed, even if the links were not covered in ice and the rain/hail stones weren't strafing you parallel to the ground, and even if the chain didn't rise too steeply as you approached the Coastel – you were still doomed.

As I approached the middle of the chain, six or seven of the bigger lads started to bounce up and down in unison on the chain at the bank end, setting up a kind of resonance that amplified to a full-blown whiplash wave by the time I was halfway over. I clung to the chain like a koala up a gum tree, lashing this way and that. It amazed me that they ever got the chain to move at all, given the weights involved. Apparently the movement, once in 'full swing' (no pun intended), could be felt on board, and it doubled as an aggravation if no one would actually walk the chain. It was icy cold and I could feel my grip on the link loosening. I pleaded with the hyenas, but this just incited them even more as they leapt up and down, now out of sync, which must have looked comical, but I had no time to enjoy that view.

I was well out over the water and had no intention of going in for a dip in these temperatures! The lads, however, had other plans. They began throwing little dolomite stones at my fingers, as my legs finally came away from my 'monkey grip' of the chain. I got a sickening feeling in the pit of my stomach as I realised they were not gonna give up till I was in the water. Too far to go back and too knackered to carry on, I resigned myself to the inevitable. The stones were really painful, like some one flicking a frozen lug.

I looked down at the 15-foot drop and gulped. My breath was shallow and made little 'ghosts' with the condensation; the lads were now in a 'Jungle Book' frenzy, like when the monkeys wanted Man's fire. They could smell the 'kill'; a couple more 'boyoings', and I was gone. Sploosh! My nuts leapt into my throat as the icy water got under my clothes; all I wanted to do was breathe in.

Still under water, my stomach cramped inward – an involuntary retch. It was quiet; I could feel the kelp against my legs, and I began to struggle. My short life flashed before me and I was bored shitless! I felt the bubbles coming out of my ears, which caused the arctic chill on either side of my neck to go from there to my throat; my stomach was still dragging my diaphragm in and out for breath. Water began to replace the air.

I thrashed out in an attempt to swim – but which way? I couldn't tell if I was swimming away from the bank, towards the Coastel or out to sea! Enough time had passed now for the hyenas to become concerned (I was told later); they stopped hopping on the chain and gathered at the edge of the bank.

'Fucking hell – he's been under ages! Where is he?'

The fun had suddenly disappeared from the stunt, and thoughts turned to 'getting in the shit'. A sergeant appeared in the doorway of the Coastel at the top of the gangplank; the rocking of the boat and the noise had alerted him to the high jinks.

'Someone's fell in!' a voice exclaimed, pointing to the water.

The sergeant ran along the walkway of the boat, staring hard into the darkness. I broke the surface of the water, taking the biggest gasp of air in my life and sounding like a cow 'mooing' in reverse. I thrashed the water to foam trying to get my bearings, with my arms like lead weights and the combat jacket acting like a sponge, dragging me back down. Time and time again it went dark and quiet; I was too numb to feel the cold any more and I could feel my strength ebbing away. The sergeant had now raced down the gangplank and scattered the onlookers like ninepins, pulling and dragging them out of the way, screaming at them to stop looking and start helping! He was sober –the lads weren't. I felt something solid under my foot and pushed off it towards the dolomite bank, flailing my arms at anything I could get hold of.

I grabbed desperately at the sharp rocks as the sergeant made his way tentatively down the steep embankment towards me. I slipped back once or twice, not knowing why I couldn't keep a hold of the rocks once I had got there. I also didn't feel the dolomite lacerating the ends of my fingers, opening them to the liver fluke. God knows, I'd swallowed enough of the water.

The sergeant says that he grabbed me by my hair as I was disappearing back under for the umpteenth time, but I can't honestly remember whether it was my hair or the collar of the jacket. Frankly I didn't care; I was just glad to be going up and not down. He dragged me onto the stones and I lay there gasping in a sort of euphoria, part drunk, part drowned and part frozen.

He bawled at someone to get a parka from the Coastel reception. One thing that sticks in my mind vividly was my rescuer picking my hand off the dolomite and looking at my bleeding fingertips and then at me, his eyes coming finally to rest on my month-old wedding ring! I don't know how long I had been in the water, but it seemed like a lifetime. My strength had gone and I was numb from head to toe; I was helpless. It never occurred to me that this could have been it!

'You stupid fucking c***! How long have you been married? What would I have to tell your wife? That you drowned in the Falklands while so many others had lost their lives defending the place?'

He was shaking me violently by the lapels of the parka, which was now around me. I'm not sure if it was the relief that I was reasonably OK or the realisation of the stupidity that had taken place, but either way it was having an effect. I began to splutter my apologies as he guided me up the gangplank and into the warmth of the Coastel. I sat in reception for a good while, thawing out, while the sergeant recorded the details of what had happened. Of course I never said anything about the lads bouncing on the chain, you understand; it just wasn't the done thing. I got lecture after lecture from just about everyone over the coming few days, and I would love to be able to say that it was the one and only time I'd been in the water during my four months in the Falklands. Alas, it was not so.

Settling into a routine quickly is vital for any service person. It takes your mind off other things. If I worked quickly and enthusiastically in my tyre bay, I could get most of the work done by lunchtime. This left the rest of the day for mischief and for making plastic penguins. The bay was a permanent building, albeit a corrugated affair with a concrete floor. It had to have the concrete floor, because into it was anchored the tyre-changing equipment – and believe me when I tell you that you needed to be built like 'Arnold Blackendecker' to change some of these tyres on your own.

The worst of them all were the Unimog tyres: a one-piece wheel meant it couldn't be split or have a rim removed. I've seen myself balancing on about six tyre levers all at once, trying to get one side of a Unimog tyre off. Most of the vehicles had inner tubes, because of the amount of punctures due to slipping off the road or being impaled on various bits of discarded equipment, and it was much easier to fix an inner tube than a tubeless tyre. I even looked after the Governor of Stanley's purple FX4 taxi, for which I was agreeably remunerated.

I had the use of a 'puddle jumper' (short-wheelbase Land Rover – see back cover) whenever a requisition order for tyres, tools, valves and of course glue and patches arrived at Stores, which were a stone's throw from the tyre bay. Nevertheless, whenever I got to use it I would disappear for hours at a time and go 'bondoo bashing' (rallying) across the soft, swampy ground. I would select four-wheel drive – low ratio – and try and follow the BV206 tracks up the steep hills, which looked almost impossible to negotiate, but negotiate I did. Up and down, down and up: and all out of sight of anyone. Caution was not entirely thrown to the winds, however, and in the back of my mind was the distinct possibility of getting stuck – which would mean a long walk and a certain bollocking. If you're stuck in the 'bondoo', there lies the evidence of what you have done, and trying to keep it quiet would be like trying to plait fog. I did get stuck, and managed to dig my way out eventually – but surely the amount of time I was missing would be noticed now? I began thinking of my excuses as the sweat ran off me like rivers, my arms shaking from the exertion of digging out.

As I rounded the bend to the tyre bay and MT yard, the Warrant Officer was standing outside the tyre bay, arms folded. The fact that I was approaching from the wrong direction in any scenario already sealed my bollocking.

'And where have you been, Novak?'

He reminded me of the huge eagle with glasses from the Muppet Show, as he towered over me with all his years of experience.

'I er, er, just, er ...'

Nothing would come, nothing at all, and my arse began to cave in. I turned and pointed behind me with a few more 'erms'. He just stood there dominant and triumphant, letting me dig a hole as deep as the 'puddle jumper' had been in.

'Popped back to the Coastel, did we, Novak?'

I was only too happy to own up to this, as it was a fucking sight lesser misdemeanour than I'd got into. But looking at the state of the Land Rover, we both knew it had been more than that. He gave me one of those all-seeing, all-knowing looks. I hated those; I would have rather been screamed at, as at least then you knew it was over, come what may. But he seemed to be saving them up, and there would come a time when I would face an almighty drop. I considered myself warned and very lucky, but it didn't stop me getting in the shit.

I unloaded the tyres and set to work on the Unimog tyre I had abandoned. I would try and manage on my own, but sometimes you just got a stubborn one that wouldn't play ball. I performed my octopus routine with the tyre levers and one escaped, smacking me right in the face and causing me to topple off the tyre – but not before the other levers had clobbered me in the knackers and the shins!

I was beside myself and launched a two-pound hammer at the wall in sheer frustration. I'd done this so many times that the Warrant Officer was forced to articulate the sentiment that the surface of the walls could be likened to that of a golf ball. He was a very likeable chap. I wondered if he didn't see a little of himself or one of his children in me, with my naivety and misplaced confidence. He was a placid guy, but it was his placidity that made me all the more nervous of him – suspicious even.

When you've been in long enough to rise to the dizzy heights of Warrant Officer (and I'm in no way being sarcastic) there isn't much about the job or the staff beneath you that you don't know. That was something else I would have to learn the hard way when I was disrespectful, derogatory and downright offensive about my Warrant Officer in Germany – something that I am still ashamed of today, and no amount of apologies would ever make it right.

❖ ❖ ❖

19. Man Overboard

Another assignment of tyres needed collecting from Stores, so I wandered over to the MT yard and asked to borrow the 'puddle jumper'. It was out, as was the Warrant Officer; the only thing left was a Unimog ready for scrapping. I could feel myself getting a 'stiffy' as I realised the FNG behind the desk didn't know I was void of an HGV licence.

'Well, I'll take it, but if it breaks down I'll be well pissed off.'

'You're a fitter, aren't you? So fix the fucking thing, then!'

It was then that I got a glimpse of his wedding ring. That's when things always changed for me; married people could always tell me what to do, like berating a child, and I would usually comply without question (see how immature I still was? – or was that respect?) He flung the keys at me: I say 'keys', but this looked like a child's 'let's see which hole this shape fits into'! It wasn't really a key at all, but it was my passport to fun: 'While the Warrant's away – Novak will play!'

I stepped up to the truck triumphantly, walking around it to make sure that some sly bastard fitter hadn't robbed the back wheels off it between my going into the office and coming out again. You think I'm joking? – I'm not.

I climbed into the cab; it took a bit of time to locate the socket that the shape fitted, to start the Mercedes engine. But when it did, I practically came in my pants – the sound of an almost perfectly designed German engine. If I'd known what 'purr' was in German, I'd have said it. I hadn't a clue how to drive it, other than the basic controls, but finally I managed to locate the handbrake and off we went, nonchalantly out of the MT yard as though 'butter wouldn't melt ...'.

I took off in the wrong direction, as I had done before in the 'puddle jumper'; it felt great, but with the added anxiety that if the boss wasn't in the office, where was he? And there was always the possibility that I'd bump into him (not literally), and I couldn't risk another bollocking so soon after the last one: even good guys can run out of patience. Up until now I had restricted my movements to the safe side of the active runway, i.e. I hadn't crossed the temporary runway that had fire-breathing McDonnell-Douglas 'Phantoms' from 23 Squadron tearing up it like there was no tomorrow.

I had no need to venture over to the forbidden side, the side with the beach, the side with the wandering minefields – but you know me by now! I just had to; it was in my inquisitive nature and I wasn't hurting anyone. I approached the runway traffic lights with a recognisable trepidation, testing myself as to whether this really was a good idea. I could still turn back, and I did – but as I did so a Phantom scorched the air as it strafed past me on full reheat, with that familiar aroma of warm paraffin that hovered in your nostrils, on its way to who knows where?

I carried my camera everywhere, and somehow knew I would never get the chance to be in a place like this ever again; maybe it was fate? Who knows? I took the 'Mog' on a 'bondoo bash' and tested its four-wheel drive; it was impressive – the wide tyres supported the weight of the truck easily on the bog and I didn't get stuck. But this was an 'off the shelf' Mog, not like MTSS's wrecker, which was more akin to a locomotive than a truck. It had winches of extraordinary power, front and back; crawler and super-crawler gears that would pull a house down as easily as picking a snot out of your nose; and although you selected from the six-speed gearbox in the conventional manner, it had a torque converter so it would drive like an automatic. I was utterly fascinated by this unique and unmatched power from such a small and ugly-looking vehicle; it had a lot in common with a Rottweiler. It was characteristic of German engineering – rough, ready and very reliable. These things were almost indestructible, impervious to the beating they were subjected to when no one was looking; I can't even remember a single 'Mog' being unserviceable the whole time I was there, except for the electrics (and the salt got into every vehicle for that). I sat at the side of the runway, just listening to its potential ticking over: normally aspirated, no turbo or superchargers. Its power sat under my right foot, even though I was on the left side of the cab, and I dabbed it gently to make it growl; it responded like a dutiful pet, reassuring me of its power.

I used to think I loved music, and I did, but in time I would come to realise that I loved 'sound' more than anything else – any sound; I used to be able to tell you what vehicle had just passed by its sound. Engines have a unique note, as do exhaust systems. My physics teacher once asked the class what they thought the definition of 'noise' was, and many individuals tried to answer the question, including me! You could learn as much about a subject from the wrong answers as you could from the right ones. Several times I interrupted, which only fuelled my exasperation at not knowing the correct answer ... which was: 'unwanted sound'.

Yeah, that makes sense. Things that you don't want to hear could be described as that. So I covered my ears with my hands and felt its vibration shake the very construction of my skeleton when the Phantom screamed past, afterburners on full reheat. Lucky bastards.

With the aircraft past, the runway lights changed to green and I swung the 'Mog' round with its power steering (which was still an expensive add-on in most vehicles) and wrestled with its power as I hurtled towards the temporary runway. As I did so, the lights changed to red! The brakes on the 'Mog' were second to none, but I'd already mounted the runway and thought the best course of action would be to continue and get the fuck out of there. As I hopped up the step to the runway, the tailgate on the 'Mog' fell off and was left lying in the middle of the runway. Oh holy Lord, mother of Christ and all things 'worryable' (eat the clag nuts out of my shit, spellchecker). Now clear of the runway, I slammed the emergency air-brake on, which stood the 'Mog' on its nose and threw me into the screen, but I didn't have time to worry about my own injuries!

If I didn't get that tailgate off the runway, I could well be responsible for trashing a million-pound aircraft, never mind the pilot – and I shouldn't have even been there. I'm not even sure if I leapt or fell out of the cab on the other side of the runway, but out I was. The lights erred on the side of caution, and it would be typical to sit there for a good few minutes before anything happened.

I looked up the runway, couldn't see anything; but then again, given the colour and the speed of these things, by the time you realise they're there it's too late. The lights were still at red and my heart was thumping in my chest; I'd been in trouble before, but nothing could replace the fear of bringing an aircraft down.

I scuttled onto the runway and began dragging the tailgate from the centre; even if I didn't clear it, I could surely get it far enough away so as not to collapse the front undercarriage of the approaching aircraft – but it was so heavy and awkward. Looking up the runway all the time, I knew something was coming – but what? And how soon? Adrenalin took over; I didn't mind getting in trouble, but this would be tantamount to manslaughter if it went wrong, and the military would not spare the horses when it came to burying an 'erk'. Drag, drag, drag; I got the tailgate to the edge of the runway and sat on the icy ground.

The lights were still at red! Nothing took off and nothing landed. It had all been for nothing; but I learned a valuable lesson that day: 'Don't try to beat the lights!' It wasn't worth it. I struggled to get the heavy tailgate back on the 'Mog' and considered myself very lucky; I decided that a 'bash on the beach' could wait until another day. Recomposing myself, I turned the 'Mog' around to face the runway lights once more, which were still at red.

I sat there for ages and a couple of vehicles approached on the opposite side, also waiting to cross. How much had they seen? Would they drop me in the shit? I was clueless. I was also jealous of the 'Mog' as it growled reassuringly beneath me; it just did as it was told. How I wished I could be like that (yeah, right!) I crossed, made my way to Stores and picked up the merchandise, went back to the tyre bay and unloaded said tyres.

Amongst the recently collected stock were a number of four-tonner tyres, which took up a considerable amount of space in my tyre bay; at least four feet high and a foot and a half wide, they had been stored one on top of another. Given their considerable weight and being stored like that, the bottom tyre had become compressed, making it almost impossible to seat on the rim. It was time for another 'paddy' and I flung various pieces of equipment around the bay until I was exhausted – but it felt great all the same.

The large four-tonner tyre provided a perfect hiding place for the Can-Am (plate 19) frame I had dragged into the tyre bay when no one was looking. I had stripped it down to its basic components and had begun restoring it slowly. The corner of the MT yard was used to store broken-down and dilapidated vehicles that had been cannibalised to the point of no return, and it nearly broke my heart when a 'Wokka' (Chinook) helicopter came and lifted them into the sky in a large cargo net to be dropped at sea.

Six or seven part-motorbikes disappeared in a single motion, and I decided that the next one that came into the MT yard would be pilfered forthwith in order to get mine running. The large tyres obscured it from view and I spent every spare waking moment getting it back together. Once it was running, it burned two-stroke oil at a phenomenal rate, creating clouds of blue smoke that filled up the bay. I had to open the fire exit; it looked as though the bay was on fire, and it attracted some unwanted attention from the GSE (Ground Support Equipment) lads next door. It was running, though, and I hurtled out of the fire exit and over the runway to the beach, where I thrashed it to death and fell off more times than I care to mention. Still, I remembered some words of encouragement from back home: 'If you haven't fell off – you're not trying hard enough!' My legs and arms were aching from all the jumps and sand dunes. I made an imaginary track up and tore around the place for hours; a couple of lads turned up in a 'puddle jumper' from MTSS and we raced around the beach, with them trying to knock me off.

Yeah, I suppose it was dangerous; but I was having too much fun to give a shit about that.

The lads disappeared and said they would be back in a while with some more petrol, if they could have a go. Sure, the more the merrier! They returned at lunchtime and hammered the bike up hill and down dale for an hour until everyone had fallen off at least once. Into the sea they rode, diving over the handlebars into the water.

They were fucking nutters; the electrics got soaked and the fuel tank was getting blocked with sand, penguin poo and God knows what else. Before they disappeared back to work I demanded the extra fuel they said they would bring; after all, they had used up almost all of the fuel I'd put in it courtesy of the fuel fairy (who was very kind indeed). They left me a jerrycan full to the brim, but smiled one of those 'fnar, fnar' smiles and I just knew something was gonna happen. I filled the bike up and put the can to one side. The fuel was kind of yellowish and I thought they'd just pissed in it; no matter, it was still running, although misfiring a tad. I roared along the beach and completely forgot about the wandering mines. The misfire got worse and worse and I thought it would be a good idea to turn back before it conked out completely. As I swung the bike around it coughed, farted, backfired and then gave up the ghost completely.

I was miles from the road. I kicked it over and over to try and restart it: nothing doing! – not the slightest inclination of a spark. I tried 'bumping' it, and let me tell you these things were by no means a pushover; they were well heavy. I pushed it back on the edge of the shore, as it was easier on wet sand. I dried the spark plug, let some fuel run out of the tank, and it ran: slower than normal, but it did run. I was puzzled. If it had sparks and fuel, providing they occurred at the right time it should go. I was gonna be late back again, and if the Warrant was waiting I'd be for the high jump. Yeah, the lads did bring fuel, but Dick '4x2' Morris thought it would be a hoot if they put a couple of bags of Tate & Lyle into it before I got it, causing lemon bonbons to 'phut' out of the exhaust like a 'Charlie Brown' cartoon. Wankers!

I thought my heart would burst while pushing it, as it sunk up to the rims going through the dry sand. If I had to push it al the way back to the tyre bay it would certainly attract attention, and I didn't even have a bike licence. I decided the best course of action was to hide it amongst the dunes and come back after work to try and fix it. I got a lift back to the bay from a passing truck. Basically, because the weather was so changeable, you stuck your thumb out and it was only a matter of minutes before someone would stop and help you out, civvies and military alike. It was an unwritten agreement.

I plotted the demise of Mr Morris a hundredfold and schemed endlessly to get my own back. Alas, there was no need, as it turned out. He clobbered a sergeant over the head with a piece of wood – hence the nickname '4x2' – during one of our many piss-ups. It was funny how it happened, really: just another case of things snowballing out of control.

People were throwing buckets of water around like confetti and everyone was soaked to some degree. Then someone pissed in the mop bucket, and that was gonna get thrown. Dick was centre stage and said forthrightly:

'If ya throw that at me, I'm gonna twat ya with this.'

It was a piece of the tea bar that had become detached in some form of scuffle. The sergeant who had the bucket threw its contents at Dick, who tried to sidestep it unsuccessfully. A sickening thud was heard and the sergeant fell to the floor holding his bleeding head, while the rest of the tea bar launched themselves at Dick, disarming him instantly and flooring him in the process.

'I told him – I fucking told him,' was all he could say while being subdued with several bodies on top of him. This was high entertainment and I laughed my bollocks off at the divine retribution; it was great to see someone else get in the shit for a change – but I drew the line at physical violence. I've only had a couple of real fights in my life and would normally try to defuse the situation with 'Well, you can eat the sweet corn outta my shit pilgrim!' in a 'John Wayne' voice or just waffle my way out of trouble.

But I've always had a strange philosophy about fighting, in as much as that if the situation has deteriorated to such a level that fisticuffs are inevitable I've gone all out, like the 'Tasmanian Devil'. Yes, you're gonna get hurt and maybe even get the living crap kicked out of you; but let me tell you this: no matter their size, age or how hard they are alleged to be, if you give it all you've got, they are much less likely to come back a second time.

'You're just not worth it' was a statement I had levelled at me after a particularly nasty skirmish.

'Bring it on, shithead.'

I was already damaged, so a few more thumps weren't gonna make any difference now! He declined the offer. Read into that what you will – but I'm only five feet seven and three-quarters.

I'd been colouring in my 'chuff chart', and every segment filled would usually be followed by writing a 'bluey' back home. I'd written loads and loads and received only a couple of letters from Jamie. It unnerved me – and with good reason, as I later found out. Her letters got fewer and fewer and I asked the 'Warrant' to send a signal back to Cranwell to make sure she was OK. Days went by, and still nothing.

The grapevine had informed everyone that all was not well at home and the piss-taking began again. I didn't mind people taking the piss out of me, or the way I walked, or talked, or sang – anything; but I did mind aspersions about my girl. It infuriated me. But I knew if I said anything in front of the blokes it would just be pouring fuel on the fire, so I collared them one at a time and explained first how hurtful it was when I'd only just been married. As it turned out, I was defending a 'slapper' and they were right all along. The signal came back reporting that all was well. Of course it was; they weren't gonna tell me any different, were they?

It didn't make any difference to the letters, or lack of them; Jamie was having a ball on my wages – nightclubs, taxis into town, entertaining my so-called colleagues back at the house. One of them was even the best man at our wedding; talk about sticking the knife in a twisting it! Oh, how I wanted that bastard dead. Still, 'it takes two to tango', as they say, and at least he was man enough to come and tell me himself what had gone on. I was just numb. What would be the point of kicking him to death now? And the allegation was that there was more than one co-respondent; if I'm being honest, there were at least three that I was certain of, two of whom were mysteriously on leave the day I got back. I just wanted off the station, so I could lift my chin off my chest and put it all behind me and move on.

But I'm getting ahead of myself, and we're still in the Falklands. Aside from the mail, the radio was your best friend and it was here I was introduced to BFBS (British Forces Broadcasting Service): a female DJ, 'Bendy Wendy' – don't ask me why, I just don't know – and the Archers, along with the shipping forecast.

I recall travelling home in the early hours of the morning with my girlfriend dozing in the passenger seat next to me when the shipping forecast came on. I began to say the names as the presenter did – Cromarty, Tyne, Dogger, Fisher, German Bight, North Utsire, South Utsire. My girlfriend opened an eye and said, 'Have you any idea just how sad that is?'

'What?' I asked, slightly startled.

'The fact that you even know those names, let alone be able to recite them in sync.'

I'd never given it any thought before. They were unusual, something you wouldn't come across in your daily routine, unless of course you were a fisherman. But eight thousand miles from home you grabbed anything and everything that reminded you of dear old Blighty. I still love the radio plays, but don't bother with the Archers any more; I suppose it's like someone reading you a bedtime story. I still find that remarkably comforting and do it for my daughter whenever she comes to stay.

The food at Stanley was decidedly average, 'same old-same old' – sausages frazzled on one side while pink on the other. I don't wanna give the cooks a hard time; I think they make the best of what they can and it's always a thankless task. Having seen some of the things that go into a meal, it's a foolish person that upsets a cook and still thinks he's not eating phlegm, jiz or worse!

'Aye, ya might laugh now, but we've all done it.'

I'm not sure whether the food was 'compo' – a kind of high-fibre stuff that blocked your insides up relentlessly, with the need to poo just once a week. It was either that or 'Galtieri's revenge', when the entire contents of one's stomach would evacuate themselves wherever you were, without notice. I've had it, seen others have it – and believe me, it's not pleasant.

On the same subject, I could not believe my eyes while queuing outside the airmen's mess for lunch one day. There on the ground was the biggest turd I have ever seen in my life; this would be akin to childbirth for a man. I don't want to dwell on it for too long, lest our more squeamish readers turn off – but this was enormous. At over a foot long it could have been laid by the Falklands equivalent of the Sasquatch or Yeti – and right outside the mess, while you were queuing for lunch? People covered it over with newspaper, but that just blew off. Day after day it glared at you, and became somewhat of a celebrity. It was the talk of the town; small flags began to appear in it (I can't believe I'm actually writing this and am having hysterics – but it happened; you just couldn't make up stuff like this).

How on earth did it get there? Had someone done it elsewhere and transported it thus? Or crouched down in the blackness of night? I was baffled. It seemed to be defiant of the elements too; rain, snow and howling winds could not shift it. Week after week it commanded respect, just lying there, changing ever so slightly. If it had a cherry on the top it could have given Damian Hurst a run for his money any day of the week.

Someone, somewhere, knows who did it, and what a claim to fame, even the perpetrator himself. (I say 'him'; God forbid it was a woman – she really wouldn't have been well at all!)

While we're on the subject of turds, I just gotta tell ya this. The RAF Police, as I've mentioned, were seen as party poopers for the most part; any police were, in fact. They would take their 'puddle jumper' and thrash it endlessly, yanking on the handbrake in an attempt to do handbrake turns. But the Land Rover's handbrake doesn't work on the wheels: it works on the transmission. Time and time again we would get the 'Piggy Post's' Land Rover in with snapped half-shafts (the bit that drives the wheels). No amount of explanation would stop them doing this, and they were hated for it. The next time it came in for repair, one of the nightshift laid a rather fruity turd on its exhaust manifold.

Because the engine was cold, no one was any the wiser. The police collected it and roared off in it as normal. It was back in the yard the following morning, with a bit of paper stuck on its window alerting people to the pong. Someone removed that and replaced it with a roll of toilet paper. It sat there for days and the 'piggies' had to walk their rounds instead of wrecking another set of half-shafts.

My claim to fame came in the form of a one-tonne Land Rover that wouldn't run; almost everyone in MTSS had tried to get it going. It was of the 24-volt type, so had screened ignition for suppression of radio interference. Battery after battery had been fitted and refitted, while it was cranked over relentlessly without so much as a fart from the engine.

Carburettors by the boxful had been replaced, cleaned and refitted, with the same outcome. I stood and watched fitter after fitter have a go at getting it running, listening intently to what had been done – and more importantly, not done. Back to basics: if it's got fuel and got sparks at the right time, there's not much to stop an engine bursting into life, or at least hinting that it might do so at any given moment. I removed all the spark plugs, turned the engine over and witnessed the deep-blue spark jumping across each gap. Nothing wrong with that, then.

I squirted a bit of 'Easy Start' (an ether-based accelerant) into the carburettor and it coughed, as if to start – so it was a fuel problem: and indeed it was. We took the carburettors off (it's a V8 engine) and inspected them closely. Nothing obvious; they were brand new and worked fine. I put my thumb over the fuel pipe and spun the engine over: yep, plenty of pressure, so the fuel was getting there.

Still it wouldn't run. Carburettors on, carburettors off. I thought 'fuck it'; get a fire extinguisher and be ready. I put my thumb over the fuel pipe again, but allowing a small gap to squirt almost neat fuel into the inlet manifold where the carburettors are mounted. I spun it over and it roared into life. Every head in the 'rub' looked around, and it was little old me who got it going. A few people wandered over and questioned me on how I'd done it.

The fuel was getting to the carburettors, but it was so diluted by the time it had passed though them that it wasn't rich enough to ignite: problem – water in the fuel! I had found the answer to a lot of vehicles misbehaving, and the fuel was tested. APFCs (air-portable fuel containers) were found to be the problem, as the difference between the temperature of the fuel and the external temperatures during flight/transportation caused condensation to form on the inside of the container, thus watering it down. 'Ta-da!' Am I a star, or what? (Don't answer that.)

So my new-found stardom had elevated my morale a little: that and the fact that I had coloured in the tits in on my 'chuff chart' and was almost halfway through my tour. I'd pestered the bosses of MTSS so much that they decided it would be easier to allow me to do the rest of my time in the hangar as a fitter, as opposed to a tyre fitter, and I swapped my 'cushy number' with someone else so I get could get my paws on the fantastic range of trucks and specialist vehicles.

One of them was an 'Eager Beaver' rough-terrain forklift truck. Again all-wheel drive, but with the addition of all-wheel steering. It was basically a chassis with a set of forks on it: as basic as that – no roll-cage or even cab. Safety equipment was almost non-existent and as usual people would 'beast' them, which usually ended up with one on its side – or worse. The only thing stopping you getting flung off the damn' thing was a tiny lap belt designed to strap your arse to the seat.

Given the weather conditions and the fact that we worked around the clock in bad light, at night, and in camouflage meant you really needed your wits about you if you weren't to get run over. Accidents were commonplace and there was usually a steady stream of injured parties being carted off to the medical centre. We got a call that an Eager Beaver had broken down near the runway, and were tasked with recovering it. We set off in the section's 'Mog' and headed off with the minimum of tools. As we approached the 'Beaver' it was lying at an angle of thirty degrees from the rear to the front, looking as though it had fallen into a deep hole. We got out of the wrecker, scratching our heads.

The back axle had come completely off as the driver had bumped up onto the runway, and was some distance away. What the hell were we meant to do with that? We went back to MTSS, got another forklift and coaxed the damaged one back to the hangar. It kept slipping off the forks, and I could here the arse cheeks of the poor sod that had to steer it slapping like a seal at feeding time. It sat in the hangar for weeks, being slowly cannibalised, and would never run again. I used to borrow these machines to pick up the bigger tyres from Stores, even though I had no licence to drive them.

No one gave a shit really, until something went wrong; then you would be ceremoniously strung up by the 'love spuds' and left to dangle, as a warning to others. Tea breaks were as much fun as ever and one poor soul was 'gotcha'd' in good style. He'd been to the mess and brought some booty back with him for rescuing one of the cook's Land Rovers. (The cooks seemed to have a knack for burying Land Rovers up to their nuts in mud, and usually at night.) He had a large tin of chocolate powder and several bars of butter. The tea bar was packed, and we all said we would give him a quid each if he dipped the butter into the chocolate powder and ate the lot! Neat. I have to say the poor lad got halfway through the first bar before blowing chunks and, to top it all, no one gave him a quid, either. He was devastated and I rolled with laughter, as did everyone else except the butter muncher. The cooks penance wasn't coming out of their pockets for dragging them out. This time it was a box of Mars Bars, and the 'Snecos' decided that this was too good a haul to be shared with us 'erks' and stole the Mars bars. This just wasn't cricket, old chap, so we staged a sit-in after marching with placards that read 'Feed the world and free the Mars Bars' and 'Liberate the Cadbury thirty-five' (which was a bit silly, as they don't make them). But it was solidarity, brothers, and we refused to move from the office until we got one each.

Even the normally placid 'Panther' was thrown, claws unsheathed, at one protester, who was mauled quite badly before kicking its bollocks out the door, where it proceeded to howl the place down until they let it back in. Justice did prevail though, and we were duly rewarded if we went back to work.

When I did get a day off, mischief was usually the order of the day and I didn't want to waste it getting hammered all day long, which seemed to be what most people did. I went exploring, firstly around the Coastel itself – onto the roof, where I found my first victim of the day (plate 35). One of the stewards – plate-slingers and coffee jockeys, as they were more affectionately known – was cleaning down the surface of the boat, to free it form rat turds and gull poo. He kept squirting the seagulls with the hose and trying to knock them out of the sky with the high-pressure jet. He was having a ball and I could hear him laughing from where I was.

I went back downstairs and collected a fine selection of pebbles and stones from the dolomite bank – pocketfuls, I had. Once back on the roof, I began dropping them on his head one at a time; I could hear him yelp as they struck his noggin from quite a height – they must have hurt. He kept looking around, completely bemused as to where they were coming from, since I kept ducking out of sight once they'd hit him. He was getting quite pissed off and began yelling and shouting – but at whom? He still hadn't seen me. Someone stuck a head out of the mess door to see what all the noise was about.

'Some twat's throwing stones at me – look!'

There was a little pile at his feet, as he kicked them over the side.

'Might be the gulls,' came the reply; and there were a couple of moments of silence while this scenario washed over the dim twat's brain.

Eventually he looked up as I was coming back out for another look-see; I was caught and he thought it would be hysterical to try and drown me with the hose. As he raised the hose the wind blew it back in his face and it was he who was dripping wet and not I. Oh, deep joy; I love it when a plan comes together.

After that little starter I decided to have a mooch into Stanley town and see what I was missing ('not a lot', Mr Daniels). One of the shops was shut, and the General Store sold all things connected to surviving in a remote location such as this. I wandered around for a bit and got my passport stamped in the 'Piggy Post' to prove I had actually been there. I have to say they were less than helpful, and I gather were fed up of people wandering in and out for a stamp: miserable gits.

When the sun did eventually come out Stanley could be quite picturesque, if a little ramshackle; it was built on a hillside overlooking a calm, blue bay. I sat under the whale ribs (plate 12) next to the church and just took in the view. The air was so clean here: no pollution or factories. It was still cold and I let the sun warm my face as I daydreamed of home. I think sheep farming was generating the mainstay of the income – and of course there were the usual gags and rumours that the 'Bennys' shagged the living daylights out of them, saying 'I tucked its back legs down the front of my wellies and couldn't stop, 'cos it kept asking for m-o-o-r-e!' (sheep noise).

'Was it a girl sheep?'

'Oh, yeah. There's nowt funny about Thackery Blodwin Woodcutter the third!'

Given that I kind of think in images, that was one that will stay with me for ever. Too much information.

My next adventure came when I hired a motorbike from the army – a Honda MTX 125cc (plate 25) trail bike for a fiver a day with a full tank of fuel; I was in heaven. I was also warned about going up to the Two Sisters mountains on it, which would not be a good idea with the weather closing in so quickly and the chance of discovering an unmapped minefield.

But you know me by now! I roared off into town and then way, way out of town towards the mountains. I passed the large satellite dish that sends signals back home, and wondered who would be talking on it at that very moment. I spared a thought for Jamie, but was too excited to dwell on it for long as I ventured into the wilderness. The road narrowed to a track and then to nothing at all. I was on swampy ground – a kind of spring mush underfoot. The bike tore it up and I was covered in it, but that was the plan anyway; you can tell a happy biker by the number of dead flies on his teeth or the amount of mud collected about his person. Higher and higher I went; it got so steep that the bike kept coming back over on top of me and I had to lay it on its side, which was almost upright anyway the hillside was so steep.

~ MAN OVERBOARD ~

I just had to get to the top: a prime photo opportunity. There were a couple of ominous-looking clouds in the distance and I was very wary of getting caught out in it. I had my Falklands parka on, but that wouldn't keep the wind-chill out.

I made it, and sat surveying all beneath me: what a view (plate 26). There was absolute stillness and silence – not another living soul within twenty-five miles or so, not even any animals. The sheer desolation of the place was both calming and worrying; if anything happened to me now I'd be well in the shit. There were no pay-as-you-go mobile phones in those days; only the poshest of the posh had a mobile. Now I'd conquered the tits (the Two Sisters' nickname) I began my descent carefully and eased off a bit on the scrambling until I was in sight of civilisation once more.

I 'bimbled' around Stanley for a while and then made my way back to camp. I paused to watch the Army try and recover a loading shovel that had sunk in the bog. Whoops-a-daisy; they tipped one over (plate 34) and got the other one stuck – harrar! There was always a good deal of inter-service rivalry and I wasn't gonna miss an opportunity like this. I returned the bike and made my way to the NAAFI for the rest of the evening, where I proceeded to get wholly paralytic while ripping the shit out of the Army lads. I'd had a brilliant day, got some great photos and gone moto-crossing, so I was on a high to start with – and it would be this night that I would end up in the water again. 'Never dare a fool,' they say! – and it has to be said it's a pretty good description of me. 'A fool and his money are easily parted' – I'm always skint. But then again, I'm not materialistic anyway; as long as I'm warm, dry, fed and watered I'm happy.

So what the fuck possessed me to jump over the side of the Coastel? 'Cos I was dared to do it – what a plonker!. I'd learned my lesson on walking the chain, but there were two of us that were gonna jump in – I would if he would. We were both standing on the railings now and did a small countdown; he feigned jumping off and I was already on the way – except he did not jump, and I landed in the water again. I cannot overstress how cold it was; my 'love tatties' disappeared into my throat, pushing the tonsils out of the way.

The lads were whooping and hollering as I clambered out of the water like a drowned rat, to rapturous applause. Yep, I'd been well and truly 'gottcha'd' this time. A head popped out of the Coastel door with the immortal words, 'Not fucking you again!'

He made me strip down to my underpants outside and wring out the rest of my clothes, lest I mess his Coastel up. I wish someone had got a photo of that: me in a pair of baggy, sodden, discoloured knickers, dickless, with me boots still on (oh, how we laughed!) I was three months into my tour now and the 'chuff chart' was looking good; thirty-odd days and I would be on the 'Gozzome Bird' I had my R & R (rest and relaxation) to look forward to, which was three days off towards the end of your tour to de-stress you. That was the plan, anyway; in reality it was a three-day bender where more teeth have been lost in fights than I care to mention.

I was due another day off and the 'chuff' was almost completely coloured in; I was almost on the flaps. I hired another bike from the Army and decided a trip to MPA (Mount Pleasant Airport) would be a suitable adventure now that my tour was coming to a close. It was a Sunday and a little quieter than usual; I assumed that MPA, like Stanley, would be a twenty-four-hour community and getting fuel wouldn't be a problem. Oh, how wrong can ya be? It was freezing as usual and the dolomite roads were rock hard and extremely slippery. But, given my skill as a competent motorcyclist, I fishtailed the little Honda along – until I fell off, ripping my jeans and a decent-sized hole in my leg to boot.

The edge of the road where the scrapers could not reach was like a thousand razors. I didn't think it hurt that much, but by gum, when I warmed up a tad it throbbed like billy-o. Still, the handlebars were only twisted a little, and astonishingly I hadn't snapped any of the levers. I stood astride the front wheel and gave the bars a tweak; close enough, I thought, and roared off once more.

The road to MPA was littered with all kinds of junk, and there were forty-five-gallon drums of Lord knows what scattered all over the place, as well as abandoned vehicles – a good deal of construction equipment that I just had to have a play with, now that there was no one around. I seem to remember the journey being about forty miles, and looking at the maps on the Internet that would seem close enough. It felt like thousands, though, and I soon got fed up of warming my hands and gloves on the exhaust, only to have them freeze up within minutes of getting back on.

The loneliness and desolation were in my mind once more and I did spare a thought for what if I'd broken a limb when I fell off? How long would it be before I was discovered? – if I ever was before I froze to death. The wind-chill factor could drag the temperature down to unbelievable levels in the blink of an eye, and when the sun went in you certainly knew about it. On and on I roared, snaking the bike through puddles à go-go and 'wheelie'-ing it through ditches, having no idea how deep they were. Come to think of it, I was a bit thick, really! – and very lucky.

As I approached Mount Pleasant, which is an ironic name as there was nothing pleasant about the place – not that I could see, anyway – the bike coughed onto reserve fuel. I trundled around a bit looking for somewhere to fill up: not a soul in sight. The place, to all intents and purposes was deserted. Oh, deep shit! How would I get back without fuel? The reality was that I wouldn't. I was astonished; Stanley was always a hive of activity, and yet it seemed that a Sunday here was just like one back home. I began to get worried as the sun began to sink in the sky and I wasn't relishing a journey back in the dark and the freezing conditions. Finally I found the mess hut, and enquired of the inmates where I could get fuel.

'Not today, mate!' was the reply; now I really was panicking. It was a bit like being on holiday; once you were out in the sticks there were no petrol stations and you just bought fuel from whomever you could. But I was flapping big-style now; the Army would want their bike back and I was due in at work next morning.

One of the cooks had overheard the conversation and beckoned me towards the door. I duly followed, not really sure of what was to come. I was still very naïve, but desperation was setting in and I would take any help that was offered. Walking away from the mess into the middle of a large, boggy, grassed area, he kept turning around and beckoning me silently; it did actually cross my mind that he may be leading me into the wilderness to give me a jolly good rogering! – so I hung back a little.

The bike was looking decidedly smaller now that we'd walked a good distance. He stopped, standing motionless in the middle of fucking nowhere. I thought, if those hands go anywhere near that zip, it'll be the fastest thousand-yard dash in history. He pointed to the ground and winked. If I was panicking before, I was practically passing out now; what could he mean? And why doesn't he speak? All this cloak-and-dagger shit really unnerved me. I'd heard tales of kinky cooks, and why it was important not to upset them if you didn't want a 'bell end' dangling in your soup. He pointed to the ground again, but this time with an accompanying 'Aye-aye: what d'ya think?' I still wasn't sure, but there was no way I was polishing his helmet for fuel – I'd fucking walk back before anything like that. He bent down and grasped the turf, which with one almighty tug peeled back like a well-rubbed orange, revealing a very neat pit which contained four jerrycans of fuel. I unclenched my arse cheeks and let out the biggest sigh to date.

'Help ya self,' he said. 'Fill it up and put the rest back, but don't bring the bike over here; there's still mines knocking about!'

I wasn't quite sure what to make of this last bit, apart from the fact that he'd walked over in front of me, so if there were any he was gonna cop it first. I watched as he painstakingly placed his feet as if he were retracing his steps exactly – what a twat.

And he expects me to carry petrol through a supposed minefield? – fuck off! But I had to if I wanted to get back. What a sight I must have looked as I padded my way back to the bike with one five-gallon can, which was more than enough to fill the bike up. I wouldn't have been surprised if there had been a sea of tiny faces watching me, who would collectively shout 'BANG!' as I approached. It's the sort of thing I would have done – so why not? But they didn't. I filled the bike to the brim and put the can back; he wanted only a couple of quid, but I was so relieved not to have been 'bum galloped' that I gave him a fiver and made a hasty retreat.

Taking the bike back to the Army so late in the day came with its own problems and everyone had gone ... to what we laughingly called home.

One of the rear indicators had smashed when I bit the dolomite, but I hadn't noticed it until now. I pinched one off another bike and swapped it over, before leaving it all nice and neat, Ta-da! I didn't hear anything more, so it must have been OK.

Lunchtimes at Stanley were usually entertaining and one had to be on one's guard not to get caught out. This was when a lot of the mischief took place and when someone might go mysteriously missing! Extra care was taken when returning to work. If the sun was shining we would play football, and had been doing so on the same spot for weeks.

The ball was kicked into the rough and someone trotted off after it, only to be halted in his tracks with a scream any girl would have been proud of: 'BOMB – FUCKING BOMB!'

~ Drop and Give Me Twenty! ~

Nestled neatly in the grass was one of our own Harrier bomblets: a small antipersonnel mine with metal fingers that stick up and trigger the device – it looks a bit like a pineapple top. Apparently short-wave radio signals would also set them off. EOD (Explosive Ordinance Disposal) or 'Redwings' (Plate 21) were called and carried out a controlled explosion of said bomb (Plate 38) – and we'd been playing football near it for weeks: phew!

So the flaps on the 'chuff chart' were well and truly coloured in – and in pink: one likes to be accurate – and I literally had a few days to do. It was time for my R & R on the other side of the island, at Port San Carlos. This time we flew in a 'Wokka' with an ISO (metal storage container) slung beneath the aircraft. The doors in the centre of the floor were open so the loadmaster could see what, if anything, was happening to the load. Even wrapped in my Falklands parka and with Inuit mittens on, it was still bastard freezing and the view through the floor of the container, swinging like a pissed pendulum, did nothing to instil confidence.

The under-gusset got another chewing and I could have held on to the bench seat with my arse cheeks alone. But hey! I'll never forget the run out of the back of the ramp, 'Rambo' style – 'ave it! After we were dropped off, the 'Wokka's' thundering blades faded to silence as it became a dot on the horizon, and once more the sheer desolation and isolation came to the front of my mind.

'What if they don't come back? What if it crashes? We'd be stuck in this shithole for weeks and I'll miss my spot on the "Gozzome Bird".'

Never mind: things were afoot. A 'toga party' was suggested by one of the Army lads who came on the chopper. There were about ten of us altogether, mixed services, and you never really knew who you were dealing with. The quiet ones were always the worst. After lunch I proceeded to get as hammered as I have possibly ever been, and I was sick in my sleep. It was a good thing I was laying on my side, or I could have choked.

The quick-witted ones amongst our group wasted no time in grabbing a sheet for their 'toga', and they were all gone by the time I'd cottoned on (no pun intended), so I was left with a bollock-itching rough blanket (Plate 18) and nothing underneath. I've got a great photo of some stranger's 'bell end' poking out from beneath his toga; it had gone largely unnoticed until I showed it to my sister – hmmm!

After the bingeing but before the sleeping, it was felt that the trampoline in one of the outbuildings – which was off limits to us while the instructor was away – should be given a thorough testing.

'All for one and ...': it didn't take much suggesting and we were off! Toga-clad drunkards in the throes of excitement, we would be flying home in three days' time – what could possibly go wrong now? Well ... two of the Army lads each lost as many teeth – one from fighting with an RAF Regiment lad, and the other from flying off the trampoline at an angle of forty-five degrees and smashing into the wall. I was in utter hysterics; there was blood and snot everywhere, and the more he bleated on about it the more and more I laughed. I even got punched for that, but I was so pissed I never felt it, really.

~ MAN OVERBOARD ~

If you put two inexperienced people on a trampoline with differing weights, sooner or later the heavier of the two catches up with the lighter and all the energy is transferred, even if they start at different ends of the bed and in a 'one-up and one-down' rhythm. This is what happened to the lad who lost his teeth. It was all going swimmingly as they tried to bounce high enough to touch the ceiling, which was actually achievable; but copious amounts of alcohol together with trampolines are surely a recipe for disaster. They were getting closer and closer together, taking lumps out of each other with mid-air 'Bruce Lee' kicks, when the heavier landed ever so slightly before the other did. The transference of the bounce happened very quickly, and the fact that he still had his socks on made it even funnier; the other lad shot off, arms and legs akimbo, like an epileptic starfish, into the wall. I laughed so hard I thought I was gonna puke. Oh, happy days ...

When I'd sobered up enough to be able to feel my lips, I decided that a wander around the place was a good idea.

'Don't go wandering,' we'd been told. 'There's a lot of ordnance still lying around' – but ya know me.

And so off I went and discovered an old 'Sanger' or OP (observational point). In it was an ammo box with live 7.62 rounds (Plates 27 and 28). Never a thought was given to the fact that it might have been booby-trapped; but this was 1985 and surely if it were it would have gone off by now? Outside the OP were a load of empty ammo boxes, strewn as far as the eye could see. I decided to leave well alone this time, but reported the rounds find to an officer – who then claimed he had found them, and got the 'Good show' for himself ... wanker!

20. Zippy

This chapter is dedicated to one of the funniest people I have ever met in the Forces. God bless him, he made the last two months of my tour fly by. I do know his real name, but without his permission I can't use it; I've tried relentlessly to track him down on the Internet using 'Friends/Forces Reunited', without success, although it has to be said that he was such a memorable chap that several people remember him from the short description I put out.

Firstly, a physical description. At about five feet two Zippy was a little round barrel with a walrus moustache and beady eyes. The long, heavy Falklands parka that had to be surgically removed (I think he may have even slept in it) almost touched the ground, making him appear to move around the place like a Dalek, and all this was topped off by a 'Deputy Dawg' / 'Benny' hat with the flaps permanently pulled down and locked under his non-existent chin. If he'd had a pair of flying goggles on he could have been mistaken for Roy 'Chubby' Brown any day of the week; he was certainly just as funny. He got his nickname from the impressions of 'Zippy' from the television programme 'Rainbow'.

The voice was uncannily similar, but with an adult spin to the text:

'Oooh look, Bungle: George has done a huge big shit right in the middle of the floor.'

He would drum his fingers over his lips and 'tache as he spoke. This was high entertainment enough, but he also did impressions of Stanley Unwin, the guy who invented a kind of gobbledygook-speak that you could barely understand, such as:

'Slip slidey through the bumhold and spanky thrashy around the earlober to tighty hold on a whiley.'

This was his description of a 'rodeo' shag, where one positions oneself 'doggy fashion' behind one's wife, then tells her that her sister is a better shag than she is and sees how long one could hold on for.

I practically wet myself; if he wasn't doing impressions, he was cracking gags. He was an absolute natural comedian and I truly hope he is using those gifts wherever he is. We were stunned to see him on stage at a CSE Show (Combined Services Entertainment), giving out the instructions of what to do in the event of a fire in true Stanley Unwin style.

I was in hysterics, as were the other couple of hundred people in the audience. I particularly remember him saying something about the ladies stilettos falling through the gaps in the stairs.

The lucky bastard was about two feet from six stunning girls dressed in white figure hugging basques and suspenders. I've got a great photo and would love to use it; I would if I could track down 'Valhalla' or their agent. Zippy was completely unfazed by most things, and decided that he would try and do the whole of his four-month tour without having a single haircut.

~ Drop and Give Me Twenty! ~

It was true the rules seemed to be relaxed a little, but Zippy was taking the piss and refused every hint from every 'Sneco' to get it cut – so much so that in the end the lads got a wooden engine crate and nailed him into it, before tying it to the forks of an 'Eager Beaver truck' and delivering him to the barber's, with a crowbar for extraction.

I've never seen so much snot and spit, as they chased after him for what seemed like an eternity, his big parka flailing like the Phantom of the Opera, while his little legs were just a blur as he made a run for it. It must have taken at least three of them to catch him and another two to get him into the box – all to the protestations of a hysterical Stanley Unwin lament at how he would wreak vengeance and set his pet python on them, once back in the UK.

Given that the snake is a master of escapology and Zippy wasn't, it's one of the funniest things I've ever seen.

Zippy did get his own back and was eventually revealed as the phantom glove-stuffer. God forbid that you took off your gloves for a second and turned away, as Zippy would grab whatever was to hand and cram it as tightly as he could into the unsuspecting gloves. I was unfortunate enough just to get pop rivets in mine, which went under my nails when I tried to put the gloves on. He was very thorough, making sure that the substance, whatever it was, got forced right down into the bottom of the fingers. Other disaffected souls got 'Copper-coat' grease, washers, nuts, bolts and split pins, 'Swarfega' (ironically a hand cleanser) – and of course the obligatory dollop of shit from Tina the turd taxi or Lawrence the log lorry.

Zippy was the only person who would work on the two trucks that were responsible for emptying the cesspits by means of a large vacuum pump at the rear of the truck. We could hear him hammering and banging at a stuck valve in 'Unwin speak', which just made it even more comical than it already was. A small crowd would gather whenever Zippy launched into a tirade at whoever his particular favourite was that day.

The two-pound hammer would be drawn up to maximum height again and again as he tried to free the valve; there was a cracking sound, then an almighty 'sploosh' as the remains of its contents shot out of the truck and covered Zippy with every kind of turd imaginable. He just had time to turn his back before he was pebble-dashed. He just stood there, with his arms outstretched, as bits of shit slid of his parka and plopped onto the metal floor.

The lads had practically shat there kidneys out laughing, but soon changed their minds as Zippy gave chase, covered in shit and trying to get a hug from everyone; he even went into the 'Snecos' office with his shitty hammer, only to have Panther flung at him. In hindsight this was not the cleverest thing they could have done, because the cat would sneak back into the office whenever anyone left the door open, and stink the place out as it lay by the electric fire. A damp feral cat smells bad enough by a fire, but one soaked in fresh poo was truly an overwhelming aroma.

There were a couple of trips out, courtesy of the 'Erics' (Bristow's helicopters – Plate 29). A Sikorsky hoisted us skyward to a King Penguin colony on the other

~ Zippy ~

side of the Island. I was like a kid in a sweet shop; I'd never flown in a helicopter before coming to the Falklands and was as nervous as I was excited.

Zippy just fastened his lap belt, closed his eyes and was off in the Land of Nod in seconds; this guy could sleep on a clothesline. We shuddered into the sky and my stomach felt as though it had fallen though the floor; I clenched my arse cheeks so tight it looked as if I was chewing a toffee with it.

I was in heaven – or at least a little closer to it. We swapped bits and pieces of our packed lunches around; I ended up with Zippy's fruit and he ate my sandwiches when he finally woke up. "Ave I missed anything?' were his first words; there was much shaking of heads. It was during this flight that we learned the penguin story of them all looking up and falling over backwards; like the twats we were we struggled to push our face at the windows, jostling for a place in case we missed it – duh! The 'Eric's' aircrew always got a giggle out of that one.

We got a brief introduction and description of the wildlife we were going to see, and of course we would have to land a good couple of miles from the nest site so as not to frighten the penguins. The ground was as boggy as ever, with deep puddles scattered around. It was only a matter of time before Zippy had found one, and the shrill shout of 'Oooh, fuckarse!' (which was his favourite saying) had us all spinning around to see Zippy up to his bollocks in mud, waving his arms around like something possessed.

We had to drag him out and it made a satisfying and fantastic 'shlurping' sounds as he came out. He was soaking: not a good condition to be in when out in the open on the Falkland Isles. We 'yomped' on and on and got lost, being led by some idiot 'Rodney' type.

'I say – over here, chaps and chapesses. I think I've located the colony!'

'In English, ya big poof,' Zippy mumbled from the back; a few of us heard and rolled with laughter, but the sound didn't travel all the way to the front, which was just as well. We split into two groups; while one group headed for the 'guins (Plate 16) the other headed for the beach to see the sea lions and walruses – and oh, how the comparisons flowed between Zippy and the walruses!

Another creature we were told of was the 'Johnny rook', a kind of Falklands vulture standing about two and half feet tall, with huge talons and a decidedly sharp beak. It was true the wildlife was not used to, or afraid of, human contact on this remote side of the island and provided you didn't stand at your full height they would quite happily come up and inspect you to see if you might be edible.

Zippy had had enough, and sat down on a clump of sea grass to eat his sandwiches. He had no sooner opened the box than a 'Johnny rook' flew at him full pelt, relieving him of the sandwiches; I was beside myself as he tried to flap this monster away without the slightest hint of success; it just stood in front of him, glaring at him.

Zippy was trying to stare the bird out, but it was having none of it. As far as it was concerned we were the intruders, and we'd brought lunch that was easily caught. Time and time again the vulture lunged at Zippy for whatever it was he was holding; you just couldn't buy tickets for this type of entertainment, as he tried to shoo it away with his 'Benny hat'. It just kept hopping around him until he gave up and left the remains of his dinner to the bird, which crowed triumphantly over its spoils. Bird one – Zippy nil!

The groups swapped over and we went to look at the walruses and sea lions. Nothing to be seen at first, but then we could just make out a basking sea lion perched on a rock. As we approached it from the rear, the two Army lads in our group were daring each other to see who could get the closest to it and get the best photo. I sort of lolled behind, a bit unsure; I knew the animals could travel quite fast over short distances, and knowing my luck it would be me who was bitten or squashed in the rush. The stone we were walking on were very slippery, which made walking a tad unsteady. The lads were only feet from the creature now and I could hear one daring the other to actually touch it. There was a loud clatter, and a large black blob shot out from a cave in the edge of the bank side (Plate 31).

Stones were being flung in all directions like confetti! It was the larger male, coming to protect his female, and the lads did an about turn cartoon-style and did their best to get the fuck out of the way before Papa sea lion got to them. I was up higher by now and pissed myself, shouting:

'Serves ya right, ya pair of knobbers!'

The lads ran in opposite directions and the big beast dived into the sea with his mate following him, but it made for a good picture; and there were real sea-lion sound effects –or there would have been if I had been brave enough to get a bit closer. Zippy was mumbling and chuntering that he was disappointed at missing the action, and that he was still wet and cold and that the 'Johnny rook' had pinched his sandwiches. We made our way back to the RV (rendezvous) with the chopper and were once again airborne, swapping stories like excited girls from St Trinian's. Zippy was off in the Land of Nod once more, as if it were a day out in the park. He used to fascinate me, as did many of my comrades; I looked to them for guidance and experience, but didn't want to appear too keen – there was the ever-present danger of being suckered into a wind-up and the dropping of a royal bollock.

We returned to the Coastel, showered and went for an extra large shlurp at the NAAFI, to tell of our journey to the 'guin colony and the twat Rodney who got us lost so we spent more time 'plodging' around the spongy bog than we had time to actually look at the wildlife. There would be no walking of the chain tonight, no leaping over the side of the Coastel, no matter how drunk I got; I coloured in the clitoris on my 'chuff chart' and would be on the 'Gozzome Bird' tomorrow. I sung my tits off in the NAAFI and was threatened with being 'done over'. I didn't care, though; I was no FNG, I'd 'got some in' – I was a Falklands veteran.

And the closest I ever came to firing a shot was when I almost had an ND (negligent discharge – when a round goes off accidentally) while guarding the fuel dump in Stanley Harbour.

I handed all my kit back in, said 'goodbye' to the room and nurtured my carefully coloured chart to show everyone else that I bumped into; it was soul-destroying to be on the other end of it. The four-tonner came to pick us up and we would RV with the same coaches that had brought us to this place four months

~ Zippy ~

earlier. The first two months were the slowest, and then it flew by. You could hear the 'Gozzome' party from miles and miles away, blasting out Peter, Paul and Mary's hit. 'V' signs, the 'bird' arses at the window and flailing genitals out of the back signalled our departure, as we bumped along the road to freedom.

Souvenirs à go-go meant we had to be searched, and the rumour machine told of weapons being confiscated before being allowed on board the aircraft. I brought a live 7.62 round with me that I found at San Carlos, and would have been strung up if they found it. I can honestly say that I have never felt such a feeling of relief as I did when the wheels rolled on the 747 once more, into the night and homeward bound – and the fucking bar was still shut!

❖ ❖ ❖

Epilogue

Thank you for taking the time to read this book.

I hope you have had as much fun reading it as I had writing it. I have read many similar books of military memoirs /autobiography and found that the books seemed to start out OK, but then got more technical as the author became more experienced in the literary world – so much so that I often spent more time with my head in the dictionary than I did actually reading the story! And then I put the book down – surely every author's nightmare.

There were so many humorous incidents, I couldn't fit them all into one book and have planned a second, entitled *Drop and Give Me 10,* because I couldn't manage twenty press-ups by then!

Cheers,
Rob